THE ESSENTIAL CONVERSATION

The

ESSENTIAL
CONVERSATION

*What Parents and Teachers
Can Learn from Each Other*

Sara Lawrence-Lightfoot

RANDOM HOUSE

NEW YORK

Grateful acknowledgment is made to Aunt Lute Books for
permission to reprint an excerpt from "To live in the Borderlands means you" from
Borderlands/La Frontera: The New Mestiza by Gloria Anzaldúa, copyright © 1987, 1999
by Gloria Anzaldúa. Reprinted by permission of Aunt Lute Books.

LIBRARY OF CONGRESS CATALOGING-IN-PUBLICATION DATA

Lawrence-Lightfoot, Sara
The essential conversation: what parents and teachers can learn
from each other / Sara Lawrence-Lightfoot.
p.   cm.
ISBN 0-375-50527-X
1. Parent-teacher conferences—United States.   I. Title.
LC225.5 .L394 2003
371.19'2—dc21   2002068213

Printed in the United States of America on acid-free paper

24689753

Book design by Oksana Kushnir

This book is for my brother and sister,
Charles Radford Lawrence III
and
Paula Lawrence Wehmiller,
who have—from the very beginning—helped me navigate
the borders of family and school
(and all of the other treacherous terrains).
Fiercely loyal, deeply devoted, endlessly loving,
they stand by my side, watch my back, tell me the truth,
and make me laugh.

CONTENTS

ACKNOWLEDGMENTS

From my point of view, there is no more complex and tender geography than the borderlands between families and schools. The parents and teachers whose voices and experiences fill this volume were generous in welcoming me into their midst, open in revealing to me their insights and perspectives, and brave in allowing me to witness their conversations. I am so admiring of their good works and advocacy on behalf of children, and deeply thankful to them for their trust, their candor, and their wisdom. Although their experiences and their narratives have been faithfully recorded, I have—by mutual agreement—altered names and places to protect their privacy and that of their students and their students' families.

As always, this project was supported by the extraordinary efforts and skills of my wonderful assistant, Wendy E. Angus, who brought her keen sensibilities and rigorous discipline to this work. Ethan Mintz, my devoted research assistant, wrote perceptive syntheses of the literature and was a great talking companion. Chris Olson-Lanier reviewed the text with an editor's discernment and a mother's passion. I am thankful to all three. Many of the ideas and insights found in these pages grew out of wandering conversations with friends, on walks around the pond or over cups of tea in the kitchen. I am grateful to Susan Berger, Tom and Kay Cottle, Jessica Davis, Jay and Helen

Featherstone, Linda Mason, Pat Graham, Michelle Pierce, Randy Testa, Bill Wallace, and Marti Wilson.

It is because of my children—Tolani and Martin David—that I felt compelled to write this book. I wanted to revisit—once more with feeling—the amazing journey I took with them through school, a journey of love and loyalty, a journey that continues and evolves, and circles back home. I thank them for their patience with my missteps and for the lessons they taught me along the way about humility, resilience, and mercy. My mother, Margaret Morgan Lawrence, was my first teacher; her grit and grace, truth-telling and restraint, I have tried to memorize in mothering my own children. I am deeply grateful for the generational echoes that nourish and guide me. All of my family, my sister and brother, their partners, and their progeny have woven their vivid and poignant stories into this essential conversation. From the beginning, my man, Irving Hamer, cheered me on, raised penetrating questions, and challenged me to amplify my voice. This family-school terrain is one he knows very well, and his intelligence and wisdom—generously and lovingly given—enriched the work.

Ike Williams, my savvy agent, believed in this book from the start. His sage counsel and strategic advocacy were a great support. Jonathan Karp, editor extraordinaire, was spare and incisive in his guidance and perfect in his timing. He knew when to pursue and when to retreat. Finally, I would like to express my appreciation to the Spencer Foundation for its generous support of this project and for its commitment to nourishing the work of researchers and educators who are building the bridges between theory and practice.

Inheritances

WHEN I WAS seven years old and in second grade at a rural two-room schoolhouse in apple-orchard country northwest of New York City, I contracted an exotic disease called Huntington's chorea. It was difficult to diagnose and rare in young children; the doctors allowed me to be treated at home—rather than in the hospital—only because they trusted that my physician mother would care for me with the double dose of a doctor's judgment and a mother's love. For three months I stayed home in bed, trying to conquer the subtle infirmities of this illness, which expressed itself in the physical symptoms of weakness and dizziness and in the emotional signs of anxiety and depression. I was nursed by my maternal grandmother, a former schoolteacher, who brought me trays of food and worked with me on my "lessons." My grandmother's home schooling in those three months was more strict and demanding than any curriculum that I have had before or since. My friends were allowed to visit very occasionally, but only if they promised to stay only for a few minutes and be very quiet. For a while, I enjoyed all of the attention—my parents' solicitousness, my siblings' anxious concern. But very soon the sedentary, quiet life got old. I missed my friends. I missed the group life at school, the hustle and bustle, the scheming and competing, the rules, routines, and public rewards for work well done. And I worried a lot about whether I would lose my place socially and academically. Slowly but surely, I recovered and returned to Mrs. Sullivan's classroom, first for half days and then, weeks later, for the whole day.

One afternoon, when my parents came to pick me up early, Mrs. Sullivan walked outside with me to await their arrival, a gesture that made me feel immediately important and anxious. I remember her hard hand on my shoulder as she steered me down the stairs. I recall the way she kept clearing her throat nervously as my parents unfolded themselves from the car and made their way toward us. Her greeting was strictly ceremonial. She moved quickly to her main point. She wanted my parents to know that my three-month absence had severely compromised my academic progress. She did not think there was any way I could make up for lost time; it would, therefore, be necessary for me to repeat second grade. But that wasn't the worst of what Mrs. Sullivan had to say. She also thought that my parents had to face the fact that I "might, just might not be college material." All of this was said in front of me (actually far above my head, so I had to strain my neck to look up at her face); her voice was stern and hard, her expression flat.

I couldn't believe my ears. My heart was pounding hard against my chest. This was shocking news, so unfair, so wrongheaded. I am sure that my parents felt the same way. But what I remember most from this story was not Mrs. Sullivan's wounding words, nor the knot in my belly as I heard them. The most vivid and lasting image was my parents' response, a reaction that lacked all of the clarity and courage that I was used to seeing from them. At that moment, they were not their usual strong selves, fiercely advocating for me. They were like I had never seen them before, tentative and awkward. They listened, demurred but didn't disagree, and made a quick exit.

All the way home I waited for their outrage, waited for their defense of me. Instead, they were silent, probably biding their time until they could find some private moments together in which to confer and come up with an appropriate collective response. By dinnertime, they had emerged from my father's study, their expressions upbeat, their outlook optimistic. They were saying that they knew I was very intelligent, capable of being a great student, and certainly capable of going to college and beyond. They knew that Mrs. Sullivan was wrong and the best way to prove her wrong was for me to do excellent work. I was not to succumb to her prophecy. I was to challenge it with the best I had. Of course, I rose to my parents' challenge, worked very hard, exceeded all of Mrs. Sullivan's expectations, and joined my classmates in third grade the next year.

My parents' primary message to me—a litany that they would repeat at crucial moments throughout my life—was that I was strong and resilient; that I could do anything I set my mind to; that I could even overcome prejudice, malice, and stupidity with good works. But the other, more surprising message I received from watching this encounter between them and Mrs. Sullivan was that school was a place—perhaps the only place—where my parents seemed off-balance and reluctant; where their activist instincts didn't serve them well; where it was hard for them to figure out the best way to protect and advocate for their daughter. Many years later, when I was trying to figure out how to protect my own daughter from what I perceived to be a teacher's subtle abuse, I remember my mother telling me that I should not do anything that would make the teacher feel angry or afraid, for that was sure to endanger my daughter in her classroom. At that moment, my mind raced back thirty-five years to that afternoon with Mrs. Sullivan. "I still feel guilty for not having done more to protect you from her," whispered my mother as our memories converged and our minds raced back to 1952.

None of this earlier uncertainty and tentativeness was there several years later, when my father responded quickly and decisively to my eighth-grade history teacher's rendering of an American story about which he was expert and cared deeply. (My father was a professor of sociology whose scholarship included research and writing on the history of black activism in the South.) In my eighth-grade citizenship education class, Miss Rogers—her pale face caked with powder, her eyebrows drawn on with black pencil, wisps of white hair escaping from under her red wig—taught us that Abraham Lincoln led the country in the "War Between the States" and that the battle had nothing to do with slavery. Her eyes rested on me—the only Negro child in the class—daring me to challenge her interpretation of history.

That evening around the dinner table my parents made the correction. It was "the Civil War" and the institution of slavery was at its very center. I will never forget my father's rage at discovering the word *barbarian* used to describe the Mayans of Central America in my social studies book. He could not resist lecturing his children on the "extraordinary" Mayan civilization—its creativity, organization, and resilience—and then immediately sat down at his typewriter to bang out a restrained but angry letter to my teacher.

Watching this scene, repeated many times over throughout my schooling, I observed the sharp dissonance of values between my home and my school. My parents' home curriculum was purposeful and subversive, often oppositional to what our teachers were preaching. When the infractions were minor—merely a matter of interpretation or honest error—then my parents would quietly make the corrections at home. They picked their battles very carefully. But when our teachers said something that my parents considered blatantly misleading or hurtful to their children, especially when they considered the message to be harmful to all of the children in the class, they would speak up. Since I knew my parents well and knew the things they cared about—peace, justice, fairness, dignity—I would occasionally hide my teachers' ignorance and prejudice from them. As an adolescent I did not always welcome their challenge and their activism on my behalf. By junior high school, when I was determined to define my independence, the fire and fury I had hoped for from them in second grade felt intrusive.

By the time my brother, my sister, and I reached high school, my parents had started an annual tradition of inviting all of our teachers and their spouses to our house for a gala end-of-the-year dinner party. Since there were three of us, with about eight teachers apiece (including coaches and guidance counselors), these were huge events. My father would make his famous strawberry champagne punch, my mother would bake her delicious apple pies, and they would both collaborate on the sumptuous meal. Every year we kids would beg our parents not to give this party. We hated the idea of seeing our teachers in our own living room, smoking and drinking and carrying on. We thought our parents were being overly generous by allowing them to cross the threshold into the intimate space of our home. But my parents were insistent, and the party was always a big success. The teachers loved the treat and the recognition (my father would always stand and offer an elegant toast at the end of the evening), and they loved being fed. For me the actual event was always easier than the anticipation of it. My teachers always seemed more human and more playful than I ever experienced them to be in class.

Looking back on the various ways my parents negotiated these family-school boundaries, it is important to recognize how atypical they were. Unlike the great majority of parents, my folks were present at all of the school events, were familiar with each child's curriculum, and made an effort to get to know the teachers. They were vigilant in their watchfulness, fully engaged, and prepared to act. But they were highly unusual in these respects. (I am sure they felt the necessity to keep a special vigilance helping their "token" black children navigate in a white world that was often unfriendly.) In those days, most parents in our community never even appeared at school. They were not made to feel welcome, and were summoned to the school only when their children were flunking their subjects or behaving badly. Except for a perfunctory open house at the beginning of the year, the school did everything to seal its boundaries and keep parents out.

The three parent-teacher scenes imprinted in my childhood memory underscore the complexity and uncertainty, the anxiety and the vulnerability, that came with the territory, all of which I absorbed as a child and incorporated as an adult. I watched the ways in which my strong, courageous parents became uncertain and tentative as they tried to protect me from the teacher's biased vision, and I heard the guilt that followed when they felt that they had not done enough. I saw the ways in which they raised their voices with clarity and courage when they worried that their child and her classmates were being corrupted by false or prejudicial information. And I saw my parents respond to their children's teachers' hunger for appreciation and support by throwing a big party to celebrate their work.

When my own two children became school-aged and I found myself participating in parent-teacher encounters, I—like most parents—felt the imprint of my early experiences as a child. Sitting in the tiny kindergarten chair, facing my daughter's teacher, I was drawn back in time, immediately made to feel small, powerless, and infantilized. But because I had spent a good deal of my own childhood watching my parents cross the family-school boundaries, I would also hear the echoes of my parents' voices. I would feel the confusing mix of tentativeness, passivity, the urge to protect, and the guilt that followed when I had not effectively advocated for my child. At other times, I would feel compelled to speak out and confront the teacher who I thought was neglecting or injuring my child. I would risk severing the fragile relationship that I had established with the teacher—risk the backlash that might befall my child—in order to fight for what I thought was right or fair. At still other times, I would feel my parents' impulse to celebrate the teachers' work, to feed their hunger for recognition and reward, not by throwing parties as my parents did, but by plying them with letters and gifts of appreciation.

What is fascinating about my experience relating to my own children's teachers is that my own hard-earned wisdom as an educator and social scientist concerned about these matters did not prepare me for the depth of emotion and drama I felt in parent conferences. It did not prepare me for the subtle institutional barriers that made me feel strangely unwelcome in my children's school—as if I were trespassing on foreign ground—even when the stated policies promoted welcome and openness. It did not prepare me for the terror I experienced anticipating my meetings with teachers, the uncertainty and awkwardness that kept me off balance during the conference, and the inevitable inadequacy and guilt I felt afterward as I reflected on and rehearsed what I had heard and said. It did not prepare me for the way in which these tiny scenes of parent-teacher dialogue seemed to play out the larger social and cultural issues in our society.

It was not unusual for me to stew for days afterward about the parent-teacher conferences that I attended. Even meetings that were full of a teacher's praise and admiration for my child were always marred in some way by a gesture, inflection, or word that would linger as a worry in my mind. In the aftermath of these meetings, I would often take pen to paper and write a letter to the teacher, offering an additional perspective, correcting my faux pas, urging greater candor, or, occasionally, drawing a clearer boundary for a future meeting. These were labored letters. I chose my words very carefully and edited endlessly, trying to capture a tone that would not sever my connection with the teacher or make it worse for my child, as I tried to find the delicate balance between defending my child and supporting the teacher. Scores of these letters fill my files (some actually mailed, others never sent); the following is one typical example. It is a letter sent to my son Martin's second-grade teacher. It has the ghost of Mrs. Sullivan, my own second-grade teacher, written all over it.

11/12/93

Dear Richard,

I left our parent-teacher conference with a heavy heart, feeling somewhat overwhelmed by the discouraging tone we concluded on. It seemed to me that by the end of our meeting, the view of Martin David had been clouded by an emphasis on his vulnerabilities, his trouble with "timing" in class discussions, his difficulties fitting in to the social scene on the playground at recess (a scene we both admitted is often tough and unforgiving for any child). I am sure that all of these concerns are valid; they certainly struck me as authentic descriptions of Martin. But after several days of feeling haunted by the tone of our conference (particularly the second half, with its focus on the challenges), I have felt the need to write to you . . . as a mother wanting to redraw a fuller portrait of Martin.

First, I want to say that I feel deeply thankful for the thorough and perceptive picture you gave me of Martin in the second grade. Your insights are wonderful, even though they are laced with car metaphors (smile)! And I feel thankful for the time and care you devoted to our conference.

Second, I am *very* encouraged by what I see as wonderful progress that Martin has made since September: by his strong, capable reading; by his journal writing; by his increasingly developed small-motor skills; by his wonderful spelling tests; by his steady progress with Laurie in his math tutorial; by his bright, smiling self-portrait; and above all, by his unflagging diligence in his schoolwork.

Third, I am pleased by what I see as his increasing willingness to express his emotions, to tell how he is feeling, to reveal his well-developed humor, and to be comfortable enough in your classroom that smiles and laughter sometimes spill out.

All of these signs are good and heartening and reflect, I think, both Martin's determination and competence and your extraordinary devotion and skill as a teacher. Let us not lose sight of this wonderful momentum Martin David has shown even as we speak candidly and clearly about those issues that continue to deserve our concern and keen attention.

> Thanks for listening,
> Sara

Often feeling utterly alone as I faced the teacher in parent conferences and then lived with the aftermath of unfinished business that was sure to follow, I always suspected that other parents were experiencing some version of my anguish, but that they too were struggling alone and making it up as they went along. There were no rituals or arenas—inside or outside of schools—where parents could come together for mutual support, for information sharing, for strategizing, or for catharsis. As a matter of fact, the opposite seemed to be true. Parents tended to be secretive and furtive about their worries. They were reluctant to admit to the preoccupation and anguish that somehow seemed inappropriate, and hesitant to reveal any information that might reduce their child's competitive advantage. But it was not only parents who felt isolated and vulnerable. I could also tell that teachers had their own deep concerns, their own sense of exposure and vulnerability. And I knew that most of them had not been adequately prepared in their professional training programs to build relationships with families as a central part of their work, nor were they getting support or guidance from their administrators and colleagues. This was a tough scene for teachers as well.

Everyone believes that parents and teachers should be allies and

partners. After all, they are both engaged in the important and precious work of raising, guiding, and teaching our children. But more
often than not, parents and teachers feel estranged from and suspicious of each other. Their relationship tends to be competitive and
adversarial rather than collaborative and empathic. Their encounters
feel embattled rather than peaceful and productive. This relational
enmity—most vividly ritualized and dramatized in the parent-teacher
conference—reflects a territorial warfare, a clash of cultures between
the two primary arenas of acculturation in our society. This book will
explore the microcosm of parent-teacher conferences as a way of revealing and illuminating the macrocosm of institutional and cultural
forces that define family-school relationships and shape the socialization of our children.

To parents, their child is the most important person in their lives,
the one who arouses their deepest passions and greatest vulnerabilities, the one who inspires their fiercest advocacy and protection. And
it is teachers—society's professional adults—who are the primary
people with whom the parents must seek alliance and support in the
crucial work of child rearing. They must quickly learn to release their
child and trust that he or she will be well cared for by a perfect
stranger whose role as teacher gives her access to the most intimate
territory, the deepest emotional places. Their productive engagement
with the teacher is essential for the child's learning and growth, and
for the parents' peace of mind. All of these expectations and fears get
loaded on to encounters between parents and teachers.

I believe that for parents there is no more dreaded moment, no
arena where they feel more exposed than at the ritual conferences that
are typically scheduled twice a year—once in the fall and once in the
spring—in schools. Although it may not be quite as emotionally
loaded for teachers, it is also the arena in which they feel most uncertain, exposed, and defensive, and the place where they feel their competence and their professionalism most directly challenged. Beneath
the polite surface of parent-teacher conferences, then, burns a caul-
dron of fiery feelings made particularly difficult because everyone
carefully masks them and they seem inappropriate for the occasion.

This book will focus specifically on the parent-teacher conference,

the ritual encounter in which the dynamics of this complex relationship get vividly, and dramatically, played out. In this ritual, so friendly
and benign in its apparent goals, parents and teachers are racked with
high anxiety. In this scene marked by decorum, politeness, and symbolism, they exhibit gestures of wariness and defensiveness. In this
dialogue where the conversation appears to be focused on the child,
adults often play out their own childhood histories, their own insecurities, and their own primal fears. In this encounter where the content
seems to be defined by individual stories, there is embedded a broader
cultural narrative.

Parent-teacher conferences, then, are crucial events because there is
so much at stake for the children who cross family-school borders, because they arouse so much anxiety and passion for the adults, and
because they are the small stage on which our broader cultural priorities and values get played out. In each of these ways, this tiny,
twice-yearly ritual takes on a huge significance that can be overwhelming for the participants. But the importance of parent-teacher
encounters does not rest solely on these qualitative measures of passion and purpose. The sheer numbers attest to our need—as parents
and as educators—to find ways of making them as productive and as
meaningful as possible. And these numbers are staggering. In the
United States, there are between 4 million and 4.4 million teachers
teaching approximately 52 million students in grades from prekinder-
garten through high school. (To give you a sense of the scale and magnitude of these numbers, compare the population of teachers to two
other professions—medicine and law—that offer their services to
families and in which good client relationships are crucial to successful work. Approximately 598,000 physicians practice in the United
States today, 200,000 of whom are in primary care as internists, pe-
diatricians, and family practitioners. Of the 681,000 lawyers in this
country, about three-quarters [roughly 510,750] regularly interact
with clients through work in law firms or private practice.) If each of
the approximately 4 million teachers has a minimum of two opportunities (once in the fall and once in the spring) to interact with students' parents, guardians, or other family members in parent-teacher

conferences, then there is the potential for parents and teachers to be engaged in more than 100 million conferences each school year.

Even though we estimate that the numbers are huge, it is of course impossible to know the exact number of parent-teacher conferences occurring each year. We know that some parents never cross the threshold of the school and that others do so reluctantly and rarely. But the absence of those families is counterbalanced by the large numbers of parents—particularly those of children in the early grades—who attend many more than two meetings per year. Their eager, frequent, and sometimes intrusive encounters with teachers are both formal and informal, scheduled and impromptu. For all of these powerful qualitative reasons, and based on the magnitude of these quantitative measures, it is fair to speak of the dialogue between parents and teachers as "the essential conversation."

I have long had a fascination with the theater of this essential conversation; with its substance and its symbolism; with its text and subtext; with its personal and public meanings. As a matter of fact, my first book, *Worlds Apart* (1978), explored the broad landscape of family-school relationships surrounding and shaping the parent-teacher dialogue. In its attempt to chart the historical and institutional intersections between these two primary institutions of socialization, my work was pioneering. It broke new ground. Up until that point, social scientists had looked at acculturation in families and education in schools as if these were separable, dichotomous domains in the life of a child. But I argued that families and schools are overlapping spheres of socialization, and that the successful learning and development of children depends, in part, on building productive boundaries between and bridges across them.

In the last quarter century, social scientists have become increasingly interested in documenting the complex interactions between schools and the communities they serve. Their work has ranged from conceptual and empirical to practical, from developing theoretical models to offering strategic advice. For example, there has been a great deal of conceptual interest in exploring the broad ecology of education, mapping the several institutions that socialize children, and charting the ways in which youngsters negotiate these realms. Within this broader inquiry has been a particular interest in studying the impact of family-school dissonance on children's development and achievement, finding out what happens to students who have to make the large shifts in their language, values, and behavior when they move from their homes to their classrooms. And almost every study of school achievement has included at least a rhetorical bow to the importance of positive relationships between families and schools, even though there has been little suggestion of how these alliances might be supported and sustained.

Researchers and clinicians have also weighed in with practical advice. A large number of manuals and handbooks—primarily written for teachers—offer specific guidance about effective ways of communicating with parents, giving step-by-step prescriptions for building a comfortable alliance. But even with the increasing attention given by social scientists to negotiating the borders between families and schools, no one has focused deeply and specifically on the parent-teacher conference as microcosm or metaphor for a broader cultural narrative, as the crucible where family-school dynamics are most vividly and personally played out, and as the place where institutional relationships work or fail.

Now, after a twenty-five-year hiatus, I am interested in returning to this fertile ground for three reasons. First, I believe that the educational landscape has changed substantially, creating a different set of conditions that have powerfully reshaped and complicated the encounters between families and schools. The major changes in family structure, the rise in the number of women employed outside the home, the rapid increase in the influx of immigrant groups into our cities and schools, the widening gap between the rich and the poor, the shifts in the power and preoccupations of teachers' unions, and the velocity of technological changes and increased access to cyberspace, to name a few factors, have all had an influence on redefining the roles of and relationships between families and schools. This book, then, will reflect many of these major societal shifts in the ecology of education, as well as in the experiences of parents and teachers as they adapt to these new realities.

Second, I want to shift my focus and purview from the broader structural and cultural intersections to the more intimate, personal encounters between parents and teachers. This new lens allows us to see the complexities and subtleties of the family-school drama from the protagonists' point of view; to hear the voices and views of parents and teachers, whose actions are shaped not only by the institutions they represent but also by their own histories, experiences, and temperaments. *The Essential Conversation* tells an interior story that seeks to capture the interpersonal and intrapersonal dynamics between parents and teachers, searches below the polite surface of adult encounters to document the often rancorous and treacherous underbelly of real feelings, and examines what gets both revealed and masked in the highly ritualized meetings between parents and teachers.

Third, as my autobiographical reflections suggest, this book is a timely and passionate self-exploration. This is an opportunity to bring to my analysis of families and schools a different perspective, one that takes full advantage of my being a parent yet does not deny the subjective filter that invariably blurs and illuminates my view. Before I became a mother, my inquiry into the overlapping worlds of familes and schools reflected the dispassion and skepticism of a social scientist somewhat removed from the fray. To the degree that my voice was revealed in the analysis, it was a voice of balance and reason, distance and discernment. But my experience as the mother of two, who are now in their late adolescence and early adulthood, has caused a dramatic change in my perspective, in what I see and hear, in the volume and urgency in my voice, in my sense of how we must join analysis with action, interpretation with intervention. Advocating for my own children and relating to their teachers has given me new insights into how hot and passionate these interactions are, how loaded with desire, ambition, and fear, and how shaped by the idiosyncratic nature of the individual child and the particular chemistry of the adult personalities. These poignant and powerful firsthand experiences have colored and enriched my view of family-school encounters and offered me a more intimate and empathic angle of vision.

For two years I traveled around the country talking to teachers and parents in city, suburban, and rural schools; in preschools, elementary schools, and high schools; and in public, private, and parochial schools. I wanted to capture as much variety as possible in the ways that parents and teachers come together. I wanted to see the similarities and differences in the meetings' structure and tone, to process and document the influence of such factors as the child's developmental stage, geography, demography, school funding (public or private), and institutional values (secular or sacred).

Although I spoke to dozens of teachers and parents in a broad variety of settings, the narratives that thread through this book focus on the experiences and perspectives of ten teachers—all female—I chose to talk to in depth, and some of the parents of the children in their classes. I chose to tell the stories of women teachers because the vast majority of teachers are women; it continues to be a female-dominated profession. And it is women—female teachers and mothers—who are primarily responsible for navigating the boundaries and developing the family-school relationships. I also chose to record the views and values of women teachers because both mothers and teachers (both male and female) experience a similar cultural disregard. In a society that claims to care deeply about children, where every other politician and public figure claims that education is the most important social agenda, the people whose primary responsibility it is to raise and teach the young tend to be disrespected and devalued. The dissonance between the public rhetoric that refers to "children as our most precious resource" and the reality, as reflected in how little we value those who nourish them, is deafening. How teachers and parents interpret and absorb these negative cultural views becomes a part of how they relate to one another.

I also chose to focus on teachers who are considered gifted practitioners, who are regarded as skilled, empathic, and caring in their dealings with parents. Their principals, colleagues, and parents identified them as unusual in the ways they reached out to and communicated with families; developed strategies and practices that honored parental knowledge and wisdom; and turned the largely symbolic parent-teacher conversations into meaningful, expressive exchanges. To say that the teachers who inhabit this book were good at sustaining relationships with parents that benefited their students is not to say their work was perfect or unblemished in this regard. As a matter of fact, all of them considered productive family-school encounters as central to their work but complex and difficult to navigate. Even though they enjoyed their interactions with parents and considered them crucial to their work with students, all of them regarded negotiating these relationships as the most treacherous part of their jobs. Each had one or two horror stories that still made her shudder with terror or humiliation.

I felt that it was important to describe the good but imperfect work of these teachers, because I think we—parents and teachers—can learn a lot more from examining examples of "goodness" than we can from dissecting weakness and pathology. We can also appreciate how incredibly complex and dynamic this work is by looking at people whose craft is well developed and whose self-reflective capacities are well honed. I also know from years of experience as a researcher that those people who feel relatively self-confident, both personally and professionally, are likely to be more tolerant, even welcoming, of my presence and the intrusiveness of my inquiry. And they are more likely to be undefensive and revelatory about those aspects of their work that might be regarded as problematic, weak, or underdeveloped. Their recognition of the imperfections of their efforts, and their commitment to improving their craft, are themselves sources of inspiration.

Not only was I able to interview parents and teachers—most of whom were also mothers and so could see the relationship from both sides—I also had the rare opportunity of sitting in on several parent-teacher conferences. I was able to watch the dynamics—both verbal and nonverbal—in a context of great intimacy and observe the subtle gestures that often reveal deep and surprising emotions. In fact, some of the most provocative insights came from listening for the dissonance between people's professed values and motivations and their actual behaviors and interactions, or from asking teachers and parents to offer their respective interpretations of particularly poignant moments in the dialogue.

Throughout my conversations with parents and teachers, the

gravity of my questions was usually an expression of my own personal experience and intellectual preoccupations, echoing many of
the ancient themes that captured my curiosity when I witnessed the
adult dance at the family-school border as a child. I pushed for depth
and detail, because I was interested in exploring the layers of thinking
and feeling, making the subconscious motivations conscious, tracing
the points of convergence and divergence between the text and the
subtext of the talk. And I wanted to move the dialogue that I had with
parents and teachers from the abstract to the specific, from the conceptual to the concrete. I was always searching for the particular story
that might reveal general patterns of motivation, insight, and behavior. I believe in the essential paradox of narrative work, recognizing
that the closer I was able to get to the specific nuances and detail of a
person's experience, the more we would be able to read it as a collective story.

Second, I was intrigued by the interplay between past and present;
interested in exploring the ways in which history—both individual
and institutional, psychic and cultural—gets imprinted on people's
values, views, and interactions; interested in examining the intergenerational connections. I listened carefully for the ways in which early
childhood narratives get recast and replayed in adults' advocacy for
their own children. I was less interested in identifying and naming
the objective facts of people's life experiences than in how these
experiences were remembered, reinterpreted, and rehearsed over
time. I wanted to know which ones survived as symbols, signs, and
metaphors for understanding contemporary action.

Third, I was fascinated by the ways in which the dialogue between
parents and teachers is shaped by larger cultural and historical forces.
I looked for the ways in which, for example, our culture's perspectives
on childhood influence the tenor and scope of the conversation between those adults primarily responsible for child-rearing; or the ways
in which the broader themes of race, class, culture, and gender get negotiated. I wanted to examine how the tiny drama of parent-teacher
conferences is an expression of a larger cultural narrative.

Fourth, I was interested in both the practices and paradigms of parent-teacher encounters. That is, I wanted to learn as much as I could about the particular strategies, tools, and techniques that teachers use in working effectively with parents, and about the specific proposals and plans of action that might be instituted immediately in schools and classrooms. But I was equally engaged by trying to decipher the larger frameworks and philosophies—reflecting deep-seated values and beliefs—that shape daily practices.

Finally, I was eager to understand how parents and teachers negotiate the treacherous and tender terrain—physical, psychological, intellectual, and metaphoric—between them, a terrain that is typically uncharted, where the roles are often complex and overlapping. I was intrigued by how teachers and parents navigate these gray areas, cope w th conflict and ambiguity, and manage the ambivalence—all of which challenge productive communication.

These interests in exploring the subterranean dimensions of dialogue, seeing the general in the particular, charting the intergenerational connections, documenting the philosophies and the pragmatics of productive family-school encounters, and examining the ways in which parents and teachers navigate the complex and ambiguous terrain that stretches between them brought focus to my interviews and illumination to my observations; they presaged the ways in which I hope readers will be engaged by this work.

It is my hope that this book will be a companion, a resource, and a source of inspiration, support, and challenge to readers, to parents and teachers, and to all who are interested in the fate of our children and the future of our society. I want readers to feel deeply identified with and inspired by the compassionate work of committed teachers and the passionate advocacy of parents. I want them to feel a resonance with their voices and views and to see the ways in which their insights might be incorporated and used judiciously and wisely. Although I do not believe that there is a single recipe or a set of discrete rules for constructing successful parent-teacher dialogues—one size does not fit all—I do believe that there are lessons here that delineate sound principles and good practices; that are applicable to a variety of settings and situations. Neither discrete nor prescriptive, these reflections and narratives are dynamic, complex, and contextual. They are parables of wisdom, combining common sense and good judgment, rich experience and discerning criticism, scholarly learning and reflective practice. The parables frame the essential conversation and offer explanation, insight, guidance, and a call to action.

THE ESSENTIAL CONVERSATION

CHAPTER 1

Ghosts in the Classroom

The Doorknob Phenomenon

The parent-teacher conference is over; the father rises to leave and heads for the door. He touches the doorknob, then turns back abruptly with one final thought that he delivers passionately. "And another thing," he blurts out, referring to a topic that was covered earlier in the meeting. "That same thing happened to me in fifth grade, and I swear it is not going to happen to my child!" His tone is threatening; his teeth are bared. His anguished outburst surprises even him. His passion explodes in defense of his child and in self-defense of the child he was.

Generational Echoes

EVERY TIME PARENTS and teachers encounter one another in the classroom, their conversations are shaped by their own autobiographical stories and by the broader cultural and historical narratives that inform their identities, their values, and their sense of place in the world. These autobiographical stories—often-unconscious replays of childhood experiences in families and in school—are powerful forces in defining the quality and trajectory of parent-teacher dialogues. There is something immediate, reflexive, and regressive, for both parents and teachers, about their encounters with one another, a turning inward and backward, a sense of primal urgency. The parents come to the meeting, sit facing the teacher in the chairs that their children inhabit each day, and begin to feel the same way they felt when they were students—small and powerless. And when the teachers offer observations and evaluations of their students, they are often using values and frameworks carved out of their own early childhood experiences. The adults come together prepared to focus on the present and the future of the child, but instead they feel themselves drawn back into their own pasts, visited by the ghosts of their parents, grandparents, siblings, and former teachers, haunted by ancient childhood dramas. These visitations and echoes reverberate through the room, complicating the conversation and filling the space with the voices of people who are not there, people who are often long gone. The "doorknob phenomenon," a typical but surprising aftershock of the visitation of ghosts during the conference, is evidence that parent-teacher dialogues are imprinted with ancient, psychological themes; that conversations between them reverberate with intergenerational voices; and that part of the power of these ghostly appearances is that they are usually hidden from consciousness.

For a long time, of course, the psychological literature has emphasized the power of early childhood experiences—primarily formed within the intimacy and potency of parent-child relationships—to the shaping of adult temperament and personality. It has also underscored the ways in which these primal relationships get replayed and reconfigured in the next generation. For example, in a famous essay by psychoanalyst Selma Fraiberg, she speaks about the unwelcome and unconscious presence of these ghosts hovering in the nursery, establishing residence at the baby's side, casting a spell on the way the parents relate to the child. She says, "These are ghosts in the nursery . . . visitors from the unremembered pasts of the parents, the uninvited guests at the christening." Although the ghosts to whom Fraiberg refers are imaginary, they are real in the emotional lives of parents. The images and stories of ancestral figures in the parents' families make a claim on their unique view of their child and on their hopes and dreams for who he/she is and will become.

In this chapter we see that these ancestral figures make their appearance in school as well. They are particularly intrusive when parents and teachers come together, each with their own autobiographical scripts. Just like the father whose parting shot echoed with an ancient pain, teachers also surprise themselves by beginning almost every conversation about their relationship to parents with emotion-packed reflections on their own childhood experiences. They speak about how their work with students and parents offers them the chance to undo early traumas in their lives or replay and enhance good memories that made them strong. They discover that their relationships with individual students—their overidentification with one, their unfettered admiration of another, or their feelings of revulsion with another—are often the result of seeing their own childhoods mirrored in their students.

These generational echoes are double-edged for both parents and teachers. They are a source of both guidance and distraction, insight and bias. They sometimes lead to important breakthroughs and discoveries in the conversation, and at other times force an abrupt breakdown and impasse. But for the most part, these meta-messages remain hidden, inaudible, unarticulated. They are the raw, unvarnished subtext to the ritualized, polite, public text of the conversation. They are the unconscious, diffuse backdrop to the precise words that fill the foreground dialogue.

What is fascinating about these generational echoes is how deep and penetrating they are and yet how easily they are uncovered. They are both subterranean and open to revelation. Given a safe place to talk about their lives and their work and an attentive, respectful listener who is genuinely curious about their experiences, people discover, often for the first time, the early roots of their current preoccupations and actions. When these long-ago tales are uncovered, their power and influence are indisputable.

Every one of the teachers I interviewed, for example, finds it necessary to begin with her life story, her perspective as a young child. For some teachers their autobiographical references capture only fragments of a story, metaphors or images that reverberate with broad and deep meaning: a father's frown of disapproval, a competitive sibling's fierce determination to earn better grades, a humiliating moment forgetting the practiced prose of a valedictory speech, a teacher's insinuating insult. For others the narratives are detailed and sequential, embedded in context and rich with emotional texture. Interestingly, most of the teachers' references to their childhood stories refer to traumatic, painful experiences rather than memories of triumph, and these have a huge impact on how they work with their students and build relationships with parents.

It is important to recognize that teachers' reflections on their life stories as touchstones for their work with students and families flies in the face of much of the scholarly literature on teachers. That literature describes them as—assumes them to be—neutral, unemotional, and static adults with no interior life, no phantoms from the past, no ambivalence, and no fears. Philosopher Maxine Greene challenges this pervasive view of teachers as bound up in their professional, rationalistic, and objective straitjackets and urges us to recognize the power of their "personal biographies." This narrow conception of teachers, says Greene, is not only a distortion of the complex, layered lives of teachers both within and outside the classroom, it also limits the repertoire of ways in which they might successfully relate to children and their families, and the range of human qualities and emotions in them that might support communication and rapport with parents.

The teacher is frequently addressed as if he had no life of his own, no body, and no inwardness. Lecturers seem to presuppose a "man within a man" when they describe a good teacher as infinitely controlled and accommodating, technically efficient, impervious to moods. They are likely to define him by the role he is expected to play in the classroom, with all of the loose ends gathered up and all his doubts resolved. The numerous realities in which he exists as a living person are overlooked. His personal biography is overlooked, so are the many ways in which he expresses his private self in language, the horizons he perceives, the perspectives through which he looks on the world.

(Greene, 1973)

Greene's statement seems to suggest a connection between an appreciation for teachers' personal biographies and their ability to fully engage the doorknob phenomenon that they see in parents. If teachers are to learn to respond to the ghosts that parents bring to the classroom, they too have to learn to recognize the autobiographical and ancestral roots that run through their own school lives.

Teachers are not only likely to be influenced by the narrow construction of their professional role that is conveyed in the literature, they are also likely to receive little if any preparation in their educational training for working with parents. None of the teachers that I spoke to, for example, mentions learning anything about working with families during their teacher training programs. Nor do they point to any lessons or guidance that they might have received as beginning teachers working in schools. Whether they were trained in the teacher training "factories" of large state universities or earned their certificates in elite liberal arts colleges, whether they were enrolled in programs that were considered "conservative and traditional" or "humanistic and progressive" in their orientation, teachers all decry their lack of preparation in the arena of family-school relationships. They speak about this lack of preparation in three ways.

First, they claim that their education did not offer a *conceptual* framework for envisioning the crucial role of families in the successful schooling of children. They were never made aware of what social historian Lawrence Cremin calls the "ecology of education," the broad map of the several institutions that educate children and their relationships to one another. Such awareness, they feel, would have given them a valuable perspective on the place and relative importance of school in the child's life, and made them more cognizant of the spheres that children and their families have to navigate each day. Second, teachers describe training in which there was no central *value* put on the crucial importance and complexity of building productive parent-teacher relationships. Yes, there was always facile rhetoric about teachers needing to create alliances with the significant adults in their students' lives, but never a realization of the enormous opportunities and casualties that such an effort would entail. Third, teachers claim that their training never gave them tools and techniques, the practical guidance that is helpful in communicating and working with parents. Lacking the conceptual framework, the valuing of parental perspectives, and the practical tools for productively engaging them, teachers feel ill prepared to face what many consider the "most vulnerable" part of their work—building relationships with parents.

One teacher did her graduate training at Bank Street College in New York, a place widely regarded as "progressive," that believes in educating the whole child (mind, body, psyche, and spirit), and that regards parents as "primary educators." She speaks of the contrasts between the college's espoused philosophical stance and what she actually learned there. She does not dismiss the importance of being exposed to the rhetoric, but she does admit its practical limitations. "Perhaps," she muses, "the dialogues at Bank Street gave me a kind of facility with the language and some developmental theories to hang the language on, but I certainly did not discover any new insights or useful strategies for working with parents." Rather, she believes that her informal training started very early; that even as a young child she was carefully observing the adult encounters at the family-school borders. "I feel as if it has been a lifetime of watching . . . I learned through watching the way my mom and my dad dealt with people and relationships in their world," she says, "but I was largely self-taught, leading with my intuition, imagination, and developing ideas. . . . What I experienced in school as a child definitely had the biggest influence."

But it is not only that teachers feel unprepared by their college programs, it is also that once they arrive in their first jobs as teachers, they get little mentoring, guidance, or support. Once again, this seems to be true whether teachers are working in rural or urban schools, public, parochial, or independent schools, rich or poor schools. Even when school administrators are responsible and rigorous in supervising and supporting new teachers, their focus tends to be almost exclusively on pedagogy—on developing and delivering the curriculum, on nurturing relationships with students—not on helping teachers navigate relationships with families. Without training or institutional support in working with parents, teachers develop their own styles and rituals and define their own goals and content, and these are largely guided by the rituals and echoes from their childhoods.

The Central Contradiction

ANDREA BROWN, THE founder and head teacher of a tiny Montessori school in Beach Head on the North Shore, is unusual in her awareness and purposeful use of her early childhood experiences as a way of seeing and interpreting her work with children and their families. In her school, which serves twelve to fifteen children (in two shifts) from three to six years of age, the classrooms and playground are connected to her house, although the boundary between home and school are made clear by the teachers. The classroom has the clarity, structure, and rituals of most Montessori settings I have visited, but it also seems to have Andrea's aesthetic and philosophical imprint. It is filled with children's art (finger paintings, drawings, wooden structures, mobiles, photographs), environmental treasures from adventures and hikes to the ocean and through the woods (shells, birds' nests, rocks, soil samples, pressed leaves), and posters related to Andrea's political interests in peace and justice. It is a child-centered environment filled with evidence of children's creativity, imagination, and perspective.

As soon as I describe to her my work on this book and the topics that I hope we will address in our conversations, Andrea journeys back in time to her early childhood. Her retrospective impulse is immediate, and her story combines a focus on the "primal and passionate" relationship she had with her parents, the "nourishing embrace" of her large and loving extended family, and the broader cultural and historical narrative of a young black girl growing up in a small segregated town in western Pennsylvania. At the center of her story is the idea of a child learning to cope with the pain and promise of "central contradictions," and of a mature and experienced teacher using those early lessons to frame and inform her work with children and their families. Many of the values and perspectives that Andrea carries into her teaching are efforts to redress and undo the haunts and anguish of her childhood. For all the things that adults did—wittingly or unwittingly—to cause her pain as a child, to undermine her self-esteem, she works to do the opposite with her students, and in so doing—as she would put it—"to heal herself." Andrea's voice weaves together past and present, the personal and the political, love and loneliness, and rage and forgiveness.

"I'll start with growing up," Andrea says definitively. "I was born into a family that was matrilineal . . . a family where my paternal grandmother was in charge. I was the beloved first grandchild of the firstborn son, and we lived in an extended family, grandparents, aunts, uncles, and cousins." Her face glows with the memory of the "love bounty." "The message I got from all of these people who surrounded me was that I was special. . . . Aunts held me close and uncles played with me." But more than the pleasure of being so beloved was the fact that their love did not have to be earned. "I didn't have to do anything to be special," she recalls appreciatively. There is something about the way she begins this story—the deep pleasure in her voice, the rich resonance of generously expressed love—that makes me feel as if there is a dark underside to these sunny memories. I am not surprised when Andrea's face suddenly shows pain and she says softly, "But my mother was cautious, tentative." Her mother's reticence was something she always "felt" as a child even if she didn't quite "know it." It is this central and primal "contradiction" that shaped Andrea's growing-up years, and, she admits, it has been "my baggage that I've carried through my life. . . . On the one hand, I always felt special, beloved . . . on the other hand, I was not quite good enough."

Andrea tells me this story not only because it is the central contradiction that has shaped her self-definition and echoed through her life, but also because she feels it has been imprinted on her work as a teacher. "My professional life has been driven by this contradiction," she says with surprise, for the first time discovering the links between these facts of her childhood and the ways in which she defines her relationships to the children in her classroom and their families. But before she is ready to speak about her professional life, she seems to want to examine the origins of her mother's tentativeness; she wants to look directly into the center of this ancient disappointment. Her insights are a mixture of tough candor and forgiveness, insights gained through "years of therapy and personal work." "I now understand my mother's response to me as being the result of the institutions that shaped her, rather than being about me or her response to me," she says. Actually, Andrea's understanding of the "institutional" forces that shaped her mother's identity and reality came less from her therapeutic work than from a growing political awareness. "I didn't really get it until I got consciously political. . . . You must see all of this in the context of racism."

Andrea's mother was half-white ("She looked white and identified as black") and greatly preoccupied with issues of status related to skin color. She used to always say to her brown-skinned daughter, "Don't drink coffee, it will make you black," an admonition that Andrea remembered "on some kind of muscular level." Andrea's father, on the other hand, was a "very black" man, and his daughter admired him in every way. There was no caution or ambivalence in their love for each other. "I always felt loved by him," says Andrea gratefully. "He was a Buddha man, a good man, a man of his time. He made the most of his life . . . climbed over whatever got in his way. . . . He thought of every moment as sacred, blessed. . . . He was not in the least bit bitter." Although Andrea inherited much of her father's goodness and generosity, she recognizes that some of the bitterness that he refused found its way into her psyche. "For some of my life, I have carried the bitterness, and my mother's unavailability and depression—the rage that shut her down—got mixed in with it." Luckily, Andrea's father's optimism and unfettered love usually won out and offered lessons in hope and endurance. Recalls Andrea, "I emulated him, modeled my life after him, and he was always encouraging to me. When I would come home from school angry at something that happened, or complaining about people being mean and unfair, he would say, 'Andy (he always called me Andy), it's not that they're bad people . . . they just don't know any better.' "

Andrea's life has taken her far from where she grew up. She tries to give me a picture of the remoteness and loneliness of her childhood. "I grew up in a little, rural, bigoted town in western Pennsylvania." Up until she was five years old, her extended family lived in "company housing," a kind of communal living for the folks who were employed by the steel company that dominated the town. In fact, even though this was rural Pennsylvania, there was a very international and interracial flavor in the communal living, with black folks migrating from the South and other workers coming in from abroad. But around Andrea's fifth birthday, her parents decided to move up and out of the company housing into a fancier place on the hill. The move from the warm embrace of her grandmother's home, from the open arms of the community, was traumatic for Andrea. More than fifty years later, she does not mask her pain at being ripped from her beloved first home. "This was a huge loss. I think I never recovered. Since that time, in one way or the other, I have been trying to reestablish that early sense of community. . . . I have been trying to find that original home." Her eyes fill with tears and her voice is heavy. Like the "contradiction" between her extended family's bountiful love and her mother's caution, this feeling of being ripped away from her extended family seems to have left an indelible imprint that has shaped her life's journey and choices.

In leaving the company housing, in moving from being in the midst of her extended family to nuclear family life, Andrea faced what she calls another important contradiction. Their new neighborhood was up on the hill, a rise in geography and status. And in this middle-class Negro community, Andrea's family was the most prominent, "the haute cuisine." Her father, who was a businessman employed by the Negro Supreme Life Insurance Company, was considered a leader in the community and was senior warden of the Baptist Church. "We were put up on a pedestal," recalls Andrea. "Our family was considered aristocratic by our neighbors." Now her shoulders slump forward and she lets out a heavy sigh. "Again the contradiction . . . on the one hand, we were at the top. . . . On the other hand, I was expected to rise above it all, become better than everybody else. There were these great expectations. I was not allowed to be a part of the culture." Her voice rises in a crescendo of exasperation.

This "being at the top" and needing to be better than everyone else left Andrea feeling lonely and isolated. "I had no black friends and no white friends. In fact, I was either too black to white folks or too white to black folks, unacceptable all around. This was very schizophrenic-making. I responded by developing a great fantasy life." She wanted urgently to leave, to escape the alienation and the isolation. Even now, she feels that she has invented a life on the North Shore that has some of these schizophrenic ingredients. This lovely "token" black woman who lives in the all-white town of Beach Head seems, to some extent, to have reproduced the conditions of her life on the hill in rural Pennsylvania. "I still don't belong," she laments. "I have had to invent and create my own community, not race- or class-based."

Andrea was a very successful student who made good grades and earned an excellent academic record. But even being a top student did not protect her from feeling isolated and unappreciated. She was often horrified by the thoughtless and ignorant things her teachers would say in class, and she could not resist speaking up to them. "I challenged my teachers, and then I refused to bend to their will." But more troubling than the conflicts with her teachers over their differences in point of view was the feeling that her blackness never allowed them to see her as really smart and never allowed her the pleasure of being fully rewarded for her academic efforts.

One story in particular still causes her pain. At the end of the school year, the principal held an awards ceremony in the high school auditorium. One of the awards was to be given to the student who had earned the highest grade-point average. Any way you might calculate the averages, Andrea should have received the award. She was devastated—but not completely surprised—when she heard another name being called and saw one of her blond, blue-eyed classmates go up to the stage to receive her recognition. Even though everything in her wanted to scream with rage at the injustice of it all, Andrea was stoic and kept her cool. The only thing worse than being robbed of her prize would have been to break down crying in front of the robbers. But as I listen to Andrea tell this tale, her eyes do fill with tears. "I didn't cry then," she says, weeping. "I was very proud. I had a strong back." But later on that day, her favorite teacher, Mrs. Jones, a Latin teacher who had become her mentor, stopped her in the hall and whispered to her words that Andrea will never forget. Mrs. Jones said, "We all know who really deserved that award today." Hearing Mrs. Jones's words—and replaying them over and over to herself— allowed Andrea to survive the rest of high school. "It was great affirmation for me," she recalls. "But when I graduated, I never looked back. . . . My father never understood my rage or my extreme need to leave."

Andrea's work with children and their parents seems to echo with some of the "contradictions" that she experienced as a child. She does not want the children in her classroom to ever feel that she is being cautious or withholding like her mother was. Nor does she want them to feel as if they have to earn her love or do something special to deserve it. Likewise, she does not want the children ever to feel isolated and alienated from the classroom community, like she felt on the hill in small-town Pennsylvania, attending school with teachers who refused to see how smart she was. So when I ask her what she hopes to communicate to parents who enroll their children in her Montessori school, she says immediately, "My message to my parents is that we are custodians of the most precious person . . . and I am thanking them for trusting me enough to give their children over to my care. I am always modeling my appreciation for that." Her words to parents are genuine and deeply felt, and she knows that they come from a long-ago place. "This is second nature to me. This is not strategy. I say these things to parents because of my great need as a child. This perspective, these values, are a given in my life as a teacher."

Andrea paints a large, longitudinal tableau, a colorful, passionate narrative about the deep connections between her childhood imprints, the values and strategies that define her work with students, and the relationships that she forges with their parents. Her brushstrokes are broad and expansive as she draws a picture of her family (both nuclear and extended), her schooling, and her neighborhood, and then traces their impact on her development as an adult and teacher.

A Sanctified Space

ELIZABETH MORGAN IS an experienced educator, a day-care-center director, a kindergarten and first-grade teacher, a principal of an independent school, and a national consultant to schools. She too refers to the ways in which her childhood experiences color her work with students and their parents. She, however, does not tell Andrea's expansive story, but instead offers a much more contained, subtle narrative, a specific lesson that was deeply etched in third grade and that has served as a guide for her ever since. It is a story of young Elizabeth feeling betrayed by a teacher who told her secret—one that she assumed was just between the two of them—to her parents. It is a story of her determination as a teacher never to betray her students in the same way. Whenever she is deciding when and where to draw the boundary lines with parents, whenever she is trying to determine what should be private or public knowledge, she refers to this "major event" in Mrs. Lake's third grade that helped to shape the way she communicates with the parents of her students.

As Elizabeth tells the story, her face takes on the look of Elizabeth the young child, innocent and distressed. "One day I had a major attack of the blues," she begins, "and Mrs. Lake was so concerned about me. She became very attentive and tried several times throughout the day to figure out what was wrong and to comfort me." Elizabeth remembers feeling the unnamed, unfocused sadness, but she also recalls the pleasure of her teacher's tender attention. "I discovered—not intellectually—that I could draw her into my space by being blue, that I could get all this wonderful comfort and attention. . . . But I wasn't really feeling *that* bad, and I really believed that this was something between Mrs. Lake and me. That is where it would end." That evening, however, Mrs. Lake called Elizabeth's parents to let them know that their daughter had had a very hard day and that she seemed strangely depressed. "I felt utterly betrayed," says Elizabeth, her voice still ringing with the surprise and outrage she felt at seven years old. "School was my space, and this was my private conversation with my teacher. My parents should not have been brought into it."

Elizabeth tells the story to underscore the importance of the "child's space" and "the complexity of the borders" in family-school encounters. "My experience in third grade became part of the fabric of how I dealt as a teacher with parents." She follows with another story about the privacy and sanctity of the child's place and view, but this time from an adult teacher's perspective. In her third year of teaching six-year-olds at Elmwood School, Elizabeth was pregnant with her first child. As her belly grew rounder, gestation and birth became the focus of a lot of classroom interest and conversation, a natural part of the curriculum. It just so happens that in this class of eighteen children, there were nine who were adopted or who had siblings who were adopted. One morning, during the ritualistic circle time, one of the kids announced, "You know, I was adopted." His pronouncement was followed by a chorus of other children who had stories to tell about their adoptions or those of family members. It was a spirited conversation, full of excitement and affirmation. After a while, Amy's soft, tentative voice cut through the din of exclamations, and Elizabeth asked everyone to be quiet so that they could hear what she had to say. "I was adopted," said Amy almost whispering, "but my parents don't know it yet."

At the beginning of the school year, in fact, Elizabeth had been told by Amy's parents that she was adopted and that they had not yet told her because the psychiatrist whom the family had been seeing had recommended that they not tell her until she was seven. And based on the therapist's recommendation, the parents had requested that Elizabeth not divulge the secret to their six-year-old daughter. But here was Amy announcing the secret to her classmates and living with the belief that she had to protect her parents from knowing it. Elizabeth felt torn. On the one hand, she wanted to honor the parents' wish that she not talk about it. On the other, Amy already knew and was living with the burden of keeping a secret from her parents and maybe even feeling that she had to hide the "bad truth" about being an adopted child. In addition, Elizabeth was hearing the echoes of her third-grade "betrayal," and she did not want to tell the parents something that Amy never intended for them to hear. "I always thought of meeting time in my classroom as a sanctified space," says Elizabeth with great seriousness. "I thought that Amy's parents should hear this, but I wasn't going to tell them without consulting Amy."

So Elizabeth talked to Amy and told her that she thought "it was not a good idea to keep such a big secret from her parents." Amy actually seemed "greatly relieved" when her teacher asked whether she could call and tell them. That evening, when Elizabeth called, Amy's mother answered the phone. When she heard Elizabeth mention "the topic of adoption," she asked her to wait a moment, as she took the phone into the bathroom, out of earshot of her child. She was stunned that Amy knew of her adoption, embarrassed by her public announcement in class, and saddened that her daughter believed that her parents "did not know the truth" of her origins. But she was not relieved. She sounded deeply disappointed, even wounded, that the counsel from their psychiatrist and their years of vigilant secrecy had not worked. She worried out loud to Elizabeth about the "psychological fallout" that Amy might experience. By the end of the conversation, she asked Elizabeth whether she would be willing to talk to the psychiatrist about "how to proceed." Several meetings followed with Amy and her parents, Amy and her psychiatrist, and Amy, her parents, and the psychiatrist; each time Elizabeth insisted that there be no more secrecy and that Amy be present.

Even though Elizabeth's subtle negotiations with Amy and her parents reflect her many years' experience as a teacher and the wisdom and clarity of a mature adult, her betrayal in Mrs. Lake's third-grade class continues to reverberate in her teaching and guide her actions. Clearly, the substance and magnitude of these events were very different. Little Elizabeth wanted the moodiness in school that had captured her teacher's tender attention to be a secret from her parents. She didn't want her parents to worry; she didn't want their probing questions. She wanted to have this special thing with her teacher, a way of being together that was just between the two of them. Amy's secret was much bigger and more burdensome, but she also saw the classroom as a place to make her own imprint. She was aching to divulge the secret of her adoption, a secret that she felt would be safe in the sanctified space of her classroom. She felt secure that her classmates would identify with her and that her teacher would not betray her trust. And teacher Elizabeth, reliving her own childhood traumas, was able to see her reflection in Amy's eyes and gain Amy's alliance in confronting her parents.

Elizabeth Morgan uses a specific experience with her third-grade teacher to instruct her in creating a classroom space that will respect the students' need for autonomy and privacy and honor the sanctity of their secrets. The connections she makes between past and present are conscious and articulated. She moves from the specific to the general, from one traumatic childhood experience to a set of values and behaviors that she negotiates each day in her teaching. Her third-grade experience stands as both touchstone and metaphor, radiating throughout her work, stretching across different circumstances and contexts.

A Blinding Vision

LIKE ANDREA AND ELIZABETH, Jennifer Austin feels the power of her early experiences in school, but she discovers her demons only as she searches for a way to interpret her "overidentification" with a child in her classroom and as she tries not to overstep her authority with the child's mother. Jennifer teaches second grade in a public school that is located in a slightly tattered working-class neighborhood. Her classroom is filled with the "locals"—largely Irish and Italian—who have lived in this manufacturing city for generations, and "foreigners," first-generation immigrants from Latin America (Puerto Rico, the Dominican Republic, and Haiti) and Asia (Cambodia, Laos, and Vietnam). Not only has the closing of local manufacturers turned this once-prosperous city into a near ghost town, but also the influx of newcomers has threatened the old neighborhood and taken away the old-timers' sense of home advantage. Despite the deteriorating economy, the tensions in the city, and the decay in the nearby neighborhood that has longtime residents and newcomers competing for the meager scraps, in Jennifer's classroom, the children—of all colors and backgrounds—have learned to live respectfully and peacefully.

Jennifer, who grew up lower middle class in an upper-class community, and who experienced the humiliations and alienation of her relative poverty, has purposefully chosen to do her "life's work" in this community. She wants to give her students the visibility and voice that she never had. She wants to offer them the sweet taste of success that she was never able to enjoy in school. She discovers the potential casualties of her passionate commitment to her students when she encounters a student who totally mystifies her. No matter how hard she tries, no matter what resources she brings to bear, or how much she cares, this child doesn't seem to be able to get it. Jennifer's failure as a teacher feels like a replay of her own childhood wounds.

Amazingly enough, this little girl shares her name. When teacher Jennifer looks into little Jennifer's eyes, she cannot help seeing herself almost thirty years ago. They do not look alike—little Jennifer has frizzy blond hair, full features, and large gray eyes—but teacher Jennifer identifies with her struggles in school. The girl comes from a poor family (a family that the school counselor has labeled "dysfunctional"). Her father, who is black, has been in jail for several years, and her mother, who is white and obese ("she weighs over three hundred pounds") is in and out of "detox" programs. Little Jennifer lives with her grandmother, but she gets almost no consistent or supportive care, and "nothing is reinforced at home." Since she arrived in teacher Jennifer's classroom as a first grader, little Jennifer has struggled to do the work. It is not that she doesn't try; it is that the "basic steps seem to elude her." "She has no phonetics," says Jennifer with frustration in her voice. But even more perplexing than her difficulties with mastering the basics is the fact that she "always looks like she *should* get it." There is a certain kind of intelligence in her eyes, an attentiveness, a desire to get it right. And that determination and eagerness both confuse and frustrate her teacher.

After little Jennifer failed a series of spelling tests that teacher Jennifer allowed her to retake so that she might improve her scores, the teacher handed the paper back with a sad face drawn on the top. Little Jennifer saw the sad face when she got home from school and "was very upset." She had tried and tried again, and failed again. She had disappointed her teacher. All she could do was weep. The next day little Jennifer's large mother made her first visit to her daughter's classroom, and she was angry. She walked straight up to the teacher and said, "I do not want you to put a sad face on her paper ever again. You made my daughter feel terrible." She was panting and gesticulating, sticking her index finger in Jennifer's chest. Teacher Jennifer was stunned to see her, and frightened by her dominating presence and the rage in her voice. And she was also surprised that she had the wherewithal to advocate for her child. But Jennifer had to admit that little Jennifer's mother was "right" and "had the right to make a stink." "It was nothing malicious," she says softly, "but I should not have done it. I could have said something like, 'I know you can do better. Let's figure out what is standing in your way.' "

Now that she is past the "terror" of this mother's visit to her classroom, teacher Jennifer reflects on the "overidentification" with her namesake that seems to have blinded her to little Jennifer's "disabilities" and that might have amplified her sense of disappointment and frustration with her. She begins thoughtfully, "There are qualities in Jennifer that remind me of myself. After all, I never learned my phonics either. . . . I could never hear the differences between my short and long vowels. I seem to want to give her what I never got . . . the kind of absolute attention and love, that belief in her strengths and gifts, that I never got from my teachers when I was growing up." Now her voice is plaintive, sad. "So I've worked very hard to make that happen for Jennifer. And the harder I work, the more frustrating it is." She pushes back from the table. "In order to be a better teacher, more objective and more discerning, I need to move away from her, not stay so close." Somehow the mother's one shining moment of advocacy for her daughter helped her teacher see that she was "crossing the line" and "getting too close" to her student. Seeing herself in her student was blinding teacher Jennifer's vision. The sad face was her own.

Although her experience with little Jennifer is the most vivid and troubling example of a "devotion" to helping a child that is "a bit exaggerated," teacher Jennifer generally feels very good about her commitment and loyalty to the children she teaches, and she knows that it reflects her own early experiences of "not getting enough." "This city, this school are exactly where I should be," she says definitively, her hands slicing through the air for emphasis. "I am here to give the children something I never got. I felt totally lost in the fancy, privileged Hillcrest school system. I don't think that my teachers ever believed in me. I could never have afforded an Ivy League school, and they thought my future was limited." Jennifer is now up on her soapbox, speaking with great passion. "I want to let my children dream! I want to let them know, with every word and gesture I make, that I believe that they have a big future ahead."

I am struck by several aspects of these teachers' stories—stories that rehearse childhood experiences and reveal their impact on how teachers view their relationships with their students and their families. First, I am impressed by the powerful emotional content of these memories and how it seems to override and overwhelm other sources of support and guidance. Professional training and rhetoric do not seem to have the same force or influence; nor do contemporary adult experiences, even those that reflect life in the families that the teachers have created. These primal, early childhood stories trump all else.

Second, I am struck by the ways in which these childhood narratives tend to focus on trauma rather than triumph, defeat rather than success. Whether it is a trust that is betrayed when a teacher gives away a small but treasured secret, or the assaults of racist teachers who refuse to reward a child's intelligence and leave deep scars, or the isolation and alienation of being poor in a classroom full of rich kids headed for the Ivy League, these memories are saturated with anguish. The voices are full of tears. Somehow the successes and achievements of childhood do not seem to serve the same function. If pressed, teachers will talk about them, but the good memories do not appear spontaneously or with the same force and detailed recall. Perhaps Andrea speaks for many when she says that teaching offers her a wonderful opportunity to heal herself. In reliving the traumas of her past, in revisiting her old hurts, she is able to make it right—or better—this time, and do it on her own terms.

The focus on trauma is connected to a third important aspect of these teachers' stories. When teachers replay the old tapes, they are not merely engaging in nostalgic perseveration or indulging their old wounds. Rather, they seem to be using their childhood experiences as touchstones that either bear reenactment or need to be changed in their teaching. As a matter of fact, they either want to repeat experiences from their childhood that made them feel strong and worthy, or they want to do exactly the opposite. And the more conscious and discerning they are about their childhood echoes, the more clear they are able to be about what should be radically changed in their teaching and what needs to be tenaciously preserved.

I offer one last example: Molly Rose, who reflects on what was good and bad, painful and productive, about her own experiences as a child in school and about how those experiences are either replayed or abandoned in her teaching and work with parents. Molly, who grew up in an upper-middle-class community in New Jersey and went to a fancy private school, now teaches at an inner-city elementary school where 85 percent of the children fall below the poverty line and everyone receives free breakfasts and lunches. Despite the huge contrasts of wealth and life experiences between her hometown and the community she serves, Molly sees lessons from her childhood that she wants to preserve, and others she is eager to change, in her teaching.

"You always bring your own history to teaching," says Molly about the ways in which her educational philosophy and practice are informed by her own childhood experiences. When she thinks of Mountain View, the private school she attended from kindergarten through the twelfth grade, the words that come immediately to mind are "homogeneous and conservative." But despite these "negative attributes," Molly mostly recalls the wonderful "feeling of being known by everyone"—by all of the teachers, children, parents, and grandparents in her school—and the "extraordinarily high expectations" teachers and parents had for all of the children. Everyone was expected to do well, and the standards were very high. With only twenty-three students in her graduating class, most of whom had been there for their entire school career, and an average class size of eight or nine, you knew everything about everyone. Molly does admit that by the time she reached high school, what had felt like a warm and familiar school community began to feel a little "stifling and claustrophobic." But that was a small price to pay for the intimacy and embrace the Mountain View community offered her for most of her school career. It is these two "privileged experiences"—of high expectations and "being known"—that Molly tries to "transport" into the underprivileged communities in which she teaches. Her voice is strong and urgent when she says, "I want to take these same resources, expectations, and care that I experienced in school when I was a child to the places where I work. That is why I do what I do."

The one thing that Molly remembers "hating" as a child was the parent-teacher conferences at Mountain View School. She sets up the scene. "Twice a year, my parents would hire a baby-sitter and they would go off in the evening to the parent-teacher conference. I was a very hardworking, ambitious student, and I always wanted to do well in the eyes of the teacher. . . . So I'd wait up until my folks arrived home, because all I wanted to hear was what the teacher said about me." Molly always felt terribly excluded from something in which she felt she should be a full participant. "I felt as if the adults were talking behind my back . . . as if I was out of the loop." She remembers pleading with her parents, asking them why she was not permitted to join them, and she never felt their responses made any sense. To not be included in the conversation about her life at school was excruciating for her, making her feel dismissed and "voiceless." As a teacher, Molly wants to do the opposite. She wants children to have a big voice at the center of the ritual, and she wants them to be the primary interpreters of their own experience. In Molly's view, parents and teachers should play the role of the appreciative and critical audience for the child who is center stage.

Traveling the Back Roads

BUT IT IS NOT ONLY the teacher's childhood stories that resonate in the structure and content of parent-teacher dialogues, it is also that parents come to school bearing the haunts of their early experiences. As one teacher observes, "During the conference, the parents are experiencing themselves as adults, but they are also reliving the time when they were in school as children. There are two channels working, past and present . . . and the generational reverberations are powerful." Parents bring these autobiographical scripts into the sessions, often making it hard for them to untangle the converging life stories and focus on their child's experience in school.

Paul Holland, a top executive in a major technology firm and the token African American to occupy such a lofty position in his company, sends his two children to North Star, an elite, "progressive" private school in Seattle, Washington. He is on the school's board of directors and—along with his wife—is deeply committed to being a "visible presence" in the school and a "fierce advocate" for his children. When he comes to the parent-teacher conference for his son Stephen, a third grader, he is filled with "an undeniable terror" that he may hear "bad news" (even though Stephen's school reports and classroom assignments have shown steady improvement) and a "particular bias" (that teachers do not recognize his son's potential and have not challenged him nearly enough). Like Paul, Stephen is a whiz in math (with an "aptitude in the stratosphere"), and yet Paul feels that his teacher has never really pushed him to achieve or celebrated his gifts. Paul's meetings with the teacher are marked by his steady insistence that his son is capable of achieving more and his urgent request that his teacher set higher standards and challenge him to meet them.

Paul's terror and advocacy, which surface at the parent-teacher meetings he attends at North Star, have a long history. They echo the relationship that he had with his own father and mirror his father's attitude and expectations for Paul's education. Paul's early education was very different from the elite private schooling that he has been able to provide for his children. "I went to an ordinary public school in Detroit," he says, underscoring the obvious contrasts. "The school was working class and completely black, except for one white boy, who was poorer than the rest of us." Paul's father was a machinist, an incredibly bright and industrious man who always worked two or three jobs to the support the family and was always taking classes and going to school "to better himself." In fact, one of Paul's loveliest memories is sitting with his father at the kitchen table late into the evening, both of them doing their homework together, challenging each other with "hard problems." Like his son and grandson, Paul's father, James, had an incredible aptitude for, and love of, math.

When I ask Paul to think back on his experiences as a child navigating the space between home and school, and watching the encounters between his parents and his teachers, he leans back in his chair and closes his eyes. "I'll tell you a story," he says dramatically, "that sits in my head as if it were yesterday." Paul's sixth-grade teacher was preparing her class for the open house that would be coming up in a few weeks. She asked her students what they wanted to show their parents that would demonstrate what they had learned during the first several months of school. Paul's hand shot up immediately. "How about showing them math?" he suggested. The teacher immediately dismissed the idea. "We don't want to do that," she said. "We'll look stupid if we do that. . . . We want to *shine* for our parents!" Paul was crestfallen; first, because he loved math and knew that he could "shine" given the opportunity, and, second, because he had been so quickly diminished by his teacher. But it turned out that none of the other kids had any bright ideas for the open house performance, so they ended up deciding on a math show.

A few days later, the teacher sent home letters to all of the parents announcing the open house and reporting on their child's abilities and grade level in math. Paul was horrified to read what the teacher had written. She claimed that he was doing math at the fourth-grade level. He knew that she was wrong, so he decided not to give the letter to his parents, so as not to risk their worry or their fury. The next day, the teacher asked the class whether they had all delivered the letters to their parents. Everyone raised their hands yes, except Paul, who admitted that he had not given his parents the letter. "I did not show it to them, because it is not true," he stammered. "My math is not on the fourth-grade level."

That evening the teacher called home to tell Paul's parents that he had been "sneaky and irresponsible" in not showing them the letter. James received the news calmly, told the teacher that he would take care of it, then immediately confronted his son. "But what she said wasn't true!" exclaimed Paul, trying to defend himself from the punishment that he knew would surely follow. Yes, his father agreed, he knew his son could do sixth-grade math, and that the teacher was very mistaken in her evaluation of his abilities. But Paul still should have given him the letter, and for that he would be punished. "That was the last time," remembers Paul shaking his head, "that I got a whipping."

When the day of the open house arrived, James and his wife took off from work, got dressed in their Sunday best clothes, and went up to the school. In fact, it turned out that they were the only parents who turned up for the open house, and they sat in the back row looking attentive and proud. As she had planned, the teacher called on several children "in the top math group" to perform at the blackboard, and she gave each one elaborate praise when they completed their problems correctly. Finally, she called on Paul, who had been dying to go up to the board "and show his stuff." But before the teacher could question him, James rose up, strode to the front of the room, grabbed the math book out of the teacher's hand, and turned to the most difficult problems in the back of the book. When the teacher protested that the class had not yet covered that material, James ignored her and read the questions to his son. Paul stood at the board, quickly working the advanced questions and getting every single one of them perfectly right. "Bam! Bam! Bam!" says Paul, making the firecracker noises that celebrated his victory. The teacher stood there stunned and silent. Finally, she found her voice. "Paul has never, ever done any of these problems before in this classroom," she said softly. "Well," responded James, "you've never *challenged* him."

Now, thirty years later, Paul is standing up in front of me in his office, his arms spread wide, crowing like Muhammad Ali. "The next day my status in the class was transformed!"

As Paul tells this story, he does not make the connections that I immediately hear between his tale of his father's fierce loyalty thirty years earlier in Detroit and his own parental advocacy for his son at the North Star conference. I am, in fact, surprised at the generational echoes I hear in Paul's stories of being both father and son. I had expected that the differences would stand out; differences between family-school negotiations in a rich school and a poor school, in a predominantly white and an all-black school, in the Northwest and the Midwest. But instead of the contrasts in race, class, status, and geography that I expected, I hear deep similarities in the ways in which Paul and James negotiate for and defend their sons. The converging intergenerational narratives are more powerful than the diverging sociocultural experiences. They each believe in their son's capabilities, and they both push the teachers to challenge them. When I point out the parallels to Paul, he says with all sincerity that he has never "made the connections." His face looks wistful and his voice trails off. "And both of these stories, I realize, are math stories," he says quietly.

Parent-teacher conferences become even more complicated when both father and mother attend, each one carrying his or her own autobiographical inheritance into the conversation. What is a "double channeling" for each parent becomes a "quadruple channeling" when both parents are present, with two family histories shaping and crowding the encounter. The various story lines and generational echoes colliding in the heads (and hearts) of parents often cause a delay, or a confusion, in their responses as they sift through the complex and competing layers of adult-child experiences.

In order to successfully communicate with parents, then, teachers need to recognize the complex, layered conversation and anticipate the parents' internal, often unspoken confusions. After all, the doorknob phenomenon is only the tip of the iceberg, an involuntary expression of the subterranean memories that have been influencing the conversation all along. Over more than twenty-five years of working with parents, Elizabeth Morgan has become acutely aware of the "many ancient relationships and experiences crowding the room," a

room that "appears to be inhabited by only a few people." Rather
than seeking to clarify and control the direction of the meeting, over
time she has learned to listen and observe more. Rather than insisting
on a clear focus or forcing rational solutions, she has learned to tolerate the inevitable ambiguities that fill the conversation, and even
learned to live with—and use—the silences that punctuate parent-
teacher meetings.

As a matter of fact, it is the silences—and the restraint and patience
that permit the silences—that are sometimes the most crucial to un-
tangling "the knots" in parent-teacher dialogue. Elizabeth refers to a
well-known strategy—called "wait time"—used by teachers who are
trying to honor the different learning styles of their students. Teachers
who are more patient in their exchanges with students, allowing them
more time to think and then respond, and permitting a range of "reasonable and right" responses, discover that they get more from their
students, who become more thoughtful, and that more of them are
able to participate in the discussion. Elizabeth believes that just as all
children can benefit from increased "wait time," so too does it help
parents who are trying to communicate their thoughts and feelings to
their teacher.

"I've grown comfortable with the silences," says Elizabeth about
an insight that has come with long experience, "and I consider it essential for productive dialogue." This use of time, patience, and silence in parent-teacher dialogues is more than strategy for Elizabeth,
however. These are understandings that have grown out of her professional and personal experiences and out of an increasing self-
knowledge about her style and temperament. She muses, "Over the
years I've learned a lot about myself. . . . I now regard it as a kind of
gift of temperament." This includes being both ritualistic and improvisational, being both purposeful and "saying things in their own
time." "I am good on the back roads. I do not worry about getting
lost," says Elizabeth about her approach, which allows conversations
to wander and weave their own shape. "I always feel that it is going
to take time for this to unravel." Although the "trip on the back
roads" is not rigidly goal-directed, that does not mean that the conversation is formless. As a matter of fact, Elizabeth believes that it is

her responsibility as attentive listener to "hear the shape" of the conversation and "give it back" to the parents. "It is difficult to say how I do this," says Elizabeth, trying to find language for an approach that by now feels natural and intuitive. "Words seem to just come to me. . . . I have the feeling of opening my mouth when it is time . . . and putting it together, usually by telling a story." Most parents feel the difference in teacher Elizabeth's style, and they give her appreciative feedback. "You're so patient with us," they will say, or "You always seem to find a way to thread things together."

Cultural Legacies

ALTHOUGH PARENT-TEACHER encounters are shaped by these interior autobiographical dramas, they are also guided by the larger social and cultural legacies that shape family-school relationships. These broader social forces resonate through the interpersonal and intrapsychic experiences of parents, teachers, and children. They reflect historical legacies that have left a deep imprint on our collective unconscious and contemporary cultural preoccupations and priorities. There is a paradoxical sense of both old and new—of both historical legacies that are long and enduring and recent cultural imprints that are often faddish and elusive.

There is no doubt that these broader social forces reverberate inside the walls of schools and have particular relevance to how the relationships between families and schools get configured. Schools, after all, have always been the arena where the central dramas of our society have been played out. Joseph Featherstone, a social historian, speaks about schools as society's "theater," the large stage on which our major cultural sagas are enacted and the opportunities and casualties of social change are most visible and vivid. We look inside schools—and at the relationships between the schools and their communities—and see, in microcosm, the struggles over how we define and enact equality, justice, oppression, and democracy in our society. We witness the dramas surrounding immigration, assimilation, individuation, and indoctrination. We hear the passionate nego-

tiations surrounding bilingualism and multiculturalism. Schools as
theater makes vivid the hyperbole of our society's rhetoric, the ambivalence in our motives, the ambiguities of our goals, and the dissonance between our professed values and our behavior.

Featherstone's notion of school as theater also points to the ways in
which schools amplify, even exaggerate, what is happening in the
communities surrounding them. They are dynamic, charged environments that bear the weight of great expectations for our children and
in which we place our greatest aspirations for society. Not surprisingly, then, they are also the institutions in our society that disappoint
us the most and are the source of our harshest criticism and blame.

Inevitably, teachers embody many of the schools' social and cultural traits; they are the human face of the institution, receiving, absorbing, and deflecting the praise and the blame. With tongue in
cheek, in his classic text *Sociology of Teaching,* Willard Waller refers
to teachers as society's "professional adults." He claims that they
have both a particular role and a unique responsibility in our society
as the guardians of virtue, the inheritors of a certain moral force.
They are expected to be more "adult" than the rest of us, more responsible and constant, less impetuous and erratic. We want them to
model for our children the values and norms that we ordinary adults
rarely enact consistently in our own lives. To some extent Waller's
view of the teacher's role in our society is anachronistic (we no longer
harbor such lofty, otherworldly expectations of teachers), but then, as
Maxine Greene's quotation suggests, the vestiges of his view remain,
and they influence the ways in which teachers and parents encounter
one another. Teachers' interactions with parents, then, are an expression of these broader forces, and like the autobiographical stories that
shape family-school encounters, many of these cultural and historical
influences are rarely conscious or articulated. They too loom large
and invisible, shaping the expectations of teachers and the aspirations
of parents.

Although I think that negotiations between parents and teachers
are very much influenced by the more formal public-policy decisions
affecting education, these are not the ones to which I am referring
here. Local, state, and federal policies regarding standardized test-

ing, high-stakes examinations, second-language learners, and special education, for example, frame the choices and regulate the behaviors of teachers and parents and are often the source of concern and conflict between them. But here I am referring to those historical and cultural influences that are not the result of formal or explicit policies. I am speaking about the informal but pervasive values and perspectives that are written into the cultural text, not formalized in legislation. I would argue that a dimension of their influence lies in the fact that they are *not* made explicit or visible. They are, as one teacher put it, "unspoken, omnipresent, and opaque."

The Forces of Change

FANIA WHITE, WHO has taught for twenty-two years at St. Joseph's, an inner-city Catholic high school, is the mother of three children—ages twelve, nine, and six—who attend St. Anne's, a nearby elementary school run in the same diocese. When she speaks about her teaching, her affect is neutral and objective; her voice is controlled, dispassionate. But when she "puts on her mother hat," her face becomes animated, her body presses forward in her chair, and her voice changes from matter-of-fact to emotion-packed. Her eyes—the place where she shows her pain—change from dry to teary. Fania explains this transformation that we both experience, in her attitude and her being, as a reflection of the vulnerability that she feels in trying to educate her children in a society "whose values have made loving and learning—the natural impulses of childhood—almost impossible." She sees the social and cultural values that shape educational priorities and practices as hostile to the healthy development of children, limiting and stressful to teachers, and distorting to parent-teacher relationships. In fact, she believes that the current cultural climate is much more influential on teachers' work and family life than "any law they could put on the books."

Before she can even begin to describe her attitude toward, and her interactions with, her children's teachers, Fania needs to describe the context and "set the stage." She sees parents and teachers as "the pawns" of a cultural shift that has made "life impossibly stressful for everyone." She says, "Today there is so much more pressure on kids, so much more is expected academically, and there is no chance for family time. It is work, work, work from the time they are very young." These exaggerated demands not only undermine children's pleasure and creativity, they also put enormous stress on parents, particularly those who do not possess the resources and skills to guide them.

"Let me tell you a story," says Fania, revving up her voice, "to make it plain." From the time she was two or three, her daughter, Angela, loved playing school. She would watch her older brothers doing their homework and she would pretend to read and write, dancing and prancing around the house spouting words that she would seem to be actually reading from the pages of her book. "She loved this school stuff more than playing with her dolls. This brought her so much joy," recalls Fania. Angela just couldn't wait to go to school. When she went with her mother to pick up her brothers after school each day, she would put her face up against the windows just so she could glimpse what was going on and beg her mother to let her sneak inside.

The night before her first day of kindergarten, she didn't sleep a wink. She almost made herself sick with all of the excitement. But when Fania went to pick up Angela at the end of the day, the girl was in tears. School was not anything like she had imagined. She had expected to feel smart and happy, and instead she felt stupid and dejected. Over the next few weeks, Fania watched as her daughter's enthusiasm melted away. "Here was a kid who loved learning, who was so excited about reading, and within a few days all the joy was gone." She was coming home with homework that Fania couldn't even help her with because the teachers just handed out work sheets without any instructions. And by the second week of kindergarten, Angela was flunking the tests that the teachers claimed that they were giving for diagnostic purposes. Fania looks at me incredulously. "Have you ever heard of a kid not being seen as successful in kindergarten?"

As she had always done with the older boys, Fania had gone up to

St. Anne's Grammar before the first day of school and visited her daughter's classroom. She was trying to acquaint herself with the teacher, the curriculum, and the requirements, trying to get the lay of the land. So when Angela started crying and failing, she immediately made an appointment to see her teacher, figuring that she had done all the preliminary work for a productive meeting. But within a few minutes, the conversation seemed destined to end in a stalemate. Fania offers a quick summary. "I tried my best to communicate my concerns and keep my emotions down. Angela's teacher became defensive, and then I laid back, retreated." Although Fania felt angry at the ways in which Angela was being made to feel stupid and inadequate so early in her school career, she could also identify with the teacher who was feeling the pressure to "produce results." As a matter of fact, the teacher, who was initially posturing and defensive, quickly escalated the conflict between them and told Fania that if she had trouble accepting the academic standards and expectations of St. Anne's Grammar, that she could find another school for her child.

Though she resented the teacher's defensiveness, Fania could see that her anxious response was part of something larger. It was not so much the teacher's fault as it was the way in which she was being forced to respond to broader societal priorities. The teacher's aggressive insistence upon high academic standards for five- and six-year-olds reflected her interpretation of the priorities of the school's administrators, who themselves were being forced to meet the escalating expectations of schools. But Fania believes these are not only unrealistic expectations for young children, they are also a distortion of the goals and purposes of education, and they rob young children of their delight in and passion for learning. She believes that the premature focus on academic and intellectual development robs children of the chance to mature socially and emotionally. "Teachers are no longer dealing with the whole person, with the *spirit* of each child," she claims. "Schools are too busy pushing intelligence, and this renders the children emotionally immature. It is as if we are no longer intentional enough in raising our children. We do not resist the distractions and bad influences of technology, television, and rap music taking over their lives, letting popular culture rule, and permitting the

developmental needs of our kids to get overlooked." Her voice is
stinging as she names her concerns at the deepest, most personal level
and criticizes the priorities and goals of today's education.

Even as she struggles with Angela's teacher and begs her to see all
of her daughter's "amazing strengths and beauty," she recognizes the
broader influences that force the teacher to act against her own will.
For example, ever since Fania can remember, the kindergarten children at St. Anne's Grammar have napped for an hour in the afternoon, a ritual that gave both the children and their teacher a
necessary break from the action. But this year the school's principal,
egged on by a group of ambitious parents, has decided that the five-
and six-year-olds do not need a nap and it would be far more productive to use that hour for intensifying the reading program. Fania
sounds frustrated and disgusted as she remarks on the ways in which
the "forces of change" have worked against the best judgment of
teachers and the well-being of children.

The Constructions of Capitalism

ANDREA BROWN REFERS TO other powerful forces in our society that
influence the ways in which she is able to engage the parents of her
young students in her Montessori school. She points to what she calls
the "constructions of capitalism" that shape the values and behaviors
of parents and that influence the goals they set and the ways they advocate for their children. From her point of view, this "value frame" is
not only about money. It is about the patterns of interaction and
quality of life that the accumulation of resources requires. It is about
competition and expediency ("going faster and farther") rather than
about wisdom or grace ("going deeper"). It is about a focus on ends
rather than means, living in the future rather than the present, and caring more about the end product than the process. All of these tendencies and preoccupations, she believes, work against creation of a space
for the kind of dialogue Andrea hopes to have with parents. She, for
example, does not see her role as one in which she lays down rules to
parents or provides them with answers. Rather, she wants to forge a

much more "fluid and organic" relationship that supports a process of mutual discovery, one that is always responsive to the individual idiosyncrasies of the child and his or her developmental trajectory.

"I see my work with parents as offering another alternative, another perspective," says Andrea about a crucial role that she plays in helping to raise the child. And she always begins with the same premise. "My assumption about the child is that they are acting out of their best selves," she says firmly. "Our challenge is to find out what is under the behavior that we don't like." She offers a few everyday examples of child behaviors that drive parents crazy—a child who refuses to eat his dinner, or get dressed for school, or leave the playground on his own at the end of the school day—uncooperative behaviors that interrupt the flow of the day and cause struggles between adults and children. "I challenge parents to figure out what this raises for them," says Andrea. She is quick to say that she doesn't know the answers to the questions she asks parents or the remedies for their troubles. She is, rather, interested in posing the questions and engaging a process of discovery. "I don't have the answers. I am in search of knowing, and I help parents sit with it," she explains. "This means learning to be in the moment, not worrying about the next year or even tomorrow. I remind parents that it is the process that is most important, not the goal . . . the way we are on the way to what we hope to achieve." Andrea recognizes that the approach she is pressing—of living in the existential present, of engaging in open-ended inquiry, of appreciating the process, of not worrying about tomorrow—is extremely difficult for modern parents, who are ambitious for their children and anxious about their futures, and who live in a society with contrary tendencies and values. It is almost as if she has to create an oasis for parents and teachers to meet, a safe setting defined by a different set of rules and dynamics, where they can slow down, relax, and attend to the mysterious, complex, and difficult process of rearing a child. Andrea seeks to challenge and soothe anxious parents, but she is always aware of working against the societal currents that consume their lives and against their wish that she offer prescriptions that will assure their child's success in his or her solitary climb to the top of the capitalist heap.

The social currents to which Fania and Andrea refer reflect contemporary cultural obsessions, attitudes, and perspectives that shape the dynamics and content of parent-teacher encounters. Andrea works to create an asylum from the rugged competition, the fast pace, and the "rampant consumerism" that define the behavior and expectations of parents and the aspirations they hold for their children. Fania rails against a "harsh, aggressive" set of values that do not allow her daughter's teachers to see her gifts and her beauty and that cause them to give up on a little girl whose only ambition was to love school.

Disfigurement

IN ADDITION TO these contemporary cultural imprints, there are also historical legacies that get channeled into relationships between parents and teachers. Elizabeth Morgan, a middle-class black teacher, tells a harrowing story of the historical legacy of slavery etched into her conflicts with parents in an elite private school in northern Virginia, "a place that feels more Southern in its subtle and deep bigotry than anywhere in Mississippi." For Elizabeth, this is not only a story with racism at its center. It is an incident that "smells" of the rituals and routines of the Southern plantation, that embodies the darkest elements of the master-slave relationship. Both teacher and parents find themselves playing out these roles despite Elizabeth's best efforts to speak out, fight back, and save her soul.

Elizabeth was relatively new in her role as the principal of the lower school when she found herself in the middle of a big controversy that seemed to explode out of nowhere. For years parents had complained about the fact that the school offered only a half-day program for kindergarten, a schedule that made it particularly difficult for two-career families. In one of Elizabeth's first administrative moves, she extended the day for one of the kindergarten classes and offered parents the opportunity to choose whether they wanted to enroll their child in a full- or half-day program.

Elizabeth assigned a head teacher and an assistant teacher to both kindergarten programs, but it quickly became apparent that the newly hired assistant for the half-day kindergarten program was "inexperienced and tentative." She also "happened to be black." Very soon the parents of the half-day program were up in arms, complaining about the mediocrity of the half-day program, even though it was clear— from the vehemence of their rage—that they were really responding to having been assigned to the classroom with the black assistant. The parental complaints came largely from the mouths of two couples, both rich patrons of the school with considerable influence over the head and members of the board. It wasn't long before the school's head called Elizabeth and said, "Take care of it."

A meeting was called with the "ringleaders," and they arrived at Elizabeth's office fuming with rage and venom. Before Elizabeth could open her mouth, the fathers were screaming in her face, while their wives were sitting back demurely, "looking satisfied and disdainful." "There was no one else in the building," Elizabeth recalls with a shudder, "and I remember feeling terrified." There was nothing Elizabeth could say to bring reason and rationality to the conversation. "They were like pit bulls out of control." It was even impossible for her to find a way to end the bludgeoning. They kept on until the afternoon turned into evening. The phone began to ring on Elizabeth's private line, and she was too frozen to answer it. "I remember feeling like a servant who was being yelled at for not following their orders. . . . Here I was, the principal, and I was older than they were, but they had made me feel mute and small." The phone kept ringing and the men kept yelling. "I kept on thinking, *This phone is driving me nuts,* but making no move to answer it."

Finally, someone knocked on the door of her office, the screaming stopped, and Elizabeth's son Reed appeared—scared and anxious— and blurted out the terrible news. His brother, Blake, had had a terrible injury in soccer practice. He had slashed his ankle and was in the ambulance on the way to the hospital. They had been calling and calling, but when there was no answer, the coaches had told Reed to run like the wind and find his mother. Elizabeth has no memory of how the meeting ended or how she made her exit. It was all a big blur.

When she arrived at the hospital, the surgeons told her the frightening news. "It turned out to be a fracture dangerously close to Blake's growth line." She screams, "He could have been disfigured for life!"

It is still hard—ten years later—to make sense of what happened that afternoon; still hard to understand the parents' unbridled fury and her impotence in the face of it; hard to understand how she was so far gone that she could not even answer the insistent phone calls on her private line. "I remember trying to use all the skills and gifts I had, but nothing—absolutely nothing—worked. These white rich people were in collusion with the head, who had given them permission to beat me up. It felt awful and dangerous, like a massacre, the worst kind of schoolyard brawl." I look at Elizabeth and there is still terror in her eyes, then tears. "It stands for me like some kind of icon. I remember feeling, there was my precious son with an injury that could have caused him permanent disfigurement, and here I was—his mother—sitting in a conference with raging, racist parents, feeling like their damn uppity slave. . . . There I was coming dangerously close to *my* growth line!"

This tale of danger and treachery reminds Elizabeth that when parents and teachers meet, it is not only that they are "listening on many channels," which carry the sound waves of generational connection, they are also experiencing—at least subliminally—the "historical legacies." As Elizabeth stood frozen and silenced, she was transported back to the horrors—and peculiar dynamics—of the master-slave relationship. "I'm feeling terrified and infantalized," says Elizabeth, "but they are also aware that they cannot run this plantation without me. That is, they are also feeling powerless and dependent." The historical memories echo with deep symbolism. Elizabeth returns to the urgent phone call left unanswered and reflects on the "overriding metaphor of a black woman who leaves her own children to wet-nurse the daughters and sons of the aristocrats." Now her face is as sad as I have ever seen it as she murmurs softly, "Sitting in the principal's office that afternoon in a white Southern school, responding to the rage of the master's family, I did not take care of my own child, who was in danger."

Recently, after giving a speech to an audience at an affluent, white, independent school in Arkansas, Elizabeth was approached by a black woman, the mother of one of the handful of black students in the school. She told Elizabeth that her message had been "inspiring" and "healing," and that it was the first time that she had felt "any connection" to the school. She told her that as a young girl, growing up in a segregated black school in rural Mississippi, each morning and afternoon she rode the bus to school, and on the way she would pass a much better white school that was just a mile or so from her home. Every time the bus rode by the white school, she would look away and hold her breath. Now, when she delivers her own daughter to the snazzy white private school each morning, the ancient feelings of "anger and sadness" return and she finds herself taking a deep breath and holding it until she turns the corner and the school is out of view. The historical echoes and generational memories conspire, making it difficult for this mother to have faith in the place to which she has entrusted her precious child.

Listening to the voices and perspectives of these parents and teachers, we begin to recognize that the complex and treacherous subtext of their dialogue often goes unrecognized and unnamed, but nevertheless has a powerful influence on what is said and not said between them. This subtext is defined by both autobiographical narratives and generational echoes, and by resonances from the broader cultural and historical tableaux. It is both deeply psychological in its content and broadly ecological. The ghosts are hovering over the family nursery and embedded in the cultural scripts and historical legacies.

Although the subtext of the parent-teacher conference tends to be hidden from view, it does not take much prodding to make it visible, to unleash the emotions, to start the storytelling. I believe that communication between parents and teachers is enhanced when there is an awareness of this subterranean content, when the adults begin to understand the forces within them and around them that shape their views of one another, their perceptions of the child, and the values they attach to education. This subtext should be seen as a legitimate and critical piece of the parent-teacher dialogue.

Recognizing the ghosts and hearing the echoes does not mean, however, that this ancient psychological material should be in the foreground of the parent-teacher conversation. It is, after all, a dialogue about the child in the service of his or her learning and development, not about adults making peace with their pasts. There is a tricky balance here between foreground and background. It demands work to make the unconscious content conscious but never letting it overtake or overwhelm the focus on the immediate moment in the child's life. It is a perilous equilibrium that must be struck between the ghosts of the past and the realities of the present, between adult retrospectives and child perspectives. And although both are important, the exploration of the former should always be in the service of illuminating and informing the latter.

To admit that this retrospective psychological terrain is important to understanding the motivations, preoccupations, and values of parents is not to say that the conference should be an arena for therapy and that teachers should become therapists. These are dangerous waters, and the distinctions and boundaries are not always obvious. Again, there is a tricky balancing act between being attentive to the emotional domain of adults as a critical ingredient of expressive and productive dialogue, and not letting emotions be the primary currency of discourse. Elizabeth Morgan's comfort on the back roads, her strategic use of "wait time," and her appreciation of the value of the "silences" reveal some of the skills and capacities that she might share, for example, with a psychotherapist. But there is a difference between what I see as the quality and focus of Elizabeth's attention and the typical concerns and interventions of a therapist. Elizabeth listens carefully and intervenes strategically; she follows the winding path of the conversation and guides it forward; she is both improvisational and focused in responding to parents. But she does all of this patient, perceptive, courageous work not merely to make the parents feel safe or more comfortable. She is primarily interested in using their growing trust and communication to support a conversation that will benefit their child. And, importantly, she knows the limits of her training and experience; she is clear about her place and purpose; she recognizes the boundary between empathic attentiveness and therapeutic work. Her dialogue with Amy's parents about their daughter's

public announcement of her adoption, for instance, leads to a conversation with the family's psychiatrist, a conversation that gives even
clearer definition to her role as teacher. She is vigilantly focused on
Amy's learning, not on the family dynamics or dysfunction. She turns
toward the future, not the past. She seeks practical solutions, not
emotional catharsis.

Creating a space where parents and teachers can build trust and replay ancient dramas that have contemporary relevance requires that
teachers both welcome and resist the broader cultural imperatives. To
some extent these teachers, who hear the psychological and cultural
subtext of the conversation and use it as a lens for interpreting and in-
tervening with parents, are also interested in developing a rapport with
parents that is not completely shaped by the societal currents and preoccupations. When Fania White tells the sad story about her daughter
learning to hate kindergarten on her first day of school and rails
against our society's priorities that cause families and children undue
stress, she calls on teachers to resist some of these unrealistic demands
on young children and instead to create an environment that will support the gradual unfolding of their maturity. She sees the stress that
teachers are under to "produce results," but she believes that they
must also, most important, do what they know is best for children. It
is a stance that recognizes and names the "forces of change," but also
finds ways—both obvious and subtle—to resist them.

Likewise, Andrea Brown believes that the pace, competition, and
ambition of our materialistic society put children and parents on
edge. She sees the parent-teacher conference as an alternative to rampant consumerism and rugged competition, a "haven in a heartless
world," an asylum where the dialogue can be more open and ex-
ploratory, a process of mutual discovery, more focused on today and
less worried about tomorrow. Both Fania and Andrea, I think, are
speaking about finding a balance between responsiveness and resistance to the broader cultural currents. The space they create in their
dialogues with parents should have permeable boundaries that permit
a connection to the broader forces and structures of society, but
also seal them off somewhat from the distortions and anxiety they
produce.

CHAPTER 2

Natural Enemies

Querencia

*O*ne of the teachers I interviewed uses the word querencia—*a term usually associated with bullfighting—to conjure up the space where, even in the face of conflict and bloodshed, one can retreat to safety. A bull's* querencia *is the place in the arena where he feels most safe, where he feels least vulnerable, and where he is likely to survive the matador's attack. This is the place where the bull moves instinctually, where he feels at home. It is this image that comes to this teacher's mind as she thinks about the passion, the tension, and the danger that seem to be endemic to parent-teacher encounters; and she reflects on the vulnerabilities experienced by both parties. Drawing out the symbolism, she says, "In parent-teacher meetings, there needs to be a* querencia, *a safe place, a face-saving stance . . . a corner in the arena where by mutual agreement we will not tread. . . . The idea is that no one should come out wounded and bloodied. . . . The idea is that— despite the inevitable discomforts and conflicts—we should all emerge whole."*

Minefields

THIS VIOLENT IMAGE of a bullfight—the danger and the vulnerability, the attacks and the retreats—is not the typical portrayal of parent-teacher encounters, which are usually seen as neutral and civilized. But most parents and teachers will admit that despite the civil tones and the polite decorum characteristic of the exterior of most conferences, the space between them is full of mines ready to explode and that bloodshed is just as likely as balm, adversity just as likely as alliance. This portrayal of primal passion is rarely described in the literature on family-school relationships, where goodwill and good manners are assumed and prescribed.

I remember my great surprise, about twenty-five years ago, when I was first introduced to *Sociology of Teaching,* a rancorous book written by Willard Waller, in which he challenged the usual view of parents and teachers in alliance and talked instead about the enmity between them. Published in 1932, Waller's book was refreshing in its passion and point of view; it seemed both anachronistic and amazingly contemporary in its representation of family-school boundaries. "Both parents and teachers," claimed Waller, "wish the child well, but it is such a different kind of well that conflict must inevitably arise over it." Referring to parents and teachers as "natural enemies," he wanted to convey the inevitable tensions between parents and teachers shaped by the different roles and functions they play in the lives of children. Parents, he claimed, have a "particularistic" relationship with their children, where the bond is deeply passionate and individualistic. Parents necessarily speak from a position of intimacy, advocacy, and protection for their child. Teachers, on the other hand, have a "universalistic" relationship with their students, which is more distant and dispassionate. They work hard to find a balance between responding to the needs and capacities of individual students and supporting the development of a classroom community in which children learn to be responsible and accountable to the group.

In other words, when parents plead with the teacher to be fair to their child, they are usually asking for special consideration for their youngster. They want the teacher to consider the unique struggles and strengths of their child and offer a differentiated response. But when teachers talk about being "fair" to everyone, they mean giving equal amounts of attention, judging everyone by the same objective, universal standards, and using explicit and public criteria for making judgments. Fairness, for teachers, ensures a more rational, ordered, and dispassionate classroom. Inevitably, said Waller, these differences in perspective produce conflicts and distrust—often masked and oblique—between parents and teachers, even though both would claim that they are laboring with "the best interest of the child" foremost in their minds.

Waller's notion of "natural enemies" has always struck me as both overly cynical and piercingly honest, as both hyperbole and precision. And the stark contrast that he draws between the perspective of parents and the stance of teachers seems both analytically productive and dangerously oversimplified. My experience as a parent and my observations as a researcher led me to challenge Waller's black-white portrayal. The reality is nowhere near as simple or as polarized. I do not think it was so in the early 1930s when Waller made his claims, and it is surely not true now, when the changing landscape, rhetoric, and politics of the last seven decades have reshaped and complicated the parent-teacher dialogue and made it more difficult to negotiate and understand. I am, therefore, less interested in examining the black-white duality than in exploring the gray area—the more troublesome, overlapping territories where most parents and teachers meet, where life is more ambiguous and uncertain.

Despite my reluctance to completely embrace Waller's either-or portrayal of parent-teacher perspectives, I am fascinated by his choice of metaphors and their unusual sound in an educational literature that tends to be monotonous and dispassionate and almost uniformly plays down any adversarial conception of family-school encounters. In fact, if you search out the other domains where the pairing of these two words—"natural enemies"—is a frequent reference, you will find a few references to international relations (the Cold War between the

United States and the Soviet Union, Anglo-French relations in the eighteenth century, and the close pairing of China and Japan, where they are referred to interchangeably as both "natural friends" and "unnatural enemies").

Most of the references to "natural enemies," however, do not pertain to interactions among human beings or countries, or to matadors and bulls in the arena. Oddly, the term belongs almost exclusively to the domain of bugs, insects, predators, and parasites, and the biological control of pests. Scientists and agriculturalists, observing the ecology and encounters of insects, describe the ways to control the growth of the agriculturally harmful insects by promoting the growth of their natural enemies. Thus the natural enemies of the destructive insects can destroy them and protect humans' agricultural interests. I suspect that Waller had no intention of provoking his readers to muse about biological pest control when he described the inevitable adversarial relationships between parents and teachers. But I think the use of a biological metaphor to describe family-school dynamics may at least lead us to ask some interesting questions. Who is the predator and who is the prey in the parent-teacher relationship? Are the parents, especially those who are aggressive in crossing school boundaries and actively advocating for their children, the "pests" who need to be controlled? Is the parent-teacher conference the school's way of engaging two natural enemies so that the supposedly harmful or annoying ones may be destroyed? Is this a flight of fancy? Perhaps. But I think stretching Waller's metaphor beyond the realm of human encounter allows us to see both the absurdity and veracity of his claim.

The one place where I was able to find Waller's notion of "natural enemies" used to refer to the experience of human beings was in a volume edited by Alexander Klein in 1969, entitled *Natural Enemies? Youth and the Clash of Generations*. In a passage about the shifting dynamics between parents and children, Klein underscores the two faces of passion—the inevitable love-hate quality that resides in intimate relationships. "In the family, parents and children, readiest targets of one another's varied ambivalent emotions, both love and hate each other—are natural allies and enemies, mutual sources of satisfaction and frustration, pride and guilt." Klein's conception of "both" in counterpoint, rather than the dissonant "either-or," offers a useful refinement to Waller's perspective and an important framework for this chapter. In complex, sustained relationships, where there is often contentiousness and antagonism, there is also compatibility, camaraderie, and teamwork. Even where there are the extremes of emotion—love and hate, hope and despair—there is the potential for alliance and complementarity.

To some extent, all of the teachers I interviewed have this complex, contrapuntal view of their relationships with parents: the good and the bad, the truth and the lies, the love and the hate. And they all speak about the passion that is the undercurrent of every encounter, the deep emotional content that often gets masked by polite language and empty ritual. The gray space stretching between families and schools is treacherous territory that has to be navigated very carefully and cautiously. A wrong move, a careless step, can easily lead to misunderstanding and distrust. However, the right words or a deft gesture can lead to new insights, deeper understanding, and mutual appreciation. Although parents and teachers feel the high stakes and vulnerability of these encounters, they also know that good communication requires a naturalness, an authenticity. They must be themselves. They must not act defensive. And to further complicate the picture, their moves—so subtle and strategic, yet so ordinary and real—must be in the service of understanding and supporting the parent's child and the teacher's student. What is most important, say all of the teachers, is creating a "safe space" and a "trusting relationship" where the adults, who each care deeply though differently about the child, can share their unique perspectives and speak the truth.

Safe, however, does not mean unsullied. And conflict does not necessarily lead to permanent injury. In fact, teachers, who are experienced and wise in their work with parents, see conflict as an inevitable dimension of successful communication. Misunderstandings, misrepresentations, mistakes in judgment, and indiscretions are unavoidable and come with the territory. As a matter of fact, one measure of candor and authenticity might be whether there is any heat, whether we see any sparks fly. If teachers and parents are speaking their minds and opening up their hearts, then it is likely that there will be contrary points of view that lead to disagreements needing to be named and dealt with. Conflict, therefore, is not to be avoided. But in the heat of battle, parents and teachers need to know that there is an asylum, a *querencia,* a place to recover and regroup, a place to save face.

Sophie Wilder, a combined fifth- and sixth-grade public school teacher who claims to "love" working with parents and is thought by her colleagues to have "a special gift" with them, tells a story of a rare encounter with a mother who, without warning or seeming provocation, "went into the attack mode." When the mom started screaming and making accusations, Sophie felt suddenly exposed and defenseless. She wanted to retreat and run for cover; she wanted to find her *querencia.* Her tale underscores the passion and the irrationality that so often arise in parent meetings, and the vulnerability and hurt that can result. Although she experienced the mother's assault as coming out of the blue, in retrospect she can see the precipitating factors.

In order for me to understand the precipitating incident she needs to "back up" and provide a bit of history. In so many ways, this has been a hard year. For the first time Sophie is teaching fifth and sixth graders, and she has still not completely found her "comfort zone." She still isn't feeling her usual sense of "solidity and confidence" in her teaching. In addition, the class that she inherited this year had a well-deserved reputation as a tough group, a class filled with a bunch of kids who were unruly, angry, and mean and disrespectful to one another. Sophie found that the only way to turn around the "negative culture" of her classroom was to go back to the rudiments of civility and decorum and actually *teach* respect. So in the opening weeks of school, she was strict and dogged in her insistence that her students act kindly toward one another and "learn how to be together as a community." She had them practicing how to shake hands correctly, how to look into the other person's eyes when you are speaking to him or her, how to share their snacks and listen to one another during class discussions.

Sophie explained her rationale for focusing on these themes of kindness and respect to the parents at the fall open house. She told the parents that she, of course, cared deeply about academic standards, but she knew that she and her students would not be able to make much progress in their schoolwork if they didn't learn how to be civil to one another. She also suspected that the parents had already heard from their children that their teacher was being very strict about these matters, and she wanted them to know why. Just as she was getting to the heart of her presentation, one mother raised her hand and leapt up to make a statement before being recognized. Her voice was sharp and condescending. "Did it ever occur to you," she sneered, "that if you believed in our children and really thought that they could do these things, that they would quite naturally do them? Why do you think that you need to continue to preach to them about these things?" Sophie did not know what hit her. She immediately felt hurt and fell speechless. The room seemed to cave in around her. You could feel the tension in the air. Somehow she managed to blurt out a response that barely masked her surprise and her anxiety. She said, very slowly, "I do care about these kids, and I'm sorry if I'm not getting that across."

Somehow, Sophie was able to look down at her notes, compose herself, recover her momentum, and finish the presentation. Afterward, as the parents were milling around the classroom looking at their children's work, she approached the mother who had ruined her evening. Again her voice was modulated, imploring. "Wow, it sounds as if you're feeling pretty upset about stuff." The mother was stone-faced, so Sophie tried again. "It sounds as if I have to do a better job appreciating your son." This time the mother reared back and said through clenched teeth, "No! No! No! You don't understand. Your problem is that you don't trust your students." They stood in the corner having this intense exchange that seemed to circle around some truth that neither was able or willing to name. Finally, the mother admitted that her son felt "unappreciated" by his teacher, and by extension, so did she. "In essence, she circled back to where I began," says Sophie, reliving the weariness she felt at that moment. "By the end of the evening, she left feeling as if she had gotten something off of her chest, but I ended up feeling raw and raging."

As Sophie reflects on this painful encounter, she still "isn't able to let it go." She goes back to the substance and tone of the mother's public statement. "Implicit in what she said—and in the way she said it—was that I didn't care about these kids." Now she is bellowing,

"Couldn't she hear that I *love* these children?" It has been months since this event, and Sophie feels that she and this mother have achieved a "decent relationship" that allows them to work together and communicate important information to each other. But it is not over for Sophie. If anything, she has grown clearer about the legitimacy of her rage and her need to protect herself. Her face shows sadness and resignation as she says, "I still don't feel a whole lot of trust. I thought what she did was completely inappropriate, a real personal attack on me. . . . I still feel raw when I am with her."

It is fairly easy to describe those encounters that lead to enmity and a breakdown in communication between parents and teachers. They are all defined by a lack of empathy, a disrespect for the other's role and perspective, and an imbalance of knowledge, authority, and power. That is, when there is an asymmetry between parents and teachers, it is difficult for the conversation to be productive and the relationship to grow. Bad things happen when teachers are made to feel like "the hired help" by powerful and influential parents. And raw feelings result when teachers flaunt their status, withhold information, and infantalize parents.

But it is not only disrespect and asymmetry that produce poor communication. Enmity is also the result of empty ritual. When meetings—both formal conferences and chance encounters—lack real substance and are designed to avoid truth-telling, when the ritual turns into mechanical, meaningless routine, then the participants will walk away feeling disappointed and cheated. An accumulation of these discomforting encounters will usually lead to a barely sublimated, unproductive hostility on both sides.

These empty and adversarial exchanges are obviously unproductive. The roots and dynamics of these troublesome encounters are easy to describe but difficult to avoid. And in too many schools across the country, too many teachers and parents fall into this catastrophic chasm. But I think rather than recite the obvious sources of enmity, it is more instructive to observe the work and hear the voices of teachers and parents who are generally—though imperfectly—successful in working together on behalf of children, those for whom a breakdown in communication feels unusual, surprising, and disturbing.

This chapter, therefore, assumes that parent-teacher encounters are rich with complexity and contradictions, that there is always the potential for alliance and enmity, opportunity and casualty, love and hate. Our primary focus will be on the ways that parents and teachers seek common ground; the ways in which they create rituals that are meaningful, candid, and supportive of the child's growth and development; and the ways in which even those teachers who generally enjoy "good enough" relationships with parents from time to time find themselves embroiled in exchanges that are undermined by distrust or escalate into confrontation.

Crossing Boundaries

BOTH PARENTS AND teachers have a sense of territoriality that shape their encounters, a map in their minds whose lines define their appropriate roles and the range of their authority. The boundary lines may refer to physical geography, to parents crossing the threshold of a classroom or to teachers making home visits. Or the lines may refer to temporal measures and limits, the frequency of encounters that feel useful and appropriate to parents and teachers. In both of these cases—the physical and the temporal—boundaries can be marked, measured, and regulated. But the terrain between families and schools is also defined by boundary lines that I would describe as both psychological and metaphoric. They are intangible and rooted in emotional content. A single gesture or image can stand for something much larger and more serious. These lines, those we cannot name or see, are the most difficult to anticipate and navigate.

How the lines get drawn is related not only to parents' and teachers' temperaments and perspectives and to school policies and practices. It is also defined by the age and developmental stage of the child. In general, parents of young children are more engaged in their schooling and have more frequent and intense contact with teachers than the families of older students. Teachers welcome their presence as essential in helping the child make a comfortable transition between home and school. As children grow older and more autonomous, the distance between families and schools increases, and the boundary lines tend to become clearer. By the time adolescents reach high school, most of them are not eager for their parents' presence inside the school. They may want them to be in the audience cheering them on, admiring their theater performances and attending their sports events. But they want their life in school with their peers and their teachers to be their domain, a place where they can establish their independence and forge their identities away from the scrutiny and intrusions of their parents. In mapping the terrain and drawing the boundaries between families and schools, teachers' and parents' interactions are, to some extent, shaped by the developmental needs of children.

Jane Cross, a revered master teacher who teaches the nursery class at Northwood, a prestigious independent school in New Haven, hopes to "erase" the boundary lines—both physical and temporal, psychological and metaphoric—and create an atmosphere where families and schools become "seamlessly joined." At fifty-six, and after nearly thirty years of teaching, Jane still finds four-year-olds fascinating. One of the reasons she enjoys teaching the "beginners" is because she loves being involved in their very first experience in "real school," and she likes the ways in which parents become engaged in the life of the classroom. "There is a wide open door, a great deal of contact with parents, and more opportunity to interact with them than at any other grade during their school career," explains Jane.

As a matter of fact, Jane sees almost all of the parents every morning, when they bring their children to the classroom and, usually, hang around for a while. She encourages this daily boundary-crossing by parents, welcoming and encouraging them to stay between 8:00 and 8:30 A.M., which she calls "choice time." During this time, the classroom is as full of parents as it is of children. Children crawl into their mothers' laps for a story and one last cuddle, or parents hang around the edges and talk to one another (a benefit of this time that Jane considers the "most important"), or they approach Jane with a question or concern. It is a very "loose and easy" time, when family and school seem to be seamlessly joined and a lot of information can be exchanged informally and "organically."

Jane recognizes that this kind of bridge-building with parents is essential for her work with four-year-olds, that it is crucial that children experience the daily connections between home and school and that parents feel comfortable leaving their children in the teacher's care. "Parents are coming to terms with a new school," says Jane sympathetically. "For the first time in their child's life, they have no clue about what is happening from nine to twelve. They are full of anxiety, very worried about whether I am going to love and care for their individual child." The ritual of "hanging out" each morning certainly eases the parents' anxiety, but Jane keeps returning to the ways in which her maturity (being an "older teacher") and experience as a parent seem to be crucial to the development of parental trust. "Being a parent is so important. It gives me authenticity in the eyes of parents, and they hear the wisdom in my words," says Jane. But this works only if the teacher herself feels a deep self-confidence. "When the teacher feels confident and can display that confidence—in her voice, in her gestures, in her decisions, in her boundary-setting—then parents begin to feel comfortable and begin to believe that their children are safe in her care."

Jane's warm welcoming of parents and her belief in the value of their presence to their children's successful socialization to school mostly led to an easy, fluid rapport, even a trust and intimacy, with them. But her notion of a "boundaryless" classroom does not always work. Sometimes, in fact, the fuzziness of the boundaries tends to encourage a parental entitlement and aggressiveness that makes Jane uncomfortable. This is particularly true at Northwood, where the philosophy and rhetoric of the school support a great deal of parent participation, the school depends on the volunteer efforts and resources of parents, and professional parents have lofty ambitions for their children. The school has a long tradition of welcoming parent voices and perspectives and relying on their support in making the school run. In this context, Jane's efforts to erase boundaries can backfire and send the wrong signal to parents.

In fact, Jane feels that the pushiness of Northwood parents and their unrealistic expectations are to some extent the fault of the teachers and administrators, who are not clear about defining lines of authority with parents and are unwilling to "take the heat" when parents are angered by the limit setting. Jane feels as if a huge amount of time is wasted engaging parents in conversations and listening to their demands about issues that should not rightly be in their domain of responsibility or expertise. She believes that administrators need to be much more explicit about the boundaries between home and school, about "what is in and what is out" in terms of parent participation. Because the school is not decisive in establishing boundaries, Jane feels that the parents are given a license to "be in spaces where they don't belong" and given subtle permission to "always argue for the advantage of their own child" rather than to consider the community of all children. "As a faculty," says Jane critically, "we have not been as clear about our expectations of what is up for discussion. Everything should not be seen as negotiable and discussable. . . . We need, for example, to tell parents that we have made a firm decision not to teach French to our four-year-olds, not sit around in endless hours of meetings talking about the pros and cons with them."

Jane's message is mixed, suggesting a subtle negotiation with parents. In order to be successful in her teaching, she—and her students— need the parents' easy and fluid participation in her classroom. She wants them to feel "warmly welcomed and completely at home." On the other hand, in the context of a school where parents feel powerful and entitled, Jane also wants to be clear about the limits of parental engagement. She wants the school, her colleagues, and her administrators to be collectively responsible for defining the spaces where parental input is acceptable and welcome and those where it is overly intrusive and a waste of time. She also believes that these messages need to be clear and unambiguous.

Andrea Brown, the founder and head teacher of the tiny Montessori school on the North Shore, also believes that the drawing of boundary lines for parental involvement is crucial in creating a space for open dialogue with them. The lines that she draws are neither literal nor straight, however. They are a paradoxical blend of bridge-building and gatekeeping, connection and constraint. Parents, for example, are not allowed in Andrea's classroom except as observers. They may come and visit anytime, without advance notice, but they must "keep their hands off" and stay on the periphery of the action. These clear limits are balanced against Andrea's generosity in reaching out to parents, responding to their questions and concerns, and being attentive to their needs. Parents need to feel that they are not being excluded from their child's experience. "My strategy," says Andrea, "is to spend a lot of time personally with parents . . . make them feel I'm not holding anything back. I bend over backwards to indulge them. . . . I have discovered that it is only when they feel deprived that they become troublesome or overly intrusive. When they are kept out, they want in. It makes them feel hungry. . . . So I tell them they are welcome anytime."

This open-door policy makes them feel as if they have limitless access, even if they decide not to take advantage of it. In fact, Andrea believes that just knowing that they are welcome may, in fact, reduce their "hunger" for more school visits or more time with her. It certainly—paradoxically—allows Andrea to draw clear boundaries about the ways they are allowed to participate in the classroom. Andrea admits that her inclusive "strategy" is primarily a reflection of her temperament and style. "I am a 'yes' person," she says firmly. "I believe that anything is possible." In all the arenas of her life—not just in school—she lives by this basic principle. It is the way she feels most comfortable relating to children and adults. "It is a pretty simple equation," she reasons. "The more I give, the more I get."

I ask whether this reciprocal generosity sometimes backfires, whether the "equation" ever gets distorted by needy people who take advantage of her caregiving. Does she ever feel as if parents are wearing out the welcome mat? Doesn't she ever get exhausted from giving so much and being so available? Her response is clear, unadorned. "No, I do not feel overwhelmed." But then she adds an important caveat, her voice quiet and self-assured, not defensive in the least: "Even though I tend to say 'yes,' I do speak up about how I feel. I don't hide it." She wants to make sure that I do not interpret her "yes" policy with parents as an invitation to be used up or abused by them. Rather, her welcome mat comes with the assurance that she is also going to take care of herself and be clear about her needs. I push further, wondering whether, given her values and her temperament, she is really able to say "no" when her "yes" is misinterpreted by overly aggressive or needy parents.

Once the parents' "hunger is fed," and they feel "truly welcome," then Andrea believes that everyone can forget about the boundary constraints ("the limits offer us a kind of freedom of expression") and teachers and parents can become allies and collaborators. "I want to invite them to share with me in the challenges the child is presenting," says Andrea. Although her language sometimes sounds ethereal, threaded through with spiritual allusion, Andrea is a pragmatist and a strategist when she works with parents. She says clearly, "I am strategy-oriented. I am always asking, 'What can we do about it?' " And as the parents and Andrea try to unravel the problem together, her questions to them are usually grounded in the daily habits and rituals of the child's family life. "I might ask the parents to describe an average day, and I'm interested in the details. . . . Who gets up in the night to comfort him? Who prepares the dinner? Who does the child sleep with?" As they respond to these ordinary questions about their daily patterns, parents often "discover the roots of their dis-ease." In these explorations with parents, Andrea is careful not to violate the family's privacy, keeping her ears open for a shift in the conversation that might cross the line from inquiry to intrusion. "The child is always my primary concern," she says firmly, "and my motivation for conferencing is to keep the communication clear and honest between home and school, and home and home."

I am puzzled by the last part of her statement. It turns out that she is referring to supporting dialogue between the child's parents, who "often feel so isolated from each other." The parent-teacher conference is one of the few places they may come to speak—and listen—to each other, and perhaps to get support and mediation from Andrea. Sometimes the remoteness and conflict between parents reflect gender differences as much as temperamental and relational conflicts. Andrea seems reluctant to make generalizations about gender differences, so she begins by underscoring that she is speaking from her own experience.

"Moms and dads come at this in a different way."

"How so?" I ask, intrigued by both her statement and her caution in making this bold observation.

"Moms are patient, and dads are impatient with the children and the dialogue about the children," she responds immediately. "And often dads express a jealousy and envy for the moms' knowledge of and intimacy with the child that gets articulated in the conference."

Parent conferences are formally scheduled for twice a year—once in the fall and once in the spring—but Andrea says that she usually meets with all of the parents at least three or four times, and some get much more attention, depending on the child's needs and parental concerns. Even though parent-teacher conferences are important opportunities for communication, Andrea is attentive to parents every day when they drop off and pick up their children at school. "I keep on checking in with them," says Andrea. "I look into their eyes and name what I see . . . I might say to a mom, 'What's up for you this morning?' . . . I always try to compliment parents and say something to affirm them." These daily encounters, which let parents know that Andrea recognizes and values them, seem to make a huge difference in building productive and trusting relationships with families. They pave a smoother path for children as they move from home to school.

But even when boundary lines are clearly drawn to create the space for parent-teacher alliances to flourish, even when teachers welcome parents each day and are attentive to their moods and needs, and even when the adults are focused on the best interests of the child, there are likely to be moments when parents or teachers—despite their best intentions and efforts—violate the ritualized norms of privacy, when one or the other feels as if the line has been crossed.

One afternoon I watched Jennifer Austin, a second-grade teacher in a working-class city school, conduct conferences with several parents. Sitting with parents at a child-size table, she situates herself so that she can look into their faces. The meetings follow the same ritualized structure. Like many teachers, Jennifer begins by saying something positive and laudatory and ends by offering words of optimism and encouragement. But she always finds a way to squeeze in news about the child's "challenges," and she doesn't mince her words.

When she has something difficult to say and hard for parents to hear, Jennifer's tone softens and becomes almost beseeching. Whether Jennifer is telling Jewel's father that his daughter has some struggles with math, that she does not always do her homework, that she has been devastated by the loss of her best friend, whose family left town, and that she seems to be taking out her pain on bullying other children, her eyes remain steady on his face. She does not fudge the message or retreat. In fact, these tough messages almost sound tender and empathic in the way that Jennifer delivers them and balances them against the good news that always precedes them. And she always ends with a question. "Do you know what I mean?" she asks, looking to see whether the parents recognize the child she is describing.

For the most part, parents nod their heads in recognition and agreement when Jennifer talks about their child's struggles. They appreciate her candor and even seem to empathize with *her* willingness to risk telling them the difficult truths. Admits one mother whose daughter, despite Jennifer's persistent and firm interventions, continues to steal things from other children, "Boy, do I hate to hear that, but I would hate it even more if you didn't tell me what was really going on. . . . The truth is hard to tell and hard to hear." But there are also moments when Jennifer's words seem particularly hard to take, when parents startle and become slightly defensive, as if some invisible line has been crossed.

When, for example, Jennifer says that Jamie, the first of five boys in his family, tends to demand a lot of attention in the class and that he is "needy," Jamie's mom's body stiffens and her jaw gets tight. She tries to keep her voice even. "He gets pretty much attention at home. We always have our private time," she responds. Jamie's mom seems comfortable with Jennifer's assessment of her son's "need to be first," but she chafes at the notion that this reflects a kind of "neediness," a point that feels suspiciously like a judgment of her parenting. Maybe the teacher thinks that Jamie is needy because his mother does not give him enough time and attention.

Jennifer seems to cross another boundary line when she tells Rory's mom about "how good he feels about himself." She describes his growth over the year, his emerging self-confidence, and the ways in which his strong self-esteem has improved his participation in class and his relationship with his classmates. But Jennifer begins by referring to Rory's size: "Even though he still has a bit of a weight problem," she says as a prelude to her main point and without any criticism in her voice. Rory's mom looks down, her face full of pain, and she says softly, "Yes, we're working on that." The reference to her son's weight seems to shadow everything else, masking the teacher's major point about Rory's sturdy self-image. Later on, when I mention to Jennifer this moment of tension in the conversation and the mom's sudden shift of mood, she looks baffled and a little hurt. "It was a throwaway line," she says sadly, "even though for this mom it turned out to be the dominant point. . . . I know she will forgive my indiscretion, but I don't think she heard anything I said after that moment."

It is during Jennifer's conference with José, the father of Jewel and a recent immigrant from the Dominican Republic, that I see the tense crossing of boundaries (or wires) that seems to mystify and confuse both father and teacher. Jennifer spends some time talking about Jewel's bossiness and her own efforts to help the girl find ways of asserting herself without manipulating and dominating her classmates. Jennifer is trying to draw the fine line between being overaggressive in getting what you want and being assertive in making your voice heard and getting your needs met. She wants Jewel to become self-confident and strong, not merely demanding and controlling. This is a subtle distinction to draw even when both parent and teacher speak the same language. But trying to convey this nuanced message to someone who is barely proficient in English is particularly difficult.

But what I see in this interaction seems to be more than a confusion over the meaning of Jennifer's words. Rather, the real break in communication seems to be rooted in a clash in cultural perspectives: two very different views that the father and teacher hold about the role of women in society, particularly in families. Jennifer admits to having a "feminist perspective" on the raising of girls and wants "gender equality" in her classroom. José, on the other hand, has a view of his daughter's place in the family—and in the broader society—that limits her to bearing children and taking care of the hearth and home.

He wants her to learn to be (or at least act) subservient to men. So when Jennifer talks about Jewel gaining strength, "discovering her voice," and telling the truth, José looks blank, then his face shuts down, as if what he understands of Jennifer's message he doesn't want to hear. The silence between them speaks volumes. "Do you know what I mean?" asks Jennifer. And for the first time José looks away and offers no response.

Later on, when Jennifer is reflecting on this moment, she says that she senses some real "cultural differences" in the way she and José see Jewel. She has heard so many stories, both from Jewel and her parents, about the household chores that conflict with her homework. In addition, she has been told that Jewel's younger brother Carlos is never expected to do any housework. As a matter of fact, Jewel is often required to clean up after him. There is an expectation at home that the daughters will serve the needs of the son. This is a definition of gender roles that Jennifer would never condone or support in her classroom.

In the silence between Jennifer and José there lurks a subtle conflict over cultural values that neither addresses openly. But at the end of the conference, Jennifer refers to a more visible value difference, which had been resolved earlier in the school year. She thanks José for letting his daughter do the "respect movements." Several weeks ago, two artists-in-residence had come to work with the children in Jennifer's class. The theme was respect, and they taught the children a series of dance movements to accompany a poem that celebrated the theme. Knowing that Jewel's parents were devout members of a Pentecostal church that does not allow any dancing, Jennifer was not surprised when Jewel said that she would not be able to participate. At the end of school that day, Jewel admitted to Jennifer—her voice soft and urgent—that she really wanted to join in the dance. Jennifer said that she would be willing to call her father to seek special permission, but Jewel knew better. No, she did not think it wise that her teacher ask her father directly, because he would surely say no. It would be better, Jewel reasoned, if she asked her father herself, then her father would ask her mother, and her mother would say yes. So Jennifer let Jewel make the moves and it all turned out fine. At the conference,

Jennifer wants to be sure to convey her thanks to José, "not to make a big deal about it and blow it out of proportion so the father might change his mind," but rather to briefly express her appreciation for his support of Jewel's life in school.

One of the things I find fascinating about this story of permission-seeking is the role that Jewel played, the way in which she navigated the family-school boundaries and value differences, knew whom to talk to and how to get what she wanted. I also am impressed by Jennifer's realization that it was Jewel who knew the dynamics best, that this seven-year-old girl understood—in a way none of the adults did—how to bring these two worlds together so she could participate without guilt in both domains.

Finding Common Ground

JENNIFER'S DISCOVERY THAT seven-year-old Jewel understood best how to bridge the cultural divide between her teacher and her parents underscores the importance of the role that children play in navigating the boundaries between families and schools. It is the child, after all, who is the only one who has an intimate view of both of these domains. He or she knows—often with great specificity and subtlety—the personalities and preoccupations of the significant adults in his or her life, and is able to read both the home and classroom scene like a complicated cultural text. Teachers who are successful in working with parents know that they must do everything in their power to put children—their strengths and their vulnerabilities, their achievements and their challenges—at the center of the parent-teacher conversation.

Keeping the focus on the child offers two important perspectives and opportunities. First, it encourages a conversation that speaks to the unique temperament and capacities of the child, seeing the "whole child" from a variety of angles ("the whole three hundred sixty degrees," as one teacher put it). It avoids a narrow view of the child, a preoccupation with only one dimension, an overemphasis on pathology, a recitation of his or her weaknesses. Likewise, it avoids frivolous, ungrounded praise or empty adulation. Second, a focus on the child permits parents and teachers to recognize his or her unique position as a witness to and participant in both his family and his classroom. Even very young children like Jewel have experience navigating the boundaries, making sense of the contrasts in values and norms between home and school, and finding a way of creating connections that make sense for them.

The Child Is the Bridge

MOLLY ROSE, a first-grade teacher in a city school that serves a largely poor, immigrant population, speaks about "the child as a bridge" between home and school and gives the child the most visible and audible role in her work with parents. In order to assure that the adults focus on the child, and in order to take full advantage of the child's singular perspective and wisdom, Molly has, over the years, developed an elaborate system of interactions with parents. This highly organized system insists upon their full attendance at several parent-teacher meetings, communicates with parents weekly about curricular issues in the classroom, and encourages—in fact, depends upon—parental input about the child that they know "better and more intimately" than anyone else.

Of all the teachers I interviewed, Molly was the one whose "system" for parental engagement seemed the most structured and highly developed. Put in place before the beginning of the school year, the system was carefully explained to, and followed by, the parents of each child. It is designed to assure a "transparency," an "accessibility," and the "experience of fairness" for every family. No one, not even the most difficult and recalcitrant parents, can be excluded from the system. In fact, such a transparent, public process allows teacher and parents to better attend to the unique and individual dimensions, the very private stories, of each child.

"Almost everything I do with parents is with the child at the center," says Molly, as she begins to describe a series of encounters with parents that she has designed and refined. In fact, Molly's description of her engagement with parents is less about a focus on the twice-yearly conferences mandated by the system and more about carefully and patiently building a bond with families that is nourished by frequent and myriad encounters.

The first communication with the family occurs before school begins, and—true to her word—it is sent to the child. In early August, Molly writes a simple letter to each child in her class telling them about her summer. "Last August," she recalls, "I wrote that 'I read a lot of good books, I went swimming, and I went hiking.' Then I drew a picture of myself hiking." Along with the letter, Molly attaches a blank page, and asks each child to draw a picture of his or her summer and have an adult help write a letter back to her. When September rolls around, the children's pictures are posted up in the classroom to welcome them on their first day of school. Molly underscores the strategy and the symbolism that she attaches to this first piece of communication. "The very first way that I'm meeting the parents is through a letter to their child." A couple of weeks later, toward the end of August, Molly sends a letter to the parents welcoming their child to her class and alerting them to some of the routines, rituals, and schedules that they will need to know.

Molly's first face-to-face contact with the parents comes a couple of weeks after the opening of school, when she schedules a short "getting to know you" conference. This meeting is specifically designed to give parents the chance to tell Molly about their child's personality, interests, strengths, and challenges and about the parents' expectations, goals, and concerns. "I try very hard," says Molly, "not to talk at all. This is purely a *listening* conference. . . . The parents are the experts, and I'm seeking their wisdom and their guidance. . . . I'm saying come and tell me all about your child." Even though Molly tries to make this first meeting "as low-key as possible," and even though she tries very hard to be welcoming and receptive, many parents seem worried and apprehensive when they come in. Some seem to feel awkward assuming the voice of authority, expecting instead that the teacher will tell them what to do, while others seem to feel nervous about "saying the wrong thing." They are understandably reluctant to reveal anything that might compromise the teacher's view of their child. So Molly must quickly disabuse them of the idea that there is a "right answer" to her queries or that they need to present a perfect picture of their youngster. "I watch them very carefully," she says about her active listening during this first session. "I try to convey to them my support and understanding," often by asking a question that allows them to be proud and admiring of their child. "What is your child good at?" Molly asks, ready to receive any and all answers. "She's good at setting the table," says one. "He's good at making friends," answers another. "She's a terrific soccer player," beams a third.

Molly shakes her head, remembering one upper-middle-class mother i·a fancy suburb where she used to teach who said her daughter was good at "nothing." She recalls feeling a sharp pain in her chest. ("Almost like *my* heart was breaking for this mother.") This seemed impossible. How could any parent claim that her child was not good at anything? What did this say about the mother, about the daughter? Molly soon realized that this mother was taking a "too narrow view" of her question, that she was probably expressing apprehension that her daughter might not be as "academically prepared" as the other children. So Molly tried to expand and rephrase the question in order "to help this mother broaden what she was looking at." Within a few minutes, the mother was able to see the good in her daughter.

Because Molly believes that these initial "getting to know you" meetings are a crucial moment for her to bond with parents, she "insists" on a 100 percent turnout. "How do you do that?" I ask incredulously, knowing how difficult it must be to legislate full participation. "I just insist," she says, punching the air. "I make myself available any time of the day, from early morning to late at night. We work through all kinds of scheduling complications." Then she underscores an "attitude" that seems to keep her going until she has achieved 100 percent attendance. "When they break an appointment or do not show, I have no problem with that. I don't take it personally. We work until we can find another time." I imagine that Molly's zeal and determination to meet them and know their child must impress even the most reluctant parents. And I suspect when they finally come and she "really listens" *to* them—rather than talking *at* them—the bridge between home and school begins to get constructed.

In addition to the face-to-face encounters with parents, Molly keeps in contact with them each week in two ways. First, every Monday, the children take a large envelope of their work home for their parents to review. On one side of the envelope, Molly writes one or two sentences about something that might have occurred during the week. She might comment, "I noticed that Eli is beginning to really learn how to share." Or she might write, "Tamara, work on practicing your counting by twos. We're almost there." The envelope is to be returned the next day with comments written by parents on the reverse side of the envelope. Molly admits that the parental response is uneven; the same parents make an effort to write something each week, while others rarely do. This year, two families have never responded, and Molly reasons that their life is just too overwhelming. "They do not have the order in their lives, or the resources or systems in place at home to check the backpack on Monday nights, look at the folders, and return them with a note." For the most part, however, the weekly envelope exchange works amazingly well, lubricating the communication between school and home, and it allows the parents to keep in touch with the "amazing progress" of their child's work. Perhaps more important, writing a specific comment on each child forces an important kind of discipline on Molly. She must be observant and attentive to their individual development, creating a written document of weekly challenges and changes.

The second weekly communication to parents comes in the form of a newsletter, called *The Rose Room News*. It is a one-page rag packed with information about trips to the planetarium at the Science Museum, or midterm progress reports that will be sent home on Wednesday, or the collection of money for the book fair. But the biggest space in the newsletter is devoted to a section called "Ask Me . . ." that Molly proudly claims as her own "invention." In this section, Molly lists ten or twelve questions that parents might ask their children about their week in school. For example, after a recent visit to the arboretum where the class "adopted a tree," Molly wrote, "How were the trees at the arboretum different from when you observed them in the fall? Why are the trees changing? How do you think they will be different when you observe them in the spring?" In this same "Ask Me . . ." column Molly suggests two "games" that parents and their children might play at home. "Write three words that begin with a vowel. Write three words that have a vowel in the middle. Write three words that end with a vowel." And "Let's play a rhyming game. I will think of a word, and you tell me a word that rhymes. Words that sound alike are often spelled alike."

Molly regards this "invention" as the most important piece of communication with parents because, she says, "it is accessible to everyone." It is also a powerful extension of the teaching and learning that go on in the classroom. "Ask Me . . ." helps children talk to their parents about what is happening in school. Laughing, Molly explains, "If you ask any six-year-old what happened in school today, they'll of course tell you 'nothing.' This gives the parents *specific* language to ask about their child's time in school, and parents continually discover, and are amazed by, how much their children know." Like the weekly envelopes home, Molly also has discovered how much she enjoys writing the weekly missive. It offers her the chance to "summarize and synthesize," to put it all together and put the week to rest. And it helps her—like the parents—recognize "the incredible amount of stuff" her students have learned.

Molly wants me to know that even with this highly organized system of parent contacts, she always leaves room for "spontaneous calls" home to report on "good things" that are happening in school. She reasons that when teachers call home, it is usually about something bad, and parents are, therefore, conditioned to fear the teacher's voice on the phone. Molly, on the other hand, "likes to call *randomly* with wonderful news." She might call Jasmine's mother and say, "Your child just wrote the most terrific thing about her baby sister! You just have to hear this," and then she might read the piece over the phone or suggest that Jasmine's mom drop by the classroom the next morning to take a look at it. Molly is grinning as she recalls the double pleasure of acting spontaneously and delivering good reports on her students.

Unique Fingerprints

MOLLY ROSE'S SYSTEM is successful in offering parents equal access, in getting them all (an amazing 100 percent, every time) to come to parent conferences, and in putting their children front and center. "The system is visible, open, and just," says Molly about its principal attractive feature. Once the child has created the "bridge," it is much easier for the parents to follow in his or her footsteps to school. Once parents have taken advantage of the open access and navigated the home-school boundaries, their success in communicating with teachers will depend on developing a mutual empathy, a genuine appreciation of the other's role and point of view.

As a matter of fact, Elizabeth Morgan, who has taught children of different ages in a variety of independent schools, sees conferences as an opportunity to give support to parents and to help parents become their child's best advocate. "As a teacher, I want to convey to parents some confidence in their parenting," she says definitively. "I want to help them learn how to advocate for their children." In order for parents to be effective advocates, however, Elizabeth believes that they must not see their children as small reproductions of themselves. They must see them as separate human beings with different strengths and vulnerabilities. "I want to convey to them that their child is not themselves . . . that every fingerprint is different . . . that each child is inventing a whole new thing." But parents not only need to see their child's singularity in order to be "fully supportive" of him or her, they also need to appreciate the different paces and trajectories of development. "I want to help them gain a sense of perspective and help to ease their anxiety," says Elizabeth. This usually requires that they "see a longer time frame."

Elizabeth recalls facing the challenge of convincing parents to let go of their need to control their child's development when she was the director of a day-care center and parents were constantly preoccupied with their child's potty training. She recalls saying to them with a knowing smile, "You have two choices. You can take two years and two weeks or just two weeks to accomplish this training," because it was only the last two weeks that really mattered. It depended almost entirely on the child's readiness to be trained, not on some arbitrary developmental clock determined by parents or teachers. When Elizabeth was teaching five- and six-year-olds—whose parents were desperate for their children to learn to read—she also worked hard to convince parents that they should relax and not pressure their youngsters. "Reading is a process of integrating. It's mysterious," she would tell concerned parents. "We have very little to do with it. It will happen in its own time if we provide the appropriate resources and conditions."

Just as Elizabeth believes that part of the teacher's work is to help mothers and fathers "gain confidence in their parenting," so too she thinks that parents should be appreciative of the teacher's role and perspective and be modest in their expectations of the meeting. For example, she warns parents not to "go in with a big agenda" to parent-teacher conferences, but be ready to "listen for how the teacher knows their child." "Hopefully," she says, "by the end of the conference, they will have learned something about their child that they never knew." And just as she suggests that teachers need to support parents in their role, she also believes that "parents need to help the teacher feel a sense of confidence." Remarks like "What an interesting idea!" or "I never thought of that"—particularly when they are spoken with sincerity—help to strengthen parent-teacher conferences. Elizabeth is talking about the power of really hearing what the other has to say, and she is underscoring the mutuality of empathy, generosity, and expressed appreciation that she believes is core to productive communication. I think that she is not suggesting that the appreciation be faked—by either teachers or parents—or that the exchange be superficial or manipulated. She does seem to be saying that if one comes prepared to "really listen," if one is "truly curious" about the other's perspective, then one becomes open to hearing something new and useful. The stance of generous receptivity goes a long way toward creating the conditions of mutuality that allow for a meaningful exchange.

But even though empathy, advocacy, and earnestness are essential ingredients of a respectful mutuality between teachers and parents, Elizabeth worries about the heaviness that can weigh down the conversation and give a distorted and exaggerated sense of its importance. Parent-teacher conferences are such serious occasions, so filled with dread and anxiety, and parents can so easily lose a sense of scale and perspective as they focus on their precious child. Elizabeth can see those difficult, dreary moments coming when the air grows stale and the temperature rises. These are the moments when she can't resist her urge to be irreverent, when her sense of humor kicks in. Elizabeth recalls one of hundreds of conversations when she felt the need to cut through the thick seriousness of the dialogue with some light humor.

Julia was the only child of late-middle-age parents who were extremely concerned with their five-year-old daughter's hygiene. "These were tight, tight, controlling parents," says Elizabeth, shaking her head. "At home the mother even monitored Julia's bowel movements, and when her daughter came to school, she expected me to monitor her trips to the toilet as well!" At a certain point in the conference, the mother said with complete seriousness, "Now, about her bowel movements. I have noticed some brown in Julia's panties when she comes home." Without skipping a beat, Elizabeth responded, her voice light and mischievous, "So whom among us has this not happened to?" With that, the mother's face softened and the father grinned quietly. There was no more toilet talk, no more expressed requirement that the teacher monitor Julia's trips to the bathroom or check her panties for brown spots.

Talking Over the Back Fence

THE BEST WAY to communicate empathy for parents, and to keep the child in focus, says Sophie Wilder, is to mine the parents' wisdom about their child, to learn all that you can about how they see their child. Like Molly Rose, she believes that teachers see only the narrowest slice of a child's capabilities and temperament, and that it is critical that teachers seek parents' insights and guidance, not in an abstract way that invites rhetoric and hyperbole but in a very specific, grounded way that provides useful evidence to the teacher. Sophie knows that parents have a much fuller, more complex, and intimate view of their children than she does and that any glimpse of their lives outside of school will enhance her work in the classroom. "I see such a small picture of these kids at school," she admits sadly, "a smaller and smaller view as they get older. . . . So every bit of information that I get from parents is always helpful in filling in the spaces of what I can't see and don't know."

Her stance of curiosity and openness helps enormously when parents arrive with concerns and criticisms about her work—criticisms that if left unchecked might lead to misunderstanding and stalemate between them. Sophie admits that her interest and curiosity are genuine. She truly wants to know what the child's life is like "on the other side"; she wants to live vicariously through the parents' subjective perspective. And she wants to use that information to do what she enjoys most: to make a successful intervention with a child so that he or she will succeed, and, by so doing, "mend a tear" in the community that she is creating in the classroom.

Several weeks ago, for instance, Malcolm's grandparents came to school and told Sophie that their grandson was very unhappy in her class, that he felt picked on by her, and that she never seemed to notice or appreciate how hard he was working. Even though they were certainly worried and anxious, they did not come in with a chip on their shoulders or speak as if they thought that Sophie was being intentionally mean to Malcolm. Sophie remembers "listening comfortably" and not feeling the slightest bit defensive. As they spoke, there were things that felt familiar and rang true. I probably *am* on his case a lot, thought Sophie. He *is* really being disruptive in class, and it really *does* bother me.

Sophie asked Malcolm's grandparents to tell her exactly what he was reporting, because she knew that the understanding and resolution of this problem would be found in the details. They reminded her of the day when she went out into the hall to talk briefly with a parent and she asked Malcolm to be the class leader while she was gone. Malcolm interpreted his assignment as a punishment, even though

Sophie had seen it as a classroom privilege. The grandparents offered several other examples of miscommunication and misunderstanding that had led Malcolm to feel picked on and resentful, *and* there were also real disciplinary issues that Sophie felt needed monitoring. But what Sophie liked about the encounter with Malcolm's grandparents was how much she learned from them and how useful the information they shared turned out to be in her developing relationship with their grandson.

In the days that followed, Sophie had lots of opportunities to talk with Malcolm, "sharing their different perceptions and admitting their mistakes." She promised, for instance, to praise him more when he was doing things right, and he said that he would be more respectful of the rules that she expects everyone to follow in the class. Malcolm relished the attention, his grandparents were grateful for Sophie's immediate and specific response, and they reported a "huge change" in Malcolm's demeanor at home.

Sophie regards this encounter with Malcolm's family as "typical" of her work with parents, and it is one of the things she loves most about teaching. "It is the place where I feel most confident," she beams. "I feel as if I am very good at and work very hard at class cohesion, at understanding the dynamics and social issues among the kids. . . . I'm eager to address that kind of stuff in the classroom." For Sophie, the sessions with parents provide her with new information and another perspective that will help her do what she does best with students, see them whole and help them grow. Seen this way, parents are an essential resource. She also recognizes that she has a "special gift" for this kind of honest communication and problem solving. "I have the tools to respond," she says matter of factly. "Somehow, when we are in the midst of these conversations, even the toughest, most difficult ones, I never feel as if my back is up against the wall. This doesn't scare me."

Telling the story of Malcolm's grandparents leaves Sophie feeling optimistic and upbeat. Despite the fact that over the years she can certainly recall searing words and tough combat with parents that have left permanent scars in her store of memories, for the most part she feels "blessed" with a perspective that allows her to "see when conflict is productive" and a temperament that enjoys "data gathering and problem solving." "With the vast majority of parents," she says, without an ounce of pridefulness in her voice, "I have great conversations and very comfortable relationships." It is not only that working with parents is a big part of what she loves about teaching, it is also that she feels "lifted up" by them. "This feeds me!" she says, smiling and rubbing her stomach as if she's had a great meal. "I am always amazed that these parents are trusting me with their most precious treasure. They must make a huge leap of faith leaving their child with me all day. This requires an enormous amount of trust, and I'm buoyed up by their faith and trust."

Sophie closes her eyes as if she is searching for an accurate image of how she feels most of the time when her work with parents is collaborative and mutually appreciative, when they have found common ground. She comes up with a wonderful metaphor that offers a stark contrast to Waller's adversarial image of "natural enemies." When parents and teachers begin to trust each other and recognize the mutuality of their concern for the child, she says, it is like "close neighbors chatting over the back fence." It is a conversation that is embracing, not adversarial; collaborative, not competitive; and a bit casual, not too proper or formal. It is a "loose kind of love" that reaches out to make connections, not the particular, jealous kind that struggles for power and ownership. I also hear in Sophie's metaphor a line from Robert Frost's famous poem that reminds us that "good fences make good neighbors." Productive relationships between parents and teachers require the marking of boundaries and some degree of separation.

Teachers who are successful in developing this "loose kind of love" recognize that the drawing of boundaries between families and schools is a complicated calculation, a subtle negotiation. The lines are neither clear nor literal; the territories are not black and white. The either-or conception of Willard Waller is useful in pointing out the different roles and perspectives of teachers and parents and the ways in which they are likely to be in conflict. But it is overly simplistic and pessimistic. Teachers are both bridge builders and gatekeepers. They are engaged in the dialectic of forging connections and maintaining boundaries with parents.

In working with the parents of her young charges at the Montessori school, for example, Andrea Brown is clear about the double message she gives to parents. It is an open-door policy with definite restrictions. The parents may visit her classroom whenever they want, but they may not participate in the activities; they must not touch anything or disrupt the natural flow of things. In general, the parents are pleased by the access and happy to exchange it for the clear limits. But it is not only that the barter works. Andrea believes that setting limits provides a structure that allows for a greater freedom of expression and more productive engagement between them. Like Andrea, Jane Cross also works to find the right balance between opening wide the doors to her classroom, making "a seamless connection" with parents, and being clear about those "spaces and discourses" where parent participation feels inappropriate and overly intrusive. She too sees the legitimacy in the double message of open access and clear boundaries—a message that needs to be made particularly clear in a school like Northwood, where affluent, professional parents have overzealous ambitions for their children and feel entitled to invent their own norms of interaction with the school.

Just as teachers mark the school boundaries and make barters with parents in order to ensure the territorial control they believe necessary for their work with students, so too must they be careful to honor the borders and privacy of families. When teachers are seeking information about a child's life at home, for instance, they must be careful not to cross the line between inquiry and intrusiveness; they must make sure that their curiosity does not turn into voyeurism. Sometimes these distinctions are hard to make, and teachers recognize that they have crossed the line only after they have trespassed into family territory. Studs Turkel, one of the great oral historians of our time, talks about the questions he chooses *not* to ask when he is engaged in "deep conversations" with his subjects. It is an admonition about trespassing and violating boundaries of privacy. His advice is deceptively simple. "Don't ask them anything that is none of your business," he says. There is a lesson here for teachers as well. Questions of parents should always be guided by the need to know, not the wish to snoop. They should reflect a concern for the learning, development, and well-being of the child, the teacher's need to know information that will help her connect more successfully with her student. Anything else is none of her business.

Beyond recognizing that the boundary lines between families and schools are dynamic and double-edged, not linear and static, we must also, I think, modify our portrayal of parent-teacher meetings as civilized, ritualized encounters devoid of passion and heat, and replace it with a much more realistic picture that admits the threats, the vulnerabilities, the wounds . . . and the need for a safe place to retreat, a *querencia*. And we must also admit that conflict is endemic to parent-teacher dialogues, that it is not to be ignored or avoided. Rather, it must be met with open eyes and open hearts, made visible and named, and worked with over time. Sophie Wilder, for example, is blessed with a temperament that other teachers would envy, one that welcomes the challenges and the clarifying dimensions of tough conversations. She sees "difficult dialogues" as invitations for problem solving, rarely takes them personally, and recognizes "conflict as productive." Anticipating these moments of misunderstanding and disagreement as a legitimate part of successful communication and admitting to the primal passions that occasionally get unleashed help parents and teachers be real with one another and create alliances on behalf of children.

But there is a difference between productive conflict and destructive assault. The former is clarifying and seeks resolution; the latter feels like combat and leaves you feeling raw. The former moves toward a symmetry of authority and mutual respect between teacher and parent; the latter is a power play designed to diminish the other. The latter was the case when Sophie Wilder was attacked by the mother of one of her students, who sneered and screamed at her during her open-house presentation and publicly humiliated her. The mother was raging and out of control. She wasn't asking a question or merely raising a concern; rather, she seemed to want to demean her son's teacher and put her in her place. And although she seemed to get relief from her cathartic outburst, the attack led to a permanent wariness and distrust in Sophie.

But perhaps the most important condition for finding common ground and supporting productive engagement between parents and teachers is the frequency of their contacts with one another. Clearly, the two prescribed twenty- to thirty-minute conferences per year are inadequate for supporting meaningful dialogue across family-school borders. Teachers who are successful in working with families create many more opportunities to get to know the parents of their students. Sometimes they call additional meetings and announce to parents their willingness to respond to requests for even more. But what seems even more critical than scheduling additional formal encounters is the way in which teachers encourage and recognize the value of the informal presence of parents: inviting them to hang out for a half hour in the classroom before school starts, greeting them and sharing up-to-date information at the close of the day, or calling spontaneously when a child has done something wonderful. The daily and weekly accumulation of these more organic and "loose" encounters helps fertilize the common ground for the more highly charged and symbolic parent-teacher conferences.

Crossing the boundaries frequently and naturally certainly helps produce the conditions for better communication, but it is important to recognize that this does not necessarily require the physical presence of parents in the classroom. Molly Rose's carefully constructed program for communication with parents is designed to assure "transparency, accessibility, and fairness" for each family. Through *The Rose Room News* and the exchange of folders each week, Molly works to keep parents involved in what is going on in the classroom and aware of their child's individual progress. She gives them a language with which to talk to their children about what they are learning. Her reporting out to parents offers them a window into their child's world in school and a rich, detailed foundation for productive dialogue with the teacher when they meet face to face. This view into the classroom and their child's place in it allows parents to see—and empathize with—the teacher's role and begins to soften and modulate the contrary perspectives that make parents and teachers "natural enemies."

CHAPTER 3

Truths the Hand Can Touch

Hiding Behind the Ritual

As he sits in the first parent meeting of the year for his son, who is in third grade, Andrew Green tries to push the teacher past her ritualistic reporting, past the usual platitudes that tend to define the first cautious encounters. In the opening minutes of the conference, he hears what he already knows and what he expects, and he grows impatient. The teacher reports that Alex is in tutoring, that he is in the third reading group, et cetera. "All they are doing," says Andrew, "is hiding behind the ritual, reciting facts." He holds up his hands above his head. "They are starting way up here, saying all the stuff that is already observable to me. . . . I am trying to get them to be more descriptive of what's going on, to move beyond the abstractions and the bland, empty platitudes. . . . In other words, I want to know what the teacher has observed that leads her to make these judgments . . . and I want to know how these judgments stack up relative to what set of expectations."

Sympathy and Sentimentality

Parent-teacher conferences are highly ritualized events, and like most rituals, the form and content can become symbolic or substantive, routine or revelatory, limiting or liberating. In other words, rituals are double-edged, offering a structure and a routine that can inhibit expression and mask feeling, or providing a framework and safe place for authentic and honest dialogue. Andrew Green recognizes both the casualties and the opportunities, and he doesn't want to leave the conference "feeling empty and uninformed." Having sat through too many conferences that were "superficial and perfunctory," he is wary of the "pleasantries and banalities" of the ritual routine that muzzles truth-telling, and he pushes to open up real dialogue with the teacher through a vivid exchange of detailed information about his son. I believe that the double edge of ritual is magnified in family-school meetings because there is so much at stake.

For parents, there is nothing more precious or more important than their child. They come to the meeting eager, often desperate, to hear good news about their child's life in school. They approach the conference with fear and trembling, with terror in their hearts. Even for parents whose children are thriving in school, who have every reason to believe that the teacher will deliver only laudatory and appreciative comments, there is always a lingering worry that they will hear about a blemish on an otherwise perfect report. And the blemish, however small, can turn a joyous encounter into one filled with disappointment, even despair.

One mother, for example—a financial analyst with a ten-year-old son—tries to convey to me just how terrifying and urgent a teacher's call feels to her. Her son's teacher had called her the day before to set up a planned follow-up meeting to their fall conference. "In other words, this call did not come out of the blue; I had been anticipating it," she admits. The early-morning call had reached her at home before she departed for her office, "totally compromising" her day and "filling it with distraction and apprehension." But even this description of her anxiety does not communicate the "raw terror" she experiences, even though she knows from reviewing the teacher's response to her son's homework and his recent test scores that her boy is making steady improvement in his schoolwork. She tries again to describe the feeling, using "the most apt metaphor" of her fear, her voice full of urgency. "It is like if your doctor called and said, I want to see you about the results of the tests that we did last week . . . and you say, 'I'm free tomorrow . . . or how about tonight!' You want to rush there as quickly as possible. You can't wait for the news."

Although teachers do not express the same terror that parents do, most will admit that they worry a lot about conferences, that this is an arena of their work where they often feel the most unprepared and exposed. As one teacher said to me, "This is the part of my teaching where I feel the most raw and the most vulnerable." Most teachers feel as if the ritual conferences are a kind of "proving ground" where their professionalism and competence are being judged by people whose judgments are inevitably biased and who do not have the experience to make sound judgments. They also know that they not only have to convince parents that they themselves are competent, they also have to develop an alliance with them and gain their trust.

With so much at stake on both sides, and with the expectation that conferences are supposed to be relatively pleasant and civilized events, this ritual can often tilt in the direction of form over substance, sentimentality over sympathy, and rhetoric over truth-telling. The ritual becomes an empty, unsatisfying event that avoids talk that reflects the authentic feelings of the participants or talk that might lead to conflict. (This was Andrew Green's fear as he waited for Alex's teacher to "get to the substance.") I believe that parents and teachers often engage in an implicit and subtle bargain with each other: to give up the potential for discomfort in exchange for pleasantries; to not speak their minds in exchange for peace of mind. But the bargain is rarely fully satisfying for either party. Rather than the ease and comfort they bargained for, parents and teachers are left feeling a chronic disappointment, knowing that they have wasted each other's time and not learned what each has to offer in support of the child.

John Dewey's admonitions about the conditions that are particularly critical to dialogues between parents and teachers, written at the turn of the last century, still ring with relevance and poignancy. Article five of "My Pedagogic Creed" (1897) warns us of two major threats to productive parent-teacher encounters and echoes the urgency of Andrew Green's lament. First, Dewey speaks about the dullness and formalism that often characterize the ritual meetings between parents and teachers: all form, no substance. His words are biting: "I believe that next to deadness and dullness, formalism and routine, our education is threatened with no greater evil than sentimentalism." The ritual routine flattens and mutes the dialogue. But Dewey argues that the dead discourse is not the only "evil." The encounters are also distorted by "sentimentalism," a false politeness and forced decorum that do not permit honest exchange.

Dewey's second warning offers parents and teachers a way to break out of the formalism and empty routines, a way to overcome their preoccupation with pleasantries and platitudes. He reminds us that the adults—parents and teachers—must stay focused on the child and his or her whole development. Claims Dewey, "Only through the continual and sympathetic observation of childhood's interests can the adult enter into the child's life and see what it is ready for, and upon what material it could work most readily and fruitfully." Parents and teachers, therefore, must observe with a keen and sympathetic (not sentimental) eye that allows them to see who the child is and what he or she needs. This caring attentiveness and careful documentation of the child's life—his or her strengths and challenges, his or her capacities and gifts—will help teachers and parents know how they can best support the child's learning and growth, and in so doing give substance and authenticity to the ritual conversations between them.

Dewey's warning of the potential casualties of routine and formalism and his reminder of the ways in which education must always remain child-centered speak to the two primary arguments of this chapter. First, in order for parent-teacher encounters to be productive, the ritual must not turn into routine. Trusting relationships between parents and teachers grow out of a freedom of expression and a truth-telling that rails against the constraints and dullness of routine. Second, successful encounters are scaffolded by close observation of the child at home and at school and a sharing of information that allows parents and teachers to gain a holistic view of the child.

Artifacts, Anecdotes, and Evidence

ALL OF THE TEACHERS I spoke with recognize the twin power of the ritual to mask or enlighten. All work to develop relationships with parents that will allow them to be discerning and honest in talking about their students, and they all talk about authenticity and trust with parents growing out of a keen focus and subtle observation of the child's life in school. They also see parents as a great resource and recognize that they have a very different point of view. They understand that parents know their children far better than they ever will, and they count on them to offer their perspective and wisdom.

Interestingly, the trust that is the bedrock of good communication between parents and teachers develops out of the exchange of very specific information about the child. Several teachers, for example, say that conferences, despite their predictable form, must never become generic. They must speak to the individuality and idiosyncrasies of the child. The best way to keep the focus on the child and feature his or her individuality is to use evidence of the child's work and progress in school. By "evidence," I am referring to specific observations by teachers of children's aptitudes and achievements, vivid anecdotes of their activities, records of their written work, even photographs taken at school or audiotapes of their voices giving reports or reciting poems. These teachers use evidence, both proactively and defensively, to support their evaluations of children and to suggest prescriptions for what students (and parents) need to do to improve the child's chances for success.

Fania White, who teaches math and business courses at St. Joseph's, an urban Catholic high school, collects all of her students' work, including classroom assignments, homework, tests, attendance records, and class participation, into a portfolio that she presents to parents at their conferences twice a year. She depends upon these materials, and her visible and fair evaluation system, to efficiently represent the curriculum that she has covered in class, to convey her concern for each individual student and her fairness to all of them, and to hold her students responsible and accountable for their work. Fania believes that this system allows parents a realistic view of their youngster's progress, helps them understand her criteria for evaluating students, and convinces them that her judgments are neither capricious nor arbitrary. But Fania believes that the portfolio of work, scored by her exacting point system, does something even more important for parents. It makes them calm down. It is a source of great relief. When parents see that Fania is assuming the primary responsibility for their children's learning—that she is holding *herself* accountable—it allows them to "let go of some of their anxiety." "These are working parents, weary from a long, grueling day, struggling to hold their families together, always living on the edge," says Fania empathetically. "You can look into their eyes and see their tiredness. But there is something about confronting the evidence and feeling my seriousness of concern that gives them relief. . . . Their eyes brighten and they are thankful."

There is an intriguing irony here. Fania uses numerical, discrete evidence to assuage the anxiety and reduce the stress of parents. They are not comforted by convivial conversation or by a teacher's general statements of appreciation and support for their child. Rather, the evidence—rational, quantifiable, transparent—lets them know that Fania is watchful and discerning, "that she is taking care of business."

But Fania's portfolio account of each student also provides a visible and convincing record when parents express suspicion or a concern that their youngster is not being treated fairly. "They can challenge me, and I never feel defensive because the tangible evidence is always right there in front of us," claims Fania about a system she depends upon for its open access and rationality. On those rare occasions when she feels the tension rising as parents begin to challenge her grade, Fania's system never fails her. "I can present the proof, and the tension always subsides."

Fania offers "proof" through the fairness, thoroughness, and objectivity of her point system. The evidence is detailed, specific, and individualized, a convincing reflection of the student's work and a record of the responsibility and accountability embedded in the teacher-student relationship. In addition to the "proof" established by the point system, portfolios display artifacts of students' work and may be excellent reference points for meaningful dialogue between teachers and parents.

Jennifer Austin, a second-grade teacher in a city school that serves a largely poor and working-class population, uses artifacts of her students' work as a way of identifying their strengths and weaknesses, and as a way of coming as close as she dares to candor and truth-telling. She always begins each conference by showing parents the best example of their child's writing and pointing out the subtle and dramatic changes that are clearly evident when it is compared to earlier samples of their work. When she met with Rory's mom, for example, Jennifer read several sentences from a recent story he had written, and she applauded his use of adjectives and the fluidity of his writing. But she also pointed to his poor penmanship and ended up giving his mother some forms on which Rory could practice his letters every night. Jennifer also exhibited a more subtle strategy; she seemed to select a sample of her students' strongest work. She wanted the parents to see their child in the best light. Even though this allowed her to underscore the positive, it also permitted her to point out the areas of weakness that needed development. There was something generous, loyal, and strategic about choosing to reveal the best view of her student for parents to see. After the glow of the good news, the parents were better able to hear her concerns and criticisms.

Although Jennifer has developed a structure and set of rituals for her parent-teacher meetings, she also thinks of each conference as a unique encounter and tries to anticipate the particular idiom and dynamics of each family. For example, when Jamie's mother showed up unexpectedly, Jennifer had to quickly gather her thoughts, not only about Jamie's experience in her classroom but also about what she knew about his parents and his life at home. "I had to remind myself," says Jennifer, "that Jamie's mom is very scattered and disorganized. There is a lot of disorder in their home, a lot of clutter. In fact, Jamie's mom admitted to me just a couple of months ago that she was totally ADD. With that in mind, I want to be very clear and focused in what I say. I only want to say a few things and underscore them in a variety of ways." Despite the "disarray" in Jamie's home life—or maybe because of it—his mom tries to create daily rituals that will make life more peaceful and enjoyable for both herself and her son. For example, Jamie loves books, and "every single night, he and his mom cuddle up and she reads him a story." Whatever else is going on, they both create the space to close the day in each other's arms, reading a book. Before the conference, Jennifer also reminded herself that Jamie's mother "is extremely overprotective" and "keeps him very young"; "she babies him" and "gets really panicked" before she comes to the conference. With that in mind, Jennifer made sure that she offered Jamie "a lot of praise, all of it deserved, but maybe slightly larger than life." She also expressed empathy for how "difficult it is to parent." In general, with all the parents she works with, Jennifer is committed to "breaking down barriers," to "letting them know that I know that they know their child better than I do and that I have a lot to learn from them," and that "all of us are fallible; we all make mistakes." Jennifer's voice rises to a crescendo as she almost sings the "most important feeling I want to convey." "I want the parents not to feel threatened by me," she says. "I don't want them to have any fear. . . . I want to speak *to* them, not *at* them."

Sophie Wilder, the teacher of a combined fifth- and sixth-grade class at an alternative public school, uses evidence in another way. Like Fania and Jennifer, she gets very specific and personal. She always tries to begin each parent-teacher conference with a vivid anecdote that conveys to the parents how well she knows their child and his or her temperament, interests, vulnerabilities, and quirks. The anecdote can be profound or frivolous, serious or nutty, but it must somehow reveal that Sophie is "really tuned in to their child." And the specific characteristic that she chooses to talk about is most persuasive when it reveals something "larger and more core" about the child—when, in the tiny example, we can discover something about the whole child. For example, Sophie might mention to Nathan's parents that she noticed him wearing his brand-new Chicago White Sox sweatshirt for five days running, and that when he really wants to concentrate, he pulls the hood over his head and hides out. Nathan's parents grin in recognition; they've seen the same thing at home. And this small picture of Nathan leads to a broader conversation about his emerging social identity in the classroom as a "baseball junkie" and his developing focus and discipline as a student.

Sometimes Sophie purposely collects anecdotes and writes them down so that she will remember them when parent conferences come rolling around. She has one saved for the conference with Mona's mother next week, for example. At the beginning of the year, Mona's mother—a self-proclaimed card-carrying feminist—had told Sophie that she was concerned about her twelve-year-old daughter "maintaining her strength and voice" in the classroom. She had read the feminist developmental literature and worried about a pattern reported in the research that shows that around the age of eleven or twelve, girls stop telling the truth about what they are experiencing and begin to mask their power and intelligence. Mona's mother was determined that her daughter would not succumb to the "female stereotype of weakness and passivity." When she expressed her concern to Sophie during their very first conversation in the fall, she was seeking her alliance and support.

At her next conference with Mona's mother, Sophie has decided to begin with this image of Mona captured a few days ago during science class. "Last Thursday, Mona was working on a science experiment partnered with an older, sixth-grade boy," she recalls. "They were collaborating quite well together, talking, disagreeing, explaining things to one another . . . until Mona began to get totally absorbed by the data she was collecting. Soon she completely forgot about the fact that she had a partner, so absorbed she was in her work. In fact, she began talking to herself. It was thrilling to see how excited she was about the experiment, how strong she was in her passion, and how uninhibited she was about showing her brilliant insights."

Sophie believes that these individual narratives offering parents a vicarious view of their child in school are convincing to parents in two crucial ways. First, they can see that Sophie knows their child in a very specific way, that her remarks are not routine, abstract, or generic. Rather, they provide the kind of discerning and empathic documentation that Dewey talked about—and Andrew Green is yearning for—that makes the ritual expressive and meaningful. Second, the parents hear the care and admiration in Sophie's voice when she lights up the conversation with a story about their child. "Parents want to know that I care about their child, that I like him or her, and these anecdotes convey that better than anything I might say," says Sophie.

But there is also an added benefit for the teacher when she searches for the specific idiosyncratic narrative of one of her students. The selection of the anecdote, the composing of the vignette, requires the teacher to focus on the individual child (not the group) and on an event or experience that might capture something more "core" about his or her life at school. It also encourages teachers to look for interpretations of behavior that are promising and strong, ones that might hold potential for the child's development. As Dewey suggests, the kind of observation that will support student learning must be "sympathetic." Looking through this lens will help the teacher discover and focus on the positive attributes of her students, even with those students whom she finds the most difficult to like and teach.

Creating narratives of children, then, helps both parents and teachers focus on the child and identify his or her strengths and potential. It helps move the conversation from the rhetorical to the real, from the abstract to the specific. The "evidence" convinces parents that the teacher sees, knows, and cares about their child. And a story well told and embedded in context allows the listener to hear the general in the particular. The specific well-chosen anecdote tells us much more about the life of the child in school. There is a powerful blend of art and science here, in the well-crafted story and the hard data, the sympathetic insights and the empirical description. I am reminded of the great storyteller Eudora Welty, who, in referring to the development of her craft, said, "I always begin with the particular, never the general." When Sophie Wilder collects the poignant anecdote to tell Mona's mother and writes down the details in preparation for their conference, she is using the medium of a storyteller. Like Welty, she knows that the general resides in the particular, that Mona's enthusiastic engagement with the science experiment speaks about something larger.

Another artist, South African playwright Athol Fugard, also sees truth as residing in tangible evidence, in grounded data. He quotes a passage from Camus that refers to "truths the hand can touch." Fugard is drawn to Camus's phrase because, he says "I'm very frightened, very nervous, about a slightly religious element in my nature, and so I always hang on to the tangible." Fugard focuses on the tangible to avoid the religious; in a way, the tangible keeps him on the earth, grounds his ideas, and keeps him grounded. I think that it is these kinds of truths that build connections and trust between parents and teachers. The teachers that I have observed and talked to provide tangible evidence to parents of the child's work and/or words to convey their intimate knowledge of the child.

Intuition and Documentation

TEACHERS USE EVIDENCE not only to convey their knowledge of and concern for the child, but also to convey the "truths the hand can touch." They also gather data and marshal evidence when they have hard truths to tell, when they have a serious concern about the child and they know the news will be difficult for the parents to hear. "When I want to say something difficult to parents, I must first observe and keep a record of what I am seeing," explains Jane Cross, a teacher of four-year-olds in an elite private school. "Intuitively I may know that I have a concern, but it is only right, fair, and just that I be able to present the evidence to the parents."

Just a few weeks ago, Jane experienced that "intuitive" concern as she watched Adam, a normally easygoing and responsive kid, "tune out and shut down." For a few days, he seemed despondent and unfocused. When Jane approached him, he would just stare at her, almost as if he were looking right through her. After watching this behavior over a few days, noting when it occurred, and jotting down notes to herself, Jane asked Adam what was bothering him. She found a time when they could be alone, curled up together in the book corner, and she asked him why he seemed sad. He said that his brother was being mean to him.

After school that afternoon, Jane told Adam's mother that he had had a difficult day and had said his older brother had been mean to him. Adam's mother was surprised; she had not seen the boys fighting. Over the next week Adam continued to be "staring, frozen, looking through people," and Jane continued both to try to comfort him and to document what she was seeing. When Adam's mother returned to talk with her about what was going on with her son, Jane was able to be very specific in her descriptions. In fact, the "evidence" helped his mother recognize that she was seeing the same behavior at home. "I felt a real sense of relief," says Jane, "not because we came up with any answer, but because I knew we were talking about the same child, and I knew that I was not doing something to him that was bringing on this behavior." In the end, they agreed that his mother needed to speak with Adam's therapist, and that it would be a good idea to have a three-way conversation that included Jane. Throughout all of these meetings, many of which were both puzzling and painful, Jane offered a valuable perspective, a view that was always supported by documentation and illustration, a voice that tried to balance concern and dispassion.

Encounters with parents that focus on understanding a child's struggles and developing a plan of action are both challenging and rewarding. Jane feels confident both about her intuitive sense, which reflects long years of experience with young children, and her powers of observation. She also feels confident about communicating both her concern and the evidence to parents. These conversations tend to be without rancor or defensiveness, as Jane and the parents work collaboratively to solve the problem.

Much more problematic for Jane are the encounters with parents that feel "nebulous" and "fuzzy" (the opposite of specific and descriptive); when Jane feels unclear about why she is being approached; when the conversation seems to be masking some other concern or complaint. This "fuzziness" is often communicated not with the words being uttered, but in the tone of voice and the presumptive attitude. At these moments, Jane finds herself becoming defensive and edgy. She even admits that these are the times when she begins to get up on her high horse. Her voice is unapologetic. "I have an arrogant assumption that I know what I am doing," she says defiantly. "I think of myself as a reasonably articulate person. I have a rich background in parenting and teaching, so I don't mind questions, but my response depends upon how they come to me."

One morning a mother arrived at her classroom well before the start of the school day. She began to ask Jane a series of questions about the writing program that caught Jane off guard. She had, in fact, chosen to talk about a part of the curriculum about which Jane feels "most passionate." Although the mother was not being explicit about what was bothering her, her tone was suspicious and critical. Why was Jane using the didactic teaching of writing with four-year-olds? Why was she pushing the kids so hard in this cognitive arena? Why wasn't she trusting that these things would naturally develop in the children?

Jane was taken aback for several reasons. First, she wondered why this mother, whom she knew well and whose older child she had taught a few years ago, would be raising these questions at this point, when the school year was almost over. Second, she was surprised by her request that there be less focus on academics, when all of the other parents at Northwood were always clamoring for more reading and writing and an accelerated academic program. Third, she felt particularly frustrated by this mother's attack on an area where she has a "big reputation" for curricular innovation. Most parents, in fact, jockey to get their kids into Jane's class because of their admiration for her writing program. Finally, she could hear that the mother's endless questions were not real—that she asked them but never listened to Jane's responses. In fact, Jane had a sense that there was no way that she could have satisfied this mother's queries. "These were not questions," she says with disgust in her voice. "This was subtle criticism. This was disapproval."

The conversation seemed endless and pointless. After all the children arrived and all the other parents departed, the mother made her exit and headed over to the headmaster's office to lodge a more formal complaint. Jane was left with an aching feeling that haunted her for the rest of the day and was already threatening to ruin a good night's sleep. She simply couldn't understand what had just happened. She thought that she knew this mother and had always felt her support. Besides, her son was a "magnificent child" who had been happy and productive in her classroom this year. What in the world would she have to complain about?

"It felt so incomplete and so unsatisfying," Jane says with disgust. "I felt terribly defensive, and you can't be creative or clear when you are feeling defensive." She is quiet for a while, and then her voice reveals the hurt. "I don't take it personally," she begins courageously, "even though I feel personally defensive." She knows from the rare times when she has experienced these "insinuating" encounters with parents that this one will be echoing through her for weeks to come, that she "won't be able to leave it alone." It will remain unfinished, incomplete, nagging, preoccupying. She knows already that it will be one of those times when she will just try to "live through it," but she will never feel any resolution. This normally restrained and understated woman balls up her fist and pounds the table. "I hate the way this feels!" she says through clenched teeth.

Straight Talk

PARENTS FEEL THE same kind of frustration that enrages Jane Cross when teachers do not talk straight, when they seem to be withholding information, and when their motives and judgments get masked behind polite and evasive language. They do not want to hear generic statements or ritual rhetoric. They come to meetings eager for the teacher's knowledge about their child and listening for the convincing evidence that is the basis of her judgments. They also want to feel that the teacher honors their perspective; that she recognizes that they know their child better than she ever will; and that their intimate understanding of their child will help her become a more effective teacher.

Andrew Green—who is wary of the abstractions and platitudes that fill parent-teacher conferences—is a father of two children who attend an elementary school with a reputation for excellence in an affluent suburban district. His wariness is reflected in the two big questions that he asks himself every time he enters a conference: "Does this teacher know our kid?" and "Can she talk to me? . . . That is, does she have the courage, the language, and the skills to communicate the information that will help me know my son's reality in school?" From the fragments he has picked up at home, Andrew already has a sneaking suspicion that his son, Alex, who is beginning the third grade, is not being sufficiently challenged by Mrs. James, that "she is not creating high enough expectations for him." He knows his son very well, and he knows that teachers tend to underestimate his skills and capacities, misinterpreting his slowness for dumbness and expecting too little from him. In fact, Alex is a very bright boy who struggles with fluency in both reading and writing. Since first grade he has received in-school tutoring and guidance from the school's reading specialist, and he has shown steady improvement. But perceptions of his "slowness" persist, and they are probably more related to his style and personality than they are to his reading level. "By personality," says Andrew, "my son moves at a slow pace. He's careful, methodical, and takes great pride in his stuff." Andrew explodes with laughter, revealing a mixture of parental pride and exasperation. "He gets up in the morning at six-thirty, and by seven-twenty he's just combing his hair," he says, shaking his head.

So when Andrew meets Mrs. James, the tutor, and the reading specialist for the first time, he enters with "deep concerns" and "clear biases." Before the teachers even open their mouths, for example, he makes known his "particular stance" about the tutoring his son is receiving. "My fear about tutoring is that the kid gets labeled and made to feel dumb," he says. Leaning into his argument, he continues, "And my other fear is that teachers do not talk to you straight about kids' problems." On the one hand, he is worried about the stigma of the labels that get attached to kids and lead to feelings of low self-esteem. And on the other hand, he is concerned about teachers' reluctance to honestly identify problems that they see, pretending to themselves that all is well or fearing parental backlash.

Andrew and his wife, Carol, are particularly suspicious of teachers who refuse to identify learning difficulties of children in their classrooms because they experienced "years of neglect" with their daughter, Beth, who is four years older than Alex. As early as first grade, when most of her classmates were already reading, many of them well beyond grade level, Andrew and Carol knew that their daughter was struggling with decoding letters. They were vigilant in questioning her teachers and expressing their concerns. But each time they raised the issue of some possible learning difficulties, the teachers told them not to worry and seemed to dismiss their growing anxiety. It wasn't until Beth reached the third grade—when most of her classmates were already veteran readers—that a teacher finally made the diagnosis of dyslexia. (Apparently, this teacher was the mother of a dyslexic daughter, and she saw the signs immediately.) When she finally named the neurological origin of Beth's struggles, it came as a great relief. "She was real, direct, and clear with us," recalls Andrew, "and as soon as we knew exactly what it was, we could take action . . . and within months she had moved ahead light-years." At the beginning of third grade she was reading at the first-grade level. But with the appropriate interventions—and incredibly hard work on Beth's part— she was reading on grade level by the time she reached the fourth grade.

The diagnosis of Beth's learning disability was complicated by the fact that she is a child that "everybody loves." "Beth," says Andrew proudly, "is instantly lovable." She is the kind of child that every teacher enjoys having in her class, the kind of student that makes teachers exclaim to each other in the hall, "Oh, you got Beth! Isn't she wonderful!" Now Andrew is shaking his head over the teachers' rapture about the daughter whom he calls "my hero." "I remember one time when one of her teachers was telling us about Beth at a parent conference. I had to stop her, because it sounded like she was giving her eulogy, like my daughter was some kind of saint." The problem with Beth being so "instantly loveable" is that the teachers' extravagant admiration for her somehow compromised their ability to identify and name her academic difficulties. The warm glow that emanated from her and made her teachers feel good and successful in her presence masked the truth they needed to see and the difficult news they needed to tell. So when Andrew enters his son's third-grade conference, he feels the echoes of his earlier struggles with Beth's teachers who "did not speak the truth" about his daughter. He wants to make sure that his son does not get wrongly labeled or categorized, and that the teachers get to know him and see both his strengths and his challenges.

At first, Andrew does not express his impatience with the teacher's "ritual reciting of facts." He hides his frustration behind a placid, unmoving face that the teachers find hard to read and that causes them some discomfort. But inside, Andrew is aware of his growing impatience and his chronic skepticism. Although their talk is reasonable and relatively pleasant, he feels that they are withholding some information that he wants and needs to know. Now he is leaning forward, his face full of intensity. "The teachers feel, to me, resistant. They don't trust me to handle the information in a way that allows them to make better decisions about my boy," he says in a way that sounds elliptical and confusing. Then he makes it plain. "You see," he says drawing an invisible line on the table, "we're in a contest for control. It's them or me. The less information they give me, the harder it is for me to tell them what to do . . . the harder it is for me to question them." His voice is now at peak crescendo as he declares his ultimate goal: "I want to have a clear and honest description of the situation, and I want them to offer a prescription for action." He gets even more specific and pragmatic. "By the end of the meeting, I want to know what we would have to do to get my son out of tutoring. What is the plan that we can create for him that will allow him the expected amount of self-sufficiency that a nine-year-old in this environment should have?"

Andrew pushes hard for a plan of action. He does not want to leave the meeting without a clear sense of the next steps, so by the end of the conference he is "forcing them to be explicit about expectations—ours of them, and theirs of my son." His voice is almost mocking as he refers to the "empty praise" teachers ritualistically offer at the beginning and the end of parent conferences. "If everyone really believes that my son is so smart," he says with a snarl, "let's make a plan. Don't massage me by telling me he's so bright. There is no news in that for me . . . unless that translates into how we interact with him." Mrs. James looks uncomfortable when Andrew insists that they be explicit in "naming the prescription and designing the intervention." She resists the formality and urgency of his approach, which she believes should be more organic and open-ended. They each finally give a little, in a subtle negotiation that softens Andrew's expectations and gives more clarity and structure to Mrs. James's proposals for action. The plan includes a ratcheting up of the teacher's and tutor's expectations, translated into higher, measurable standards for Alex, a careful monitoring of his progress, and another conference scheduled in a couple of months to "review the bidding."

When they reconvene in early November, the news is good on every front, although Andrew admits that his anxiety almost doesn't let him hear what the teachers are saying. The tutor begins by reporting that Alex is reading faster and comprehending more. He recently wrote a book report and read it very nicely in front of the class. The teacher taped it, so his parents are able to hear his voice, strong and sure, even funny in spots. Actually hearing his son's voice is the "most convincing evidence" of his progress. It is now his writing that needs special attention. Although his penmanship has improved, the teachers say the writing remains slow and labored. Knowing by now that Andrew wants a measuring stick, the tutor reports that if the class is given twenty minutes to write something, Alex will get 75 percent of the way through the task.

The main thing Andrew notices, however, is how the tutor describes "the intervention," the plan that they had prescribed at the last conference. The tutor offers an example of how she has begun to push Alex. "Look," she says, "you're at seventy-five words, let's see if you can read eighty-seven words next time." As his parents had predicted, Alex rises to the challenge, and "it seems to energize him." As Andrew listens to the tutor's satisfied exclamations, he watches Mrs. James carefully and notices her lack of enthusiasm. He hears her say—not once but three times, and in a voice that sounds slightly disapproving—"but this requires so much effort from Alex." After the third repetition, Andrew becomes a little suspicious. He tries to keep his voice quiet, but his question probes for her meaning. "What am I to take as important in your statement?" he asks, looking directly at her. "Is this a good thing or is this a problem?"

Mrs. James turns pink and appears a little flustered, but her voice is steady. "No," she says, "I'm *complimenting* him."

"Now," says Andrew dramatically to me, "enter my wife, Carol, the good cop, who tries to smooth things over by saying that we—that is, she and I—have these same kinds of problems with communicating at home."

But Andrew does not want things smoothed over. For some reason, at this moment, the masked talk is unbearable. "No," he says, correcting Carol in front of the teachers, "this may be uncomfortable, but it is our attempt at *good* communication. We're trying to figure out what is really being said here."

"By contrast," he explains to me, "poor communication would be if I did *not* ask what Mrs. James *really* meant, and then I went home and thought maybe she was really saying that challenging our son was a bad thing because he was getting overstressed and over-heated . . . or I went home and worried maybe she was just bullshit-ting me and I had not caught her doing it."

It has been less than twenty-four hours since the conference, and the memories are raw and fresh. But I am struck by Andrew's vivid recall of the nuances of expression and language, and by his awareness—even as he sat there—of the text and the subtext of his conversation with the teachers. I am also impressed by his determination to find the real meanings of the words that usually pass for communication during these rituals. He is unwilling to "leave it alone," even though his urgent interrogation makes everyone—including himself—slightly uncomfortable. He will risk conflict and discomfort in order to move the ritual beyond rhetoric to something real.

Empowering the Child

IN ONE WAY or another, teachers and parents who want to avoid the "dullness" and "sentimentalism" that Dewey rails against must be willing to risk the discomfort of truths grounded in evidence. They must challenge the platitudes and pleasantries, the formalisms and rhetoric of empty ritual. The challenge needs to be in the service of seeing the child more fully and clearly, keeping the child in focus. Molly Rose believes that having the child in their midst is the only way to make sure that parents and teachers come together on behalf of the child and remain focused on his or her needs. To have the child physically present reminds the adults why they are there. But Molly goes a step further toward ensuring that the child will be a full participant. In her first-grade classroom, in a city school that serves a largely poor, immigrant population, the six-year-old children not only attend all the parent-teacher conferences, they actually lead them. "These are," Molly says grandly, spreading her arms wide, "child-led conferences." Moreover, Molly's first graders actually evaluate their own progress and grade themselves. *They* produce the "truths the hand can touch." And in learning how to gather the evidence, make informed judgments, and report their self-evaluations to their parents and teacher, they develop the skills of documentation and discernment. They learn how to talk about what they see and feel, and how to present their own perspective on their experience in school. In the process, their parents begin to see their children in a new and different light.

Molly shows me an example of a large portfolio that serves as the text for the parent-teacher conferences. It documents the student's work and self-evaluations at three intervals during the school year—fall, winter, and spring—along with the child's changing self-portrait. Before the conference, Molly meets with a small group of students to introduce and interpret the checklist of categories they will use to evaluate their own work. The progress report includes checklists in reading, writing, math, social studies, and personal growth ("I tell the kids that this is the most important page," says Molly), and the children are asked to rate themselves with an "M" (most of the time), an "S" (some of the time), and an "N" (not yet). After reading each of the items out loud to the children (by the end of the year, they no longer need her support reading the words), she talks to them about the approach they should take in filling out the forms. "I say to them, 'You really should be thinking about who *you* are, not comparing yourself to other people or trying to compete.' " Even though over the years she has watched her six-year-olds rise to the occasion, she still sounds awestruck when she says, "It is amazing how serious they are about doing this . . . how absolutely thoughtful, reflective, and honest they are about setting goals and measuring their progress."

Once they have filled out the forms, the children come to the conference ready and eager to show their work and their appraisals to their parents. "It is quite a sight to behold," exclaims Molly, "to see this little kid taking charge, explaining his work, and making informed and clear judgments about his progress." The parents often listen in amazement. They have never heard their child speak with such authority. And by the end of the year, Molly becomes a mere observer, sitting on the sidelines admiringly and saying very little. The portfolio grows over the year and documents the trajectory and development of the students' work. Most of the time, children look back over the pages and note the "dramatic changes" in their work. "I used to write like that!" they say incredulously, looking at the primitive scribbles they made in the fall. Everyone can watch the changes as "the scribbles turn into letters, then words, then voice, then ideas." Throughout the year, Molly is always taking photographs of the children, which are also pasted in their portfolios, recording the "amazing changes" in their physical development as well.

At the very end of the conference—in a gesture that feels almost like an afterthought—Molly gives the parents their child's report card. "By the time I give them the report card," she says, "it feels superfluous. It almost has no meaning. The real information, the authentic work and assessments, are all in the *child's* report. . . . I have never had any parent complain about the grades on the report card.

They've already heard the evidence." As Molly reflects on the child at the center of the parent-teacher conference, she underscores a principle that shapes all of her interactions with parents. "I'm very reluctant to talk with parents if their child is not there." Sure, there are the occasional exceptions when there is a family situation that the child does not know about, or when a parent just seems too awkward speaking in front of her child. "I would never *insist* that we not talk alone," claims Molly, "if this made the parent feel very uncomfortable." But she does everything in her power to smoothly draw the child into every conversation, and when she feels she has to defy her principle of inclusion, she does so with reluctance and guilt. It feels like a defeat, like she is being disloyal to the child.

Very occasionally—even with all of the coaching and preparatory work with children—the conference ends in disaster. Before she tells me her "worst ever" experience with a parent, Molly reiterates the goals that always guide her conferences. "Most of all," she reminds me, "I want to work with kids to take ownership and responsibility for the conference, *and* I want to always communicate to their parents how much I respect their child and how well I know him. This is not a generic conference." But all of these lofty goals broke down one day during a scary conference with Marcus's mother.

Marcus was a very difficult child. "Sneaky and manipulative," he was mean to other kids: hitting and kicking them, ripping up their papers, stealing their lunches, and bullying anyone who dared to cross him. Some of these transgressions he did openly and without apparent remorse. But other acts of delinquency and vandalism he performed surreptitiously. One afternoon when she was about to leave school, Molly found her soiled winter coat stuffed underneath the stairs in the hall outside of her classroom. She immediately suspected that Marcus had done it, but she decided to "let it go." Several days later, however, Molly actually saw him stuff Jasmine's coat underneath the same stairwell. This time she confronted Marcus directly and called his mother to arrange a time for her to come to the school so the three of them could talk.

In anticipation of his mother's visit, Molly worked with Marcus to get him to reflect on and take responsibility for his behavior. They made a lot of progress; he began to tell the truth and "take some ownership" of his actions. He even seemed prepared to admit his guilt in front of his mother. But at the meeting Marcus's mother interrupted her son as he recounted his story and began screaming at Molly. How dare she accuse her son of wrongdoing? How dare she humiliate and victimize her boy? "She lost it on me," says Molly with fear in her eyes. "There she is, this huge woman, standing over me, gesticulating and blaming and roaring around." Molly was terrified, but she also felt angry. "I felt she was doing a very bad thing. She was undermining me in front of Marcus. . . . I'm not a confrontational person. I was not blaming him or being accusatory. I was only trying to empower Marcus. . . . I was trying to say, 'We're going to solve this problem together, and I am going to support you.' "

But none of Molly's appeals or reasoning could halt this ranting woman who seemed to have spun out of control. Molly acted quickly to remove Marcus from the line of fire. She settled him in a nearby classroom, out of earshot of his mother's screaming. When Molly returned, the mother was still "raging and blaming," still making wild accusations. (Afterward, she found out that this mother had a big reputation around the school for being scary and disruptive. Her colleagues recounted similar tales of her terrorizing and told Molly about a screaming match she'd had with the principal in the hall right outside his office.)

Although she never spoke the words explicitly, Marcus's mother seemed to be raging at Molly's whiteness, at the image of her black boy being abused by this white teacher. Molly's voice is tentative as she works to unravel the dynamics of this encounter. Was it this mother's snarling threats that seemed to carry a racial insinuation? Was it her memory of the time in class when Marcus told her that his mother "hates all white people"? Or was it something in Molly that was frightened just because the woman was big and black? Her fears—even as she sat there with this woman towering over her— were laced with these questions, causing her guilt and indecision. But one line resonates most clearly in her memory, one line that stood out from all the background noise and hyperbole. "I remember the moment as if it were yesterday," says Molly dramatically. "I even remember what she was wearing; tight sweatpants and a green sweater." Marcus's mother said words that stunned her. "Okay, we can be friends again," she said at the end of the terrifying encounter, her voice suddenly conciliatory. Molly recalls feeling that her words felt "genuine and real," but she mostly remembers thinking how odd her comment sounded and how off the point it was. "I wasn't even thinking that this was what we were doing here. We were not about making friends. We were about finding a way to support and empower Marcus." Molly's face still registers disbelief. "I wasn't working to be her friend!"

Things never got much better with Marcus or his mother. Marcus continued to misbehave, and his mother continued to rage and blame the teacher. "The whole notion of empowering the child just broke down," says Molly sadly. This defeat still causes her pain.

Listening for Truths

When teachers speak of telling the truths about their students through the vivid recall of an anecdote, through data gathering and documentation, and through the presentation of artifacts, they also know that a one-way presentation of information will never produce the trust that is the bedrock of productive parent-teacher encounters. Truth and trust grow out of a dynamic interaction in which listening for truths is just as important as telling them. When Dewey speaks about "adults entering into the life of the child" in order to better support and nourish the child's growth and development, he is referring to the value of multiple perspectives, to the rich information that combines the teachers' and the parents' perspectives and wisdom. Teachers who are successful in working with parents, then, always stress the value of listening to their accounts of their child's life outside of school. They know that the parental view will be more holistic, more intimate, more subjective, and more passionate than theirs. And rather than dismissing their perspective as "overinvolved or biased," they see it as an essential complement and counterpoint to their own.

Molly Rose, in fact, calls her first encounter with parents a "listening" conference, and she urges them to do all of the talking. When they look to her for her opinion or ask for her evaluation of their child, she is quick to circle back to them and ask the questions that will encourage them to retake the lead in the conversation. Like Molly, Jane Cross comes to her first conference with parents ready to offer her view of the child's experience, but much more eager to listen to theirs. She wants to know how they see their child and what expectations and goals they have for him or her, and she wants their "detailed description of the child's life at home." Although Jane wants to listen to the parents' views, they usually come to the meeting eager to hear what she thinks. Their different expectations sometimes produce a moment of tension, before both Jane and the parents "each give a little" and a "back and forth" conversation emerges where information is shared. Jane is clear about the single most important criteria of a successful conference. "I judge it to be successful," she says, "if we feel that we are talking about the same child." She also hopes that there will be a "meeting of minds"; that, despite their very different perspectives, that they will be "working from the same page."

If Jane really listens hard, she can sometimes hear the dissonance between the goals parents are willing to "claim out loud" and those they actually "hold in their hearts." For these parents, whose children attend an elite, progressive, independent school, the former is always more "politically correct" and "restrained" than the latter, which Jane hears as "primal and needy." Jane has learned to be alert to both messages—the overt and the covert, the text and the subtext—but she knows that the truths she hopes to hear are likely to be found in the subtext.

It is not an exaggeration, then, to see trust between parents and teachers as being the result of truth-telling and truth-hearing. In his book *The Call of Stories: Teaching and the Moral Imagination*, Robert Coles makes a similar point when he describes the storytelling that is central to good medical practice. He recalls an early lesson taught to him by one of his supervisors during his medical residency. "The people who come to us bring us stories," said his mentor. "They hope they tell them well enough so that we will understand the truths of their lives. They hope we know how to interpret their stories correctly. We have to remember that what we hear is *their* story." Coles reminds us that trust—between doctors and patients, teachers and parents—comes from both the telling of truths through stories and the hearing of truths through stories. The story is expressive and subjective, often personal and passionate. It challenges the dullness and routine of empty ritual. And if teachers really listen, they may hear in the particular story something with which they can identify. Like patients seeking counsel from their doctors, parents come to teachers with the hope that they will hear their stories and comprehend their truths. The trust that parents feel for teachers is built on the teachers' hearing and understanding.

Of course, in order for teachers to benefit from the parents' perspective, the parents must be willing to communicate their point of view. They must be willing to offer their version of the truth about their child. Sophie Wilder, who counts on parents to speak to her candidly and specifically about their children and uses the information to help her be a better teacher, feels great frustration when parents are withholding and evasive in response to her queries. "Very occasionally," she says sadly, "parents are reluctant to give me a full picture of their child, either because they are embarrassed about their lives at home or because they do not trust me with the information. . . . Mostly these parents see their role as listening, or just enduring our time together. They sit there and then they leave." Sophie claims that this is often the case with low-income parents (particularly those who either flunked out or were pushed out of school themselves), who feel diminished just sitting in the classroom and have a huge suspicion of the institution that gives the teacher her legitimacy to make judgments.

Sophie recalls a painful visit with Aisha's mother, a single mom who lives in the projects, is on welfare, and never made it beyond the eighth grade. Sophie had spent weeks calling her, trying to convince her to come to the meeting. When she finally arrived, she sat across from Sophie looking tense and awkward. Aisha was "struggling enormously" in school, and Sophie hoped that her mother might provide information that would give her some clues about how to work with her daughter more productively. But every time Sophie asked her a question, she would either be evasive or straight out lie. When, for example, Sophie asked about how Aisha was managing her math homework, the mother claimed that she saw her daughter doing it faithfully every afternoon and that she never had any trouble completing the assignments. Even though Sophie could show Aisha's mother the portfolio, in which there were many missing and incomplete assignments, she still claimed that everything was fine, there was nothing to worry about. "It was as if she thought that *she* was being graded," says Sophie sadly. "This must have brought back to her all of her own humiliating experiences in school. Talking to her felt really delicate, really difficult."

It was not that Sophie even cared about the many lies and cover-ups this parent told. It was just so sad that Aisha's mom felt the need to relate to her in that way. "I began to think that this is the way that Aisha's mom has probably gotten by all of her life . . . that she has had to lie to welfare and to all the bureaucracies she has to deal with. She does not see us as having a relationship. She just wants to get it done, to get what she needs." Even as Sophie sat there trying to be non-threatening, trying gently to draw something out of Aisha's mom, she kept on thinking how hard it must be for her to be there. "I'm thinking to myself that there are so many levels of distance between us. How will we ever bridge the chasm?"

The chasm seems overwhelming to Sophie, who understands some of the reasons for this mother's resistance and alienation but is frustrated by her unwillingness to tell the truths that might help her daughter. Despite her best efforts, Sophie cannot undo the rage born of Aisha's mom's cruel history of failure and humiliation in school, or her distrust of institutions and bureaucracies that judge her harshly. Even though Sophie will continue to chip away at the woman's brittle façade and continue to remind herself not to "take this mom's anger personally," she does not expect to make much progress by the end of the year. She does not expect to develop an easy rapport with her. But she does believe that listening, even listening to lies, is a first step. And she does remind me that after numerous telephone calls, missed appointments, and even her offer to make a home visit or meet in the park, Aisha's mother did, in fact, come to the school and sit in her classroom. For her, that was a big step.

Sophie believes that listening is "the first act of empathy," and empathy is the only human gesture that just might begin to bridge the chasm that seems so vast and overwhelming. If she can put herself in this mom's place and see the situation from her perspective, she will not feel like such a stranger. With parents whose values, histories, and life circumstances are more similar to the teacher's, this trading of places is easier, more familiar, and natural. For others, the teacher needs to listen harder—to the text and subtext—of what is being said and stretch to make an empathic connection.

In her book *Fires in the Mirror,* performance artist Anna Deavere Smith talks about the ways in which she inhabits the characters she plays. She makes an interesting distinction between "getting the character to walk in the actor's shoes," which is the acting tradition that Smith herself was trained in, versus "getting the actor to walk in the character's shoes," which is what she is aiming for in her own work. The difference is both subtle and huge. In the first instance, the method leads to characters that reside within the experiences and parameters of the actor. By contrast, in the second instance, the actor travels outside his or her range to find the character. Smith says that "the spirit of acting is the *travel* from the self to the other." Smith is on a search for truth in her work—truths about events, truths about people and relationships, truths about "the American character." She finds these truths by moving outside herself, outside her frame of reference, and traveling the distance to "the other." And Smith's transformation into characters so different from herself is never an abstract process. It is grounded in nuance and subtle detail, it is conveyed through vivid storytelling. It is palpable, visceral, and expressive.

Smith's description of her art offers an intriguing image for teachers and parents—like Sophie and Aisha's mom—who want to stretch across the chasm of experience. It helps us draw a clearer image of the relationship between empathy and truth. Smith seems to be saying that empathy requires that teachers step out of themselves and travel the distance (metaphorically and emotionally) to where the parents are; they must find ways of adopting their frame of reference and walking in their shoes. This requires a rapt, undiluted attention and empathic listening to each other's narratives.

And the ultimate point—as Molly Rose would remind us—is not necessarily for teacher and parent to become friends. The stretching out to meet each other must be in the service of the child. In fact, the place where they might recognize—and ultimately appreciate—each other, however large the chasm of difference, is in their mutual concern for the child.

The wisdom drawn from the experiences of parents and teachers in this chapter is surprisingly and refreshingly specific and prescriptive. At the center of their litany of lessons is an intriguing paradox. On one hand, trust and empathy grow between parents and teachers when they share descriptive, behavioral evidence about an individual child's experiences at school and at home. On the other, abstract rhetorical talk, even general expressions of appreciation and approval, breeds suspicion and distrust. The generic conference—which "hides behind the ritual," using formalism and routine as mask and barrier—is unsatisfying and unproductive. Dialogues between parents and teachers are best, then, when they are focused on the specific strengths and capacities of the individual child, providing descriptive evidence of progress or weakness.

When parents hear the teacher capture the child that they know, they feel reassured that their child is visible in her classroom—that the teacher actually sees and knows him or her—and they get the message that she really cares. Parents yearn to hear that the teacher appreciates their child, and that is conveyed through a vivid portrayal of his or her life in the classroom, not through platitudinous praise or saccharine sentimentality. (In fact, there are few things more upsetting to parents than to leave a conference feeling that the teacher does not "like" their child.) Likewise, when the teacher practices the discipline of seeing the individual student in the foreground, against the backdrop of the group, she often discovers strengths and gifts in him or her that she never anticipated or noticed before. As Dewey suggests, this kind of "sympathetic observation" of "childhood's interests" allows for a more responsive, supportive pedagogy and more productive interactions with parents.

There are at least three specific skills that teachers need in order to do this subtle and highly individualized work. First, they need to be trained in the art of observation; they must learn to see things clearly, notice the nuances of interaction, and read body language and nonverbal cues. They must become students—even connoisseurs—of human behavior. Second, they must be trained in the skills of record-keeping and documentation. They must develop the daily discipline of note-taking and journal-writing; they must follow their intuitions with careful records that either confirm or challenge their earlier suspicions. And, third, they must learn to listen—to really hear—the voices and perspectives of parents. Just as they need to be able to offer up the specific details of their students' lives in schools, they must be receptive to the parents' stories about their children. The "listening conference" that begins Molly Rose's series of encounters with parents immediately signals to parents that she needs their intimate knowledge of and insights about their child in order to be a successful teacher. It also conveys her genuine respect for them. I believe that these three skills—observing, recording, and listening—are at the core of good pedagogy and effective work with parents. They are skills that must be taught in teacher training courses in colleges and universities, and developed and honed over time through practice, supervision, and dialogue with colleagues in school settings.

Certainly skill development and practice are essential to articulating "the truths that the hand can touch," but there is an art to this as well that enriches teachers' communication with parents. When teachers think of themselves as storytellers—when they search for the compelling narrative, select an anecdote or illustration that reveals a core truth about a student, even jot it down for retrieval at the parent conference—they are using the modality of an artist as well as the skills of an empiricist. Hearing the story well told, parents can see the general in the specific, and they can also begin to feel identified with that part of their child's experience that resides inside them. The circle of empathy is joined.

Not only does good "evidence"—grounded in disciplined observation—lead to better communication and trust between parents and teachers, it also helps teachers tell hard truths, and it helps parents hear them. In other words, parents recoil at negative appraisals of their children that are not grounded in "artifacts, anecdotes, or evidence." Such generalized statements make them worry that the teacher doesn't like their child or is unfairly picking on him or her, and parents are likely to feel diminished or become defensive. Yet when teachers are able to embed their concerns and criticisms in an evocative illustration or concrete evidence from student work, then parents may experience discomfort or disappointment, but they are better able to hear and respond to the teacher's concerns. They and the teacher can begin to problem-solve together

Finally, there is no better, more convincing evidence of a child's progress than to have him or her present and participating when parents and teachers come together. It is safe to say that parent-teacher conferences that are held without the child being present exclude the most valuable voice, the most knowledgeable perspective. When children are invited to the conference, however, it is crucial that they be seen as authentic participants, not passive bystanders, and teachers must help prepare them for their real role in the conversation. Molly Rose's experience with her first graders helps us recognize that even very young children can hold their own in the three-way dialogue. This is not a practice that should be limited to middle school– or high school–age students. In fact, Molly's six- and seven-year-olds don't just participate, they lead. They become the interpreters and evaluators of their own experience, and in so doing, the authors of their own stories.

CHAPTER 4

Inequalities and Entitlements

Polar Opposites

Molly Rose, a first-grade teacher, describes the striking contrasts between two polar opposite schools; as she moved from her first job in Winston, a rich suburban school just outside of Boston, to a brand-new charter school serving poor black children in Cleveland. The differences in these schools and the communities they served were reflected most vividly in the ritualistic open houses scheduled for the beginning of the school year. "In Winston," says Molly, "open house was a classic event. You know," she says, hoping that the description will strike recognition in me, "the classroom looks beautiful, perfectly decorated for the parents.... I write a script for my opening talk, then rehearse it until I know it by heart, so I won't need to refer to it, and so it will appear completely natural.... I stand up and present for an hour. The parents listen and take notes. I dread every moment of the evening. They ask some pointed questions, thank me when it's over, leave, and talk about me afterward." In a few short sentences, she has captured the tenor of the occasion for the teacher, so filled with anxiety, tension, and stage fright, and so focused on establishing her legitimacy in the eyes of the parents.

The open house at the charter school in Cleveland could not have *been more different. The school opened a week late that year because the building was not yet ready for occupancy, and the open house took place in a huge empty space that would one day be a combination gym and auditorium. There were no chairs, and the parents arrived with all of their kids in tow. The noise was deafening, ricocheting off the unfinished cement walls. Standing at the microphone, the principal was finally able to bring the room to some semblance of order as she welcomed the families and made a few opening remarks. Her last sentence, however, led to unbelievable chaos. "Now," she instructed the parents, "you can go and meet your child's teacher." But the parents had no idea where to go. They had not been given a map of the school, nor were they told where their child's classroom was located. So everyone sort of staggered around the halls—frustrated and confused—in search of their children's classrooms. Even though Molly had prepared a welcome talk for the parents, she soon realized that it would be absurd to stand up in front of the classroom and try to give a presentation with people floating in and out, tugging noisy, tired children behind them. Now she is laughing at herself. "The fact that I thought I was going to speak was totally ludicrous."*

Odds and Opportunities

MOLLY'S MEMORY IS one of "culture shock" as she moved from the rarified, affluent suburban school where she delivered practiced prose to an elite audience of judgmental parents to a poor, struggling city school where the chaos and confusion of opening night made it impossible for her to offer a "proper welcome." She moved from a perfectly decorated and manicured setting full of shiny desks, modern computers, and the latest curriculum materials to a room in a converted factory where her classroom supplies consisted of twenty-five chairs (for twenty-seven children) and there were no books, pencils, or paper. Molly's journey highlights the wide variations in encounters between parents and teachers that reflect differences in race, social class, educational background, and immigrant status. It is almost as if rich and poor families inhabit different planets, so remote are their experiences in building relationships with their children's schools. In the first three chapters, I explored dimensions of parent-teacher relationships that prevail, in varying degrees, in all settings: in city, suburban, and rural schools; in rich and poor communities; in private, public, and parochial schools. In each setting parents and teachers come together haunted by the ghosts of their early family and school experiences; they are engaged in passionate struggles over boundaries, rights, and issues of responsibility and accountability; and their ritual meetings are richer and more productive when they are focused on the child, grounded in evidence, and express a mutual appreciation of each other's perspectives and wisdom. But despite all of these shared experiences across social and cultural contexts, there are also striking differences in parent-teacher encounters, reflecting inequalities of status and station, of access and opportunity, of resources and entitlements.

At one end of the spectrum are privileged parents who bring the power of their money, their status, and their influence to school with their children. Their expectations are high, their demands rigorous, and their sense of entitlement assumed. At the other end are poor parents, often parents of color or newly arrived immigrants, who feel uncomfortable coming to school or approaching their child's teacher, who have no idea how to negotiate the institutional bureaucracy, and who tend to see the teacher as the ultimate authority and rarely question her judgment. Affluent parents' behavior toward teachers is characterized by frequent aggressive encounters and a fierce, determined advocacy; by contrast, poor parents appear withdrawn, uncomfortable, and passive.

Even though rich and poor children have vastly different odds and opportunities that are rarely undone by their schooling, I believe that *all* parents hold big expectations for the role that schools will play in the life chances of their children. They all harbor a large wish list of dreams and aspirations for their youngsters. All families care deeply about their children's education and hope that their progeny will be happier, more productive, and more successful than they have been in their lives. Each generation asks for more. I believe that this is just as true in Cleveland as it is in Winston, despite the huge contrasts in material and cultural resources. And all parents see the school as the primary vehicle for mobility in our society. They see a direct link between their child's achievement in school and his or her chances for a better life. Despite what I regard as the universal yearning of all parents—whatever their educational or vocational background—there are striking differences in the expectations, aspirations, and demands that parents make on schools, and in the ways in which they advocate for their children. These parental aspirations shape the quality, intensity, and scope of their encounters with teachers.

There is something peculiarly American about the extraordinary aspirations that we citizens—whether rich or poor—have for our schools. There is no other society that holds up such lofty goals for the role that schools play in the development of children and the building of society as does ours, and no other society that, as a result, expresses as much disappointment and dismay when those goals are not reached. The great expectations lurk at the borders of families and schools and shadow encounters between parents and teachers. The parent-teacher conference becomes an arena for—perhaps a metaphor for—our high ideals and our dashed dreams, for navigating the shoals of our deep cultural disappointment in schools.

Half a century ago, French sociologist Jacques Barzun observed the brash optimism that Americans hold for their public schools. A Frenchman raised and educated in an explicitly stratified, elitist school system, Barzun experienced his own version of "culture shock" as he observed the American educational agenda. Using the European educational system as his reference point, he was amazed by what we expect schools to accomplish and by the range of individual, familial, social, and cultural goals for which we hold schools accountable. He seemed to be only half-joking when he described our long wish list.

> Sociologists and the general public continue to expect the public schools to generate a classless society, do away with racial prejudice, improve table manners, make happy marriages, reverse the national habit of smoking, prepare trained workers for the pro-

fessions, and produce patriotic and religious citizens who are at
the same time critical and independent thinkers.

(Jacques Barzun, 1945)

Barzun's list also underscores some of the contradictions embedded
in our bold expectations: that children should be both accommodating and critical of what they are learning; that schools should be
breeding grounds of both civility and romance; that schools should
eradicate class and racial hierarchies and be the primary vehicles of
social selection. And Barzun believes that our high hopes for school
inevitably lead to dismay and disapproval. There is no way that
schools—or any single social institution, for that matter—could possibly fulfill our aspirations. Our schools' failure to do so leads to a
chronic disappointment that can grow into an unproductive public
cynicism. His appraisal suggests that we need to be more modest, circumscribed, and realistic in the goals we set.

Historians of education help us understand the sources of our cultural desires and our discontent. Americans, they say, have always
looked to schools as mechanisms for improving society. We have regarded schools as our major engines of social reform and advance-
ment. At the turn of the century John Dewey's words burned with an
optimism shared by most of his countrymen: "I believe that education
is the fundamental method of social progress and reform." Horace
Mann's voice was even more impassioned when he claimed, "It may
be safely affirmed that the common school, improved and energized
as it most certainly can be, may be the most effective and benign of all
the forces of civilization."

As the nation's priorities have shifted over the last century, our expectations of schools have expanded and intensified. Historian Patricia Albjerg Graham traces the changes in the goals we set for our
schools and helps us interpret the contradictory and extraordinary
demands that Barzun cites as remnants of our shifting cultural views.
Graham documents four shifts in our nation's priorities from the early
part of the century. "Assimilation" of the children of immigrants was
the goal (1900–1920) until the progressive education movement

gripped the nation and "adjustment" became the primary objective (1920–1955). In the 1960s and 1970s, schools opened their doors wide, and universal "access" was the priority. Today schools are expected to "increase the achievement of all students," and "leave no child behind." In this century-long march, Graham sees an ever expanding, increasingly demanding agenda for schools: "from assimilation to adjustment, access to achievement."

But it is not only that we Americans have historically lifted the bar of expectations, making increasingly greater demands on schools as our primary mechanisms for access, assimilation, opportunity, mobility, and social cohesion. It is also that schools are the template upon which our societal ambivalence about the meanings and measures of equality get imprinted. In his book *Inequality*, sociologist Christopher Jencks describes the contradictions embedded in our legal and philosophical definitions of equality, contradictions that find their way into our expectations of schools.

> Most Americans say that they believe in equality. But when pressed to explain what they mean by this, their definitions are usually full of contradictions. Many will say, like the Founding Fathers, that 'all men are created equal before God' and that they are, or at least ought to be equal in the eyes of the law. But most Americans also believe that some people are more competent than others, and that this will always be so, no matter how much we reform society. Many also believe that competence should be rewarded by success, while incompetence should be punished by failure.
>
> (*Christopher Jencks, 1972*)

Jencks observes that Americans have a deep commitment to the notion of equality but that we share an equally strong view that people should be rewarded for their industry, their achievement, even their good luck, and that this differential reward structure inevitably leads to just inequalities. As long as we provide people with equality of opportunity, that is as much as the law can possibly ensure. Beyond that, people must negotiate their places on the social and economic pyramid, a hierarchy based on hard work and achievements.

Jencks's analysis, however, primarily focuses on the ways that these contradictions, embedded in the American public's rhetoric and views about equality, are most dramatic and visible in the goals we set for schools. On the one hand, schools are thought to be the great equalizer. Everyone—despite his or her family origins, racial and ethnic background, or social class—is given the opportunity to achieve. On the other hand, schools are thought to be our primary sorting institution, the first place where we distinguish the winners from the losers. And, in reality, the sorting usually corresponds with the social class and racial hierarchies of the broader society. If you are poor, black or brown, or if your parents were uneducated, then it is likely that you will find your place at the bottom of the pyramid. Likewise, if you are from a white, affluent, well-educated family, it is likely that schooling will reinforce and assure your family station. To paraphrase Jencks: If we know the social class and racial background of a child before he or she enters school, then we can successfully predict his or her achievement in school and his or her likely success in society after he or she becomes an adult.

There is certainly evidence of *individual* achievement through school, heroic stories of individuals who have climbed the ladder of success through meeting and exceeding the high academic hurdles. But Jencks reports that there is no evidence that schooling supports group mobility, that education serves as a vehicle for raising up a whole category of people and causing a major alteration in the social arrangements of society. The American rhetoric speaks of a benevolent government providing opportunity for all, but in reality schools serve to reify existing status hierarchies. As Billie Holiday sang, "Them that's got shall get, them that's not shall lose."

Our great expectations of schools—forged in our history and enlarged over time—shape parental expectations and influence the ways relationships are negotiated between families and schools. It stands to reason that if our aspirations for schools are complex and exaggerated, then our views of teachers—who represent and embody these institutions—will also be charged with desire and disappointment. Our expectations of schooling in America are further complicated by our complex views of equality, by the role we see schools playing in achieving a just society, and by the dissonance between our values, our rhetoric, and our actions. We believe in equality of access and opportunity through schooling, but we express an equally powerful commitment to rewarding the talent, hard work, and privilege that produce differences and hierarchies among us. Again, these contradictory expectations of the school's role—in leveling the playing field and producing winners and losers—have a huge impact on parental demands and teacher expectations.

In this chapter we will witness the ways parents and teachers navigate the social class, racial, and ethnic borders between families and schools; the ways in which they negotiate the chasms of culture and experience between them; the ways in which bias, prejudice, and ignorance distort and confuse productive encounters; the ways in which goodwill, empathy, and forgiveness create paths for communication and understanding. Parent-teacher meetings offer an excellent lens for examining the larger tableau of culture and class in American society. They make vivid the inequalities of power, knowledge, and resources, and they reveal the contrasts in values, expectations, and dreams for our children that shape the essential conversation between families and schools.

The Pressures of Privilege

TEACHERS WHO WORK in elite, privileged environments speak about both the benefits and the drawbacks of working with parents who are well educated and ambitious for their children. They admire and depend upon the parents' interest, engagement, and participation in school events, their support and advocacy of their children, and their shared views about the value of education. The teachers can also count on a common vocabulary and an ease of communication. But they often experience affluent parents as disarming and difficult. They notice how easily their advocacy for their child can slide into an overbearing intrusiveness, and how their lofty ambitions put a heavy stress on their youngster that can inhibit and distort learning. Teachers are then in the awkward position of trying to protect students from their parents' unrealistic demands. And, in the presence of high-powered and influential parents, teachers often feel diminished and disrespected, relegated to the role of servant or hired hand.

Carol Steele, a special education teacher who directs the Pilot Program at Summit High, an elite suburban high school renowned for its academic excellence, describes the "peculiar culture" of a community where parental "power and sense of entitlement" both energize and threaten their adolescents' education. Her work with the most vulnerable students, those who crumble under the academic and social demands at Summit, allows her to see just how fierce the pressures are, even for "ordinary kids." "This is an upper-middle-class community," begins Carol, "full of well-read, intelligent parents who know their rights and responsibilities but care more about their rights." There is not an ounce of cynicism in her voice as Carol underscores the aggressive advocacy that is at the core of parental interactions with the school. "They want the best for their kids, the best school that will ensure success and status, and they have the resources to make that happen." This kind of extreme pressure from parents, claims Carol, creates a pressure cooker for their children who become single-minded, competitive, and anxious in their pursuit of academic achievement. "In this context," explains Carol, "academics take on a whole new life. . . . Kids want desperately to succeed, sometimes at any cost, including cheating. It is not unusual to see a kid crying in the hall because she got an eighty-nine instead of a ninety." Carol's tone has now changed from evenhanded observation to exasperation. "How many tutors can parents hire to keep their son in honors math . . . four or five?" She offers several examples of what she considers to be the extreme measures to which parents will go "to land their kids at the top of the heap," and the competition that gets acted out, and the stress that gets absorbed by their children. It is a story of privilege, pressure, and pain, and of the inevitable frustrations, disappointments, and casualties that follow this kind of shrewd, calculated pursuit.

This kind of high-pressure, high-stakes activity also has had an impact on institutional values, priorities, and programs at the high school. A few years ago, for instance, the technical arts programs that used to be a special feature of the school were dropped because the children (at the urging of their parents) stopped signing up for the classes. So courses in business, accounting, woodworking, and electronics were eliminated and replaced by such fancy and esoteric courses as Modern Chinese History. "This means that there is no downtime for students," says Carol, "no time for daydreaming, cooling out, letting go." She recalls one of her favorite courses when she was in high school: "You know, I used to love accounting because it was sort of mindless, and I could cool out and have downtime."

As Carol concludes this brief description of the institutional culture of the high school where she has taught for the past eleven years, her voice is a mixture of critique and admiration. She both loves and hates the striving and the standards, and she sees both the opportunities and the casualties of such a high-powered educational environment. "This is the best place I've ever seen academically, and the most committed teachers with long tenures," she says in praise. "But what gets lost is an appreciation for different styles of learning. There are a whole lot of talented kids who are not able to show their full strengths in this environment. We do not fully support their gifts."

Carol admits that the pressure intensifies and the stakes get raised for high school students as they anticipate the narrowing paths to elite colleges and universities. By the time they reach high school, most of the students at Summit are "building their resumés" for college, composing their academic and extracurricular schedules so that they will be attractive to the most selective colleges. All of their efforts and strategies are pointed toward the future; there is little energy left for enjoying or engaging the present. Parents are their youngsters' eager sponsors, protecting, demanding, and pushing for better performances from their adolescents. And to ensure success for their children, parents enlist the teachers' full cooperation and compliance. Says Carol, "This puts teachers under enormous strain, takes our attention away from the essence of teaching and learning, and makes us feel as if we have to produce results."

But it is not only adolescents who internalize the ambitions of their parents and feel the pressures of the pursuit of excellence. The demands for achievement also reach down to the very youngest children. Jane Cross, a veteran teacher of the nursery group at Northwood, an elite independent school, complains of the ways in which her sense of authority and professionalism is undermined by parents who want her not to just teach their children, but also to "produce results." Jane, who is the daughter of professional parents and was herself educated in fancy schools, chafes at the ways in which the parents of her students "talk down" to her and treat her like a "servant." She describes the ways in which the parents see the nursery year as their child's first step in the long journey to Harvard or Yale or Stanford, and they expect that the school's high tuition and elevated status will "buy them that result." Every conference is colored by the parents' desire to see and hear evidence of their child's precocious pursuit. He or she must not be "average" in anything; only "exceptional" and "advanced" will do. The teachers' ordinary descriptors become inflated as parents wait to hear extravagant praise and are disappointed when they don't. "Their child is their most valuable *possession,*" says Jane, her voice both sympathetic and cynical, "as well as a reflection of who *they* are."

Without any urging, all of her students' parents show up for conferences, and Jane is always moved by their eagerness, earnestness, and commitment. She tries to hold on to that positive view of them, but more often than not, "something seems to turn in the conversation that threatens their kid's advantage, and they become competitive and demanding." Jane spends a good deal of her time gently and strategically resisting what she feels are the unrealistic and distorting expectations of aggressive parents. In her conversations with them, she tries to strike a balance between being didactic and reassuring, as she speaks to them about the natural developmental progression of children and urges them to honor the "wonders of childhood." "I'm often telling them," says Jane, shaking her head in exasperation, "that children must talk before they can write. . . . You want to assure them that it is okay for their children to play a lot, and that they will, in time, learn to read." Jane knows that parents, in fact, are aware of these things; that they understand the developmental appropriateness of play; that they know that talking comes before writing. But she is also clear these are "intellectual understandings" that rarely correspond to their emotional yearnings or their actions.

Parents seem to be most concerned about their children's fluency in reading, even though they are just four. They have huge anxiety about their child learning to read before kindergarten. In a class where many children arrive already reading, this is the major yardstick of aptitude and intelligence, the lightning rod that fires up parents and makes them competitive. Jane recalls one difficult conversation in the fall when a mother came in to complain that her daughter had learned to read when she was three, but that now that she was in school, she wasn't reading anymore. The mother was both confused and accusatory, acting as if something Jane had done might have "sabotaged" her child's early achievement and proficiency. Jane did not feel defensive. By now she is used to both children losing their interest in reading after an early start and the parental disappointment and anxiety that follows. She explained the phenomenon to the mother, who seemed resistant and dubious. "These things take a lot of time to unravel with parents," she says, recalling her efforts at explanation and the mother's perseveration. "There are so many complex forces that must be understood." It is not unusual that these kinds of hard conversations do not lead to a "meeting of the minds." But over the years Jane has learned to be patient. She realizes that these struggles cannot always be resolved in one sitting, and she does not take it as a sign of failure or as a reason to retreat. Rather, she regards it as progress and sets up another time to continue the conversation. "With experience, I have learned that parent meetings are never completely unsuccessful. Even if we are not saying or seeing the same things, at least we're talking."

Rich and Poor, White and Black

THE "PECULIAR CULTURE" of affluent, high-achieving, predominantly white schools is made vivid when we see it in comparison to schools attended by children from poor, largely uneducated black families. The contrast reveals dimensions of both settings that shape the ways in which parents and teachers encounter one another and marks the boundaries that define family-school territories. Molly Rose—whose tale of the two open houses begins this chapter—felt the "huge sea change" between the suburbs and the city, between rich and poor, between blacks and whites when she left Winston and moved to Cleveland. In Winston, at the affluent suburban school, Molly confronted parents who felt they "owned the place, defined the standards, and ruled the roost." In the new and struggling urban school, Molly had to work hard to convince parents that they "were welcome and belonged there" and that they should "have a voice in their children's education." In the rich school, Molly tried to impress the parents with her intellectual sophistication, her innovative curriculum, and her creative pedagogy. In the poor school, she tried to find ways of engaging parents that did not depend solely on language.

When Molly arrived in Winston she was an idealistic young teacher who had just finished her master's degree in education from Teachers College at Columbia University. Even though her goal was always to be an "urban teacher," she chose to start her teaching career in an upper-middle-class suburban school system because she wanted to "get her feet wet" in a place that she "*perceived* to be more stable than city schools." She thought that in Winston she would have more resources with which to work, more collegial guidance and support, and a community that valued education. I also suspect that Winston felt familiar to Molly; it was not unlike the privileged community in which she grew up in suburban New Jersey.

Molly arrived at Winston with an unbridled eagerness and a "huge commitment" to educating children. "In Winston," she says, smiling at her idealism and innocence, "I had a passion for kids but no teaching philosophy." In the early days, she found herself focused more on her performance for parents than on the development of children. "I always felt like I had to defend what I was doing, and the audience was always the parents," she says, remembering the vulnerability she felt in relation to the privileged parents of her students. When she would send out her weekly classroom newsletter to parents, Molly would pack it with fancy-sounding, intellectually appealing items that she hoped would impress them. "The newsletter was more like a promotional tool," admits Molly. "It was like I was saying, 'Look at all that we are doing in *my* classroom. We're being so productive, and your children are being exposed to so much.' " She lets out a long sigh, recalling the emotional exhaustion that was the result of this "performance mentality."

By the time Molly moved to Cleveland, her teaching philosophy and practice had evolved. "I realized," she says, a little bit apologetically, "that the children were not there to defend what I was doing." Rather than viewing teaching as a performance piece for parents—a stance that made her feel constantly exposed—she grew to believe that it was all about "empowering kids," a perspective that allowed her to relax and focus her attention on "really teaching."

Despite the poverty and the terrible lack of resources, the charter school was a place that the parents had chosen for their children. They had fled the dreadful public schools in Cleveland, where their children were languishing from inattention, and come to the charter school determined that their children become achievers. Molly explains, "These parents were deeply invested in their children's education, but they didn't express it in the same way as the Winston parents . . . and they did not feel as welcome or as entitled, nor did they know very well how to negotiate the system on behalf of their kids."

It turned out that the open house was just the first sign of "culture shock" that Molly experienced at the charter school. "I was a stranger in every way," she says, describing both her sense of being "other" and her isolation. To this all-black, poor, Midwestern city school came Molly from her predominantly white, privileged, suburban, Northeastern background. Most of her colleagues, who never fully accepted her and refused to learn her name, called her simply "the teacher from out of state." She was given a classroom in the far corner of the building at the end of a long hall. "At first," she says, "I hated the isolation. . . . Then I grew to see the physical separation from the other teachers as a kind of protection for the innovations I wanted to make." The principal, always somewhat suspicious of

Molly's motives, insisted that she turn in her lesson plans each week. She would dutifully submit the plan book, "and then turn around and do the opposite." This duplicity was no problem, since the principal never visited her classroom. "I was completely, utterly isolated," says Molly sadly.

But she brightens up immediately as she begins to describe her "love" for the children. "The passion for the kids" always felt deeply familiar and comforting to her. She is laughing remembering the first challenge of learning all twenty-seven names and faces in a school where the children wore uniforms and had such "wonderful, exotic names." There were four girls, for instance, whose names were almost indistinguishable. "In that class," says Molly, smiling and spelling each name out for me, "I had Monika, Marika, Mooteeka, and Mafiqua." And to complicate it even further, "this was at a time when hair extensions were the big thing." So just when Molly was finally figuring out who was who, one of the girls would appear the next week with an entirely new hairdo.

Although Molly used the same system that she had developed in Winston to work with parents—the "getting to know you" meeting, the weekly folders sent home, the newsletter, and the child-led parent-teacher conferences—the quality and dynamics of her encounters with parents often felt very different. She draws out the contrasts. In Winston, the parents were much more comfortable being in the school, and they felt much more entitled to make demands on behalf of their kids. In Cleveland, the parents were, by and large, much younger, and although they clearly wanted the best for their children, they were often reluctant to make their voices heard. Molly remembers trying to make the parents feel welcome. "I was always trying to help them feel like the school was *their* place, like they could ask questions and make demands, like we really needed them as our partners."

The parents' apprehension and reluctance seemed to ease, however, when their children were present. In the child-led conferences, Molly noticed a shift in the "power dynamics" that had seemed before to get in the way of real communication. In these meetings children would often show their parents the learning games that they could do at home together. "This was the place where I had to get very resourceful," says Molly. "With no materials, I'd create these very simple hands-on manipulatives—like a paper cup with beans where they could count by twos—where kids could show, and explain, their learning during the conference." This kind of active and participatory conference not only made parents feel more comfortable and allowed children to demonstrate their schoolwork, it also tended to be much more engaging than meetings that relied purely on talk.

Even though Molly remembers learning how to "communicate beyond language" with the charter school parents, by using the children as "the best translators of their experience at school," she also recalls times when her interactions with families caused her fear and confusion; when she did not know where to draw the boundaries between home and school; and when she would occasionally yearn for the more familiar "cultural and class" demands of Winston. When I ask her for an example, her eyes fill with tears. The memories still cause her pain. Molly's difficulties with parental attitudes showed themselves most visibly—and disturbingly—in their approaches to discipline. "At that time in Cleveland," says Molly, aware that she is making a "huge generalization," "kids got whippings with a belt."

She remembers a very troubled boy named Sekou, who, at six, was already showing signs of serious delinquency. He'd bring in marijuana from home and try and sell it to his classmates, or he would hang around school with older accomplices and beat up little kids. When Sekou did not respond to any of Molly's appeals or threats, she called his grandmother, who came in the next morning, grabbed her grandson, hauled him back to the coatroom, and proceeded to give him a long, hard beating with her belt. Sekou's bloodcurdling screams mixed with his grandmother's fierce expletives. She would not stop the beating, she screamed, until Sekou stopped his "baby crying." This probably lasted for only a couple of minutes, but Molly remembers that it felt like an eternity. Horrified and scared, she had no idea what to do. "I remember," she says, with the fear still etched on her face, "trying to keep the other kids engaged and busy . . . not letting them run back to the coatroom, insisting that they stay in their seats. That was my primary concern."

This felt to her like one of those impossible situations where any action felt wrong. Her head was a jumble of confusion. She knew that Sekou deserved and needed to be punished, but the beating made her want to protect him. She felt embarrassed that she could not handle this herself and that the grandmother's entry into her classroom somehow "eroded her authority" and communicated values that were in conflict with everything she was trying to teach her students about "how to handle their anger and their disputes." On the one hand, if she had not called the grandmother in, then Sekou would have continued to disrupt and endanger her class. On the other hand, when Sekou's grandmother came at her request, it meant that she had to be ready for her to take care of it in her own way, a way that was violent and abhorrent to Molly.

Culture and Class

FAR AWAY FROM Cleveland and Winston, in a small town in Maine, Audrey Pierce, a sixth-grade teacher, also observes huge contrasts in her relationships with rich and poor parents. The Maple Street School, where she teaches, is one of three elementary schools in town that house grades kindergarten through six. With about three hundred students in the school, there are two classes at each grade level. Although it is not considered a "poverty school," it has been designated for Title 1 funds, and a significant percentage of the children come from "destitute rural families." Actually the socioeconomic mix is fairly broad, with a few professional, middle-class and upper-middle-class families at one end and illiterate welfare families at the other; with families living in manicured country estates with breathtaking vistas, and families crowded into trailers with broken cars and debris all over the lawn. "There are no really rich families here," says Audrey, "but this is a town where families with some resources will decide to send their kids to public school, rather than always choose a private school.

"Maine is one of the whitest states in the Union," says Audrey in explaining the fact that "race doesn't figure in a big way" with her relationships to parents. In this year's class, for example, there are only two students who might be regarded as "culturally different"—one from Argentina and the other from Korea—and both of them are academically gifted and extremely successful in school. Marcello, a light-brown boy from Argentina, just learned English a couple of years ago, but he is already a fluent speaker, a good reader, and a sensitive writer; he mixes comfortably with his peers. His mother has never come in for a conference despite several reminders from Audrey. Each time Audrey calls, she sounds cordial ("not disinterested"), but she seems reluctant to come because she is embarrassed by her halting English. Paul, a Korean boy, was adopted by Korean parents and raised in the United States. His father, in fact, was born in this country, moved to Korea as a young man, and married a Korean woman. "He clearly has American tastes and sensibilities," says Audrey, "while his wife is much less comfortable, much more withdrawn." When Paul was still a baby, they moved back to the United States.

When Audrey thinks about the potential for cultural misunderstandings between teachers and parents, she immediately thinks about a recent interaction that she had with Paul's father at the first conference. As in all of her other parent-teacher conferences, she began by telling Paul's dad (his mother never appears at school) what she saw as a primary goal for the year. She started gently, by praising his son's "brightness," "attentiveness," and "respectfulness." Then she told him that Paul was a "reluctant writer," reticent about expressing himself on paper, and that he had earned "only a C" for his portfolio of essays. As she looked into his face, she could tell that Paul's father was growing increasingly uncomfortable, maybe even angry. She thought to herself, *Why am I having so much difficulty reading his face?* His response surprised her; his tone was clearly defensive. "I think that you want my son to be perfect in everything," he said coldly. "You obviously have a stereotype about Asian parents. You think we all want our kids to do everything right. You think that we are overambitious for them." Audrey was completely taken aback by both his haughty demeanor and his misinterpretation of her message. "I was totally blindsided," she says, shaking her head about one of the rare times she was caught off-guard by parents. "I had no idea that this is how he would take this!" An uncomfortable silence followed, interrupted finally by a whispered comment by Paul's father. "I also had a hard time writing myself. I still do."

Audrey could see immediately that Paul's dad was defending himself *and* his son, but she still felt baffled by his charge of cultural stereotyping. Tripping all over herself, she tried to say that Paul was doing very well, and that no one was perfect or expected to be. She tried to tell him that this was Paul's only struggle, the one thing that he needed to work on. Although he must have heard the sincerity in her voice, Paul's dad continued to shake his head, finally holding up his hand in a gesture that seemed to say, "Stop trying so hard, you've made your point." But Audrey went away from their meeting feeling confused and unsuccessful, and she reports that—even now—she feels an unsettling wariness when Paul's father drops by for a conversation after school or calls to ask a pointed question about the math curriculum.

If crossing the cultural divide is rare at the Maple Street School, it is not unusual for Audrey to negotiate extreme social class differences in working with poor families. She can identify several children in her class who live in "extreme poverty," whose parents are barely literate, and who come from "dysfunctional families where there is incest, abuse, violence, and malnutrition." Rural poverty "feels different from urban poverty, but it is just as brutalizing to the kids." With students coming from impoverished environments, it is often hard for a teacher to know where to draw the line. "You want to help, but you also know that there is only so much that you can do," says Audrey flatly. "Sometimes I feel so despairing and inadequate. Other times I feel, Why bother? It just feels so hopeless."

Most of the time, Audrey tries to take a kind of "neutral" and "benign" position, in which she works to "meet parents where they are," "give them as much knowledge as they can absorb," and "help them become advocates for their children." With parents who are "barely educated," for instance, she tries very hard to "break things down" and "demystify the scene." In seeking to make things simple, however, she must be careful not to talk down to them. This balancing act between making things plain and being respectful is particularly diffi-

cult when parents are faced with major bureaucratic and legal procedures. When, for example, the school does an evaluation for a special-
needs child to determine whether he or she is eligible for special
education and related services, Audrey knows that she will lose parents and create defensiveness if she tries to go through the specifics
and language of all the rules and regulations. Instead, she tries to talk
about the general ideas and let them know "how they can best advocate for their kids" to get them the most appropriate placement. Audrey shakes her head and smiles. She actually enjoys "decoding" the
bureaucratic regulations and legal language for families who would
otherwise be lost without her interventions. She actually relishes the
role of supportive translator.

In fact, Audrey admits that her work with poor families usually
feels more "natural and rewarding" than her interactions with the
more affluent parents. She immediately reassures me that there is
nothing in her style or temperament that enjoys "saving or rescuing"
poor folks, no subtle sense of noblesse oblige. Rather, she admires the
poor parents' realism and their pragmatism. When they approach her
with a question or a concern, it always feels "real and tangible" to
Audrey; and they are usually asking for "what should be justly theirs."
Audrey's experience with rich parents—though "these are not very
wealthy people," she reminds me; "poverty is always relative, and
these folks look and feel rich compared to the other families"—has
been somewhat less satisfying and more troubled. She readily admits
to "a prejudice which I can't seem to shake" that "supereducated"
parents tend to be demanding and overambitious for their children.

Some of her prejudice comes from her own experience as a child
growing up in a family of privilege and prestige in Chicago; her father
was a very successful lawyer and her mother a devoted homemaker.
They were a family that "pushed education hard" and hoped that their
three daughters would rank at the top of their class. Audrey remembers her older sisters accommodating their parents' wishes; they were
straight-A students. Audrey, on the other hand, was never an enthusiastic or successful student, and she always felt like a great disappointment to her parents. Now, when she sees parents—particularly
wealthy, ambitious parents—pushing their children to be at the top of

the heap or asking her for special favors, she is reminded of the ways in which, even as a young child, she "felt stressed out by [her] parents' expectations and sometimes embarrassed by their sense of entitlement."

But echoes from her childhood do not account for all of the wariness she feels in relation to the "relatively rich" families that she works with. Even if she didn't have these ancient demons that feed her prejudice, she would still smart when these families take up more than their fare share of her attention. This year the worst offender, by far, is Allison's father, a child psychiatrist who both expects his daughter to be an excellent student and is preoccupied with assuring her emotional health. From Audrey's point of view, he is "unbelievably intrusive," constantly "invading his daughter's space" and "violating the boundaries" between home and school. It is almost as if he carries around some sort of emotional barometer, a stress meter that he places on his daughter's heart. When the meter rises above some point, he is at the classroom door or on the phone to Audrey at home in the evening, trying to find out what might have gone wrong during the day. Not only is this close scrutiny bad for Allison, who has learned to depend upon her father's constant intervention, it also undermines her learning, which "inevitably, from time to time, will be stressful and difficult." To protect your child from all pain is to limit the risk-taking and challenges that are central to her optimal development. So Audrey spends a good deal of time trying to calm Allison's father down and "create a buffer zone" between home and school. Audrey lets out a roaring laugh as she reflects on "the most difficult category of parents." "I think the shrinks are probably the hardest to deal with. They are always identifying all kinds of problems—too subtle for the rest of us to see—with their kids."

Immigration and Assimilation

IF "SUPER-EDUCATED AND ENTITLED" parents are at one end of the continuum in terms of their expectations and the demands they place on schools, then immigrant families—in particular first-generation immigrant families—are at the other. It is impossible, and misleading, to generalize about the characteristics and contrasts between these two group experiences. But as I listen to the voices of teachers, I hear the same descriptors again and again. Affluent parents are omnipresent, eager, earnest, ambitious, and entitled. They cross the family-school boundaries frequently and with ease; they feel as if their presence and their demands are legitimate and that teachers are there to serve and respond to the needs of *their* children. Immigrant parents may have big dreams for their children; they certainly hope that schools will give their youngsters the skills and strategies that will help them achieve and make it in their new country. But they are wary and uncertain in their interactions with teachers. Their reticence is born of not knowing the language, customs, or idioms of the new country; not knowing the norms, rules, and rituals of classrooms; and not feeling welcomed by a school bureaucracy that seems opaque and impenetrable. Not knowing all of these things makes them stay away from their children's classrooms and leaves their offspring to negotiate the school on their own.

When historian Patricia Albjerg Graham observed that the early twentieth century was a time when Americans looked to schools as the primary mechanism of assimilation, she anticipated this period in our history when another huge wave of immigration would lead to similar expectations of the role schools would play in the lives of newcomers. Again, large numbers of immigrant families—this time immigrants of color—are looking to schools as the great cultural incorporaters, and they have, like their predecessors, passionate and mixed feelings about turning over their young to them. Immigrant parents definitely appreciate the access and the opportunity schools afford. But they also know that if their children are to succeed, they must learn a new set of norms and behaviors that may undermine the precious traditions of their own families and cultures. They see the trade-offs, and they live with their ambivalence. Teachers who work with the children of recent immigrants, then, experience a complex set of responses. They observe and are often frustrated by the immigrant parents' wariness and reluctance. Teachers occasionally even admit to enjoying the autonomy and authority that the parents' reticence and abdication of responsibility allow them. But they also understand the ways in which most schools do not make these parents feel welcome, and they work hard to reach out to them and make them feel as if they belong and have a legitimate role there.

For twenty years Fania White, a lay teacher, has taught math and business courses at St. Joseph's High, a Catholic city school that serves 240 students, most of them first- and second-generation immigrants from Haiti, Puerto Rico, the Dominican Republic, and Mexico. She sees the school as an asylum and a portal, a "kind of Statue of Liberty symbol," that receives, assimilates, and educates newcomers. "It is a welcoming place where we are all God's children," she says proudly. Over the years this shiny symbol has lost some of its luster. St Joseph's has obviously seen better days. The large brick building is immaculate but very old, with crumbling stone stairs at the entrance, poorly lit corridors, worn linoleum floors, paint peeling from the walls and ceilings, heavy wooden desks arranged in neat rows, and ancient bathrooms. While I am there, a group of men in dark blue suits, with clipboards in their hands, arrive from the central diocese office to evaluate the physical plant for things that need immediate attention and repair. The only part of St. Joseph's High that feels contemporary are the students, who are not wearing the parochial school uniforms that I had expected. Instead they are dressed in typical teenage garb: baggy pants, long shirts, and sneakers.

Fania remembers back to the time when she first arrived and the school had almost twice as many students, most of them "refugees from Asia," Vietnamese and Laotians looking for a "safe haven." The Asians have all but disappeared from the school, and Fania reasons that they no longer need the protective environment of a Catholic school because they have been largely successful in integrating into the "mainstream" public system. The families that now come to St. Joseph's are mostly black and brown, working class and poor, most of them recent immigrants, and the majority are not practicing Catholics. Most of the parents of students struggle and sacrifice to pay the $3,000 tuition, or they are fortunate enough to receive one of the scholarships funded by the diocese and government subsidies. Like the Asian immigrants before them, they too are looking for a "safe haven," a strict and disciplined environment and set of religious values and rituals that will instill in their children just the right amount of fear, duty, ambition, and loyalty.

Fania recites the first sentence of the school's mission statement: "We are a people of faith, and we believe in the gospel values." And she claims that these words are not simply rhetoric at St. Joseph's. They are embedded in the "culture of the place," symbolized in the crucifixes and Virgin Marys that hang in every classroom, echoed in the student-led prayer said over the public-address system during first period every morning and woven into the Masses at Christmas and Easter and during Lent. Even though it is neither expected nor required, Fania begins every one of her classes with a prayer. Sometimes she just recites a few phrases from the Scriptures or offers a short meditation on something that concerns her: "swear words" she's heard from her students' mouths, bullying that she has witnessed in the halls, or students who are being disrespectful of one another. Occasionally, students will come in asking to lead the class in prayer. Fania wants me to know, however, that these daily prayers never feel forced or contrived. "It is free and natural," she says, "a moment for a quiet reflection."

When I ask her about teachers' relationships with parents at St. Joseph's, I am surprised when Fania begins with the negative, by describing the routines and rituals around student discipline. There is an elaborate system of demerits that teachers must follow when students misbehave. If a student gets forty demerits, the administrators in charge of the disciplinary center will contact the parents, both by telephone and in writing, letting them know that their child has been put on a one-year probation. Fania describes for me how quickly these demerits can add up. For example, a student will receive twenty demerits for class disruption, seventy-five for fighting, and sixty-five for acting disrespectfully to a teacher. If the misbehavior does not "cease and desist," the student will be put on "final probation," the last stop before getting expelled from school. Fania believes that the great majority of parents like this disciplinary system, are glad to hear from school officials when their children are in trouble, and are likely to be unquestioning in their alliance with teachers.

Fania also knows that, compared with public school parents and the rich parents of private school kids, the families at St. Joseph's are relatively easy to please. "Parents in those high-class private and suburban schools are more demanding. They hold teachers more accountable and require more of the school education-wise," says Fania. She adds, somewhat disparagingly, "They put in more money, so they want to get more back." But at St. Joseph's the parents come with no such pretensions or feelings of entitlement. They are not college graduates, many never completed high school, some are illiterate, and they see St. Joseph's as the door to a better life for their children. They must trust that the teachers will instruct their children in the decorum and the skills that they will need to make it farther, and do better, than their parents. They have, in fact, chosen to send their kids to a Catholic school, not only because it embraces the discipline of a religious education, but also because the school will demand the rigor and civility needed for their sons and daughters to climb the next step on the social rung. "They are," Fania says again, "looking for a safe haven, but also a quality education and a clear set of values." Rather than the defensive way they might approach a public school, always distrusting and challenging the teacher, Fania thinks that St. Joseph's parents come eager to trust the teachers, ready to put their children's fate in the teachers' hands. It also helps that the school is small—in fact, it has shrunk by half since Fania first arrived—and everyone knows everyone else, so that parents feel as if their son or daughter is "really known as an individual."

Less than ten miles away, in a relatively impoverished community with a predominantly Latino population, Maria Lopez, a Puerto Rican woman, teaches a bilingual third-grade public school class filled with the children of newly arrived immigrants from the Dominican Republic, El Salvador, Costa Rica, and Mexico. Like Fania, Maria enjoys the trust and admiration of her students' families, and she struggles with finding a meaningful role for them to play in their children's lives at school. Only four or five parents show up for open houses at the school (where the principal addresses the parents in English with no Spanish translator present), and most of them—despite Maria's pleading—never make it to the conferences. They are, however, quick to respond to Maria's phone calls alerting them to their child's misbehavior or missed homework, and then they are quick to inflict punishments that are much harsher than any that she might impose. For the most part, the parents look to Maria for guidance, trust her judgments unquestionably, and see in her a beacon of hope for their children.

Even though Maria has taught school for only four years, she "has great empathy" for the families of her students; for their "struggles, their confusions, and their vulnerabilities." Before changing her profession to teaching at the age of thirty-eight, she was a social worker trained in family counseling, giving her a clinical and therapeutic perspective that has greatly influenced her work with parents. As a matter of fact, Maria has grown to believe that "the action" for these parents is not at parent-teacher conferences. Most of them will never feel comfortable enough to show up at the school, nor do they believe—however much a teacher might urge and plead—that their presence will benefit their children or enhance their achievement.

"Partly it is cultural," says Maria sympathetically. "Latino culture is a very family-oriented culture, and parents see me as family . . . a wise aunt or a meddling sister, or maybe an all-knowing mother who knows the ropes." So Maria has designed a way of relating to parents that appreciates their "hard lives of poverty and struggle," understands the sources of their reluctance, and seeks to offer them support and guidance in acclimating to their new country. She sees herself as both a teacher of her students (who she hopes will become "truly bicultural," fluent in the language and idioms of both cultures, fluid in making the translations between home and school), and a teacher to their parents (whom she wants to socialize to healthy habits of family life that will ultimately support their children's success). Maria is both optimistic and unabashed about her dual ambitions, and she believes that her work is filled with the deepest respect for the people she calls "my families." "There is not an ounce of patronizing in what I am doing," she says convincingly, aware that many might regard her work with families as "inappropriate or wrongheaded" or, worse, born out of superiority or arrogance.

"The first day of school is the most important day of the year," says

Maria with a flourish. It is "most important" because it is the only time in the whole year when every single parent comes to the school. The "symbolism of this moment" is so moving to Maria; she sees it as the time when parents look in her face, deep into her eyes, decide whether they can trust her, and "pass off the torch." On that first day, everyone stands in the school yard. Maria holds up a big sign that reads—first in Spanish, then in English—MRS. LOPEZ'S THIRD GRADE. The children and their parents wend their way through the crowd and form a circle around her, flashing smiles, shaking hands, giving hugs, and saying good-bye at the sound of the bell. Before the parents leave, Maria makes a point of speaking to each of them individually, even if only for a moment. This is the last time that Maria will see them, many of these parents, even though throughout the year she will talk to them several times on the telephone.

During the first week of school, Maria sends home a long letter (usually about three pages) in Spanish that officially welcomes parents, urges them to come and visit at any time, and introduces them to the rules and routines of her classroom. In this letter, she also wants to convey her behavioral expectations and academic standards for their children; her attitude toward unfinished or sloppy homework and tardiness (both of which she will not tolerate under any circumstances). Maria is sure to spice her letter with lessons that she has learned as a mother herself. She speaks about her two sons (one a teenager and the other a first grader), the mistakes she has made along the way, and the lessons that she has learned. Above all else, Maria believes that it is her wisdom and experience as a mother that give her legitimacy in the eyes of her students' parents.

Even though only a handful of parents appear at the twice-yearly conferences, Maria has learned not to get discouraged or fret. Instead she has innovated another institutional practice that seems far more attractive and beneficial to them. Four or five times a year she holds workshops for parents in the early evening after work. Typically, the workshops draw a crowd of forty or fifty people. The last one occurred in the midst of a terrible snowstorm, and Maria watched from the classroom window as a long parade of parents and their children made their way down the icy sidewalk from the subway stop a few blocks away. Parents are invited to bring their children, all of their children, of all ages, and Maria gets her paraprofessional to provide child care. Everyone is fed, a "big Puerto Rican spread." "They are so hungry," says Maria, referring to both their "physical and emotional hunger," and she works to create the conditions that will provide nourishment for the parents. In turn, she believes that when they feel fed they will be better able to give healthy nourishment to their children. "Their presence at these events," Maria surmises, "is less about enhancing their children's work in school and more about responding to the parents' needs for support and guidance in making a healthier home environment for their kids . . . and in making it in the new country."

The workshops combine Maria's experience as a social worker, counselor, educator, and mother, and they are designed to cover issues of family life that Maria believes are particularly important to the healthy development of children. This year, for example, she has given workshops on "Effective Communication in the Family," "Problem-Solving Skills," "Disciplining Your Child," "Male/Female Relationships," and "Conflict Resolution." The two-hour sessions are always lively and interactive. Although Maria admits that she hopes to "get certain values across," she does not believe that they are best conveyed through "traditional, didactic" teaching. So the hours pass quickly as the parents (mostly mothers and grandmothers) participate in role plays, skits, and monologues, all in Spanish. The workshops have been so successful that it is not unusual for the parents of children Maria taught last year or the year before to come again to partake of the offerings.

Parent Education

ONE OF THE fascinating things about the contrasts between rich and poor schools, black and white schools, and schools that serve old residents and newly arrived immigrants is that in all of these diverse settings teachers see themselves as engaged in some form of "parent education." Certainly most teachers do not organize the kinds of parent workshops that Maria has institutionalized at her school. But many speak about the "education of parents" as an important part of their work and as crucial to building productive family-school relationships. Jane Cross, for example, tries to mute the unrealistic expectations of the private school parents with whom she works by talking to them—gently and patiently—about the developmental needs of young children and the idiosyncratic trajectory of each child. For parents who are intent upon their child reading at the second-grade level in kindergarten, for example, she tries to convey the value of "play" and the "interplay" of cognitive, emotional, and social development. Although she works hard not to sound overly didactic or defensive when she tries to reshape parental values and views (she knows that a teacherly tone will surely turn them off), she definitely sees this part of her role as "pedagogy for parents."

Like Maria Lopez and Jane Cross, Andrea Brown, the founder and director of a tiny Montessori school on the North Shore, sees parent education as a crucial part of her work. She thinks, however, that it is important to distinguish between her expectations and goals for parent conferences and what she sees as the agenda of "parent education." For Andrea the contrasts are clear. Conferences are nonjudgmental, generous, and supportive exchanges focused on supporting the development of the child. The two-hour parent education meetings that she schedules every other month, which parents are expected ("required would be too strong a word") to attend, Andrea calls her "political work."

From seven to nine in the evening, mothers and fathers sit in a circle in small chairs in their children's classroom and talk about issues that Andrea sees as crucial to her students' healthy development: conflict resolution, violence, respect and self-respect, autonomy, the role of rituals and celebrations, et cetera. (Although Andrea's students come from families that are mostly middle class and professional and would probably describe themselves as "liberal," it is interesting that the topics they examine in their meetings are not unlike the ones Maria talks about with her Latino parents.) In calling the meeting and setting the agenda, and in her line of rigorous questioning, Andrea purposely adopts a different stance in relation to parents, one in which she reveals her "philosophical beliefs" and her "ideological biases."

One recent meeting, for example, was devoted to talking about television, a source of huge conflict between parents and children. Andrea's position is clear: She believes that television is bad for children, that the violence and materialism of the programming and the passivity of watching for long hours are not good for children's creativity and healthy development. She does not express these views openly at the beginning of the meeting. Rather, she poses questions to parents and then listens attentively as they describe their concerns and experiences. They report the daily fights they have with their children over the programs they want to watch, and the battles that ensue when they insist the television be turned off. Inevitably, the parents' stories unmask their own struggles with establishing limits ("usually one of *them* is hooked on it") and their ambivalence in charting a clear course for their children. In contrast to the parent-teacher conferences, where Andrea primarily asks questions, listens, supports, and strategizes, in these bimonthly group meetings, she proselytizes. She makes her values explicit; she reveals her point of view. "I end it by saying, 'Get the television out of your life!' "

Andrea does not expect that the parents will necessarily share her values, or even be sympathetic to her point of view. Rather, she hopes that in declaring her values she will help them be reflective about, and critical of, their own. "In working with parents in this setting, my values are out there," says Andrea. "I want to have a conversation that will allow them to see and take responsibility for the consequences of their actions. . . . How do you give your kids pretend guns and at the same time say that you are for peace? . . . I am asking them to define their values. I don't feel rigid or dogmatic. . . . I just want them to be clear about where I stand and why."

Andrea describes this part of her agenda as "explicitly political," as "referring to the whole context of history, culture, and power that shape parents and children, not just individual behaviors." In fact, she believes that parent-teacher relationships are very much defined by the "social, political, and economic realities of a capitalist culture" and that parents' concerns are the reverberations of those "construc-

tions of capitalism." "I see those pressures being acted out in their relationships," claims Andrea. The group meetings, then, allow parents
to begin to see the contexts within which they are making their decisions about and forging their relationships with their children. And
they allow them to unmask some of the larger forces and "constructions" that get expressed in their individual interactions.

Although a big part of the agenda of Andrea's parent education
meetings is political, another current of the conversation seems to be
deeply self-reflective and psychological. The political dialogue seeks
to make parents' ideological values transparent, but this second
agenda searches for parental behaviors and attitudes that are shaped
by their individual life stories. When Andrea opens the discussion
with a "relevant" question, she almost always asks them to examine
their own childhoods. "How were you respected or not respected as a
child?" she asks them. "I always reach back into their childhood and
urge them to reach back." The rehearsing of childhood dramas and
traumas begins to illuminate parental attitudes toward the rearing of
their children, and Andrea believes it also allows them one more
chance to "heal" the ancient wounds that they carry themselves. Andrea's voice is full of hope when she talks about the challenges and
opportunities of these adult journeys "home." "Here is the opportunity for this child that we are talking about to help us heal ourselves,"
she sings.

I suspect that part of the equation of Andrea's relationship to the
"liberal" parents with whom she works is defined by her race, by the
white parents' perception of their child's black teacher. So I ask point-
blank what part, if any, race plays in how the parents respond to her
parent education agenda? True to form, Andrea offers up a surprising
twist that underscores the positive repercussions of their stereotypic
image of her. "Because I'm black," she muses, "I'm seen as safe by
these white parents . . . sort of a hangover from the 'Black Mammy'
caricature. That is their first impression of me, and then they soften.
You see, everything feels in its place when they give me that role. . . .
Of course, this is not anywhere near anybody's consciousness." Andrea's observation of the historical and cultural legacy that still seems
to shape perceptions on the North Shore is not offered out of bitter-

ness or complaint. She seems to understand, maybe even empathize with, these parents' views of her. She has certainly learned to capitalize on it as she builds relationships with them. Andrea says knowingly, "It helps me to be conscious of their views of me, but I don't seek to change them."

The Currency of the Classroom

ALTHOUGH JANE AND Maria's schools, and Andrea and Fania's schools seem to represent the extremes of parental engagement—aggressive and passive, hard to please and easy to satisfy, highly engaged and disengaged, entitled and accommodating—the contrasts seem even more pronounced when students from a wide spectrum of backgrounds inhabit the same school. In these more diverse settings, teachers must daily confront the inequalities and the colliding expectations among their students' families. The Field School, an alternative neighborhood public school that serves children from families that range from welfare recipients to upper-middle-class professionals (and everything in between) is a rare school where no group can claim majority—or token—status. Founded ten years ago as a parent-teacher cooperative, Field has as one of its central goals the building of an authentic partnership between parents and teachers. Parents were not to be relegated to the periphery as cheerleaders or critics. They would be critical allies in supporting and participating in a quality education for their children. And teachers were not to be related to as distant professionals or as lowly servants, but as respected and equal collaborators in a joint enterprise. A decade later, everyone—parents, teachers, administrators, and children—still stands by this view of a strong family-school alliance. However, most admit that their rhetoric is some distance from the reality they have achieved and that developing a productive and comfortable role for parents at Field has been a mixed bag, exciting and difficult.

When Sophie Wilder, a fifth- and sixth-grade teacher who has been there for four years, describes the central features of the Field School, she points to the "central role" of parents and "their deep involvement" in the school. She quickly lists the numerous roles that parents play in the life of the school: organizing field trips, potluck suppers, pizza parties, art auctions, and phone trees for snow days; assisting in the classrooms, the front office, and the library; writing grant proposals to private foundations to raise funds for special projects. For the past few weeks in Sophie's class, for instance, five parents have given several hours of their time to help students edit their long autobiographical term papers. The list goes on, but before she is through, Sophie hesitates and amends her earlier statement: "Actually, it is more accurate to say that *some* parents are very active and engaged, and that there are pros and cons to the ways in which they become involved." Not surprisingly, in a public elementary school with a diverse student body, it is the relatively affluent, highly educated white parents who tend to be the most actively involved and the most demanding of teachers, while the poor and working-class minority parents are much more reluctant to become engaged in school events or to advocate aggressively for their children.

"This pattern of parent involvement always makes me think of that notion of the 'currency of the classroom,' " says Sophie, referring to the current education lingo used to describe the unequal distribution of resources—social, intellectual, and material—in schools. "In Field, some people get more currency than others, and the inequities tend to fall along race and class lines." She admits that these inequalities have been a primary preoccupation of the Field faculty. As a matter of fact, at a recent faculty meeting there was a long and difficult conversation about one manifestation of the inequities: many of the more vocal, privileged parents want to decide who their child's teacher will be next year. Sophie offers a blunt summary of the almost-three-hour meeting. "We talked about how to curb the parents who are too pushy about their child's placement . . . how to tell parents that it is not okay to tell the principal what class he or she should be in."

Sophie does not want me to think that this was an "us against them" antiparent discussion. In fact, she remembers her colleagues taking great pains to argue both sides. "We recognized that it is our job as teachers to be thinking about *all* of the kids, and it's the parent's job to advocate for their own child. But somehow we needed to appreciate each other's perspective and find a way to resolve these tricky territorial issues." Ultimately, the faculty decided to send out a fairly open-ended questionnaire to all of the parents, asking them to describe their child's learning style, interests, personality, and relationships with peers, and promising to take their input seriously when putting together next year's class lists. There were a couple of messages embedded in this strategy. First, the questionnaire was to be mailed out to *all* parents, not just the vocal minority who felt entitled to select their child's teacher; and second, the form asked for descriptive information about the child that would become *one* element in the decision making. It was not a request for parents to state their desires or to name particular teachers, and it was clear their views would not be determinative.

This recent faculty meeting punctuates an issue of great concern for Sophie this year. "This is the first year," she says, "that I'm really trying to look carefully at this issue." Disturbed by the disparities in "classroom currency," she has pushed her thinking further to consider what she might do to address these inequalities in her classroom. "I now recognize the need to remember that I must *mentally advocate* for the kids whose parents are not here. . . . Now I try to always be disciplined in thinking, I've now heard the views and demands of the vocal parents, what would the other parents say or need if they were here?"

This kind of calculation is not always clear-cut. Most of Sophie's responses to parental requests for special favors for a child involve complex negotiations. One of the more active, vocal parents, for example, recently approached Sophie with the request that her son Jared's assigned seat be changed. The mother claimed that her son was feeling isolated and lonely; his loneliness had been exacerbated by his grandfather's and his hamster's recent deaths and by the fact that his older brother had suddenly entered adolescence and was no longer willing to hang out with him. All of these losses, his mother argued, meant that Jared needed to be closer to his special friends at school. She, in fact, had a specific recommendation, one boy whom Jared especially liked. They talked for a long time, both about Jared's mood (Sophie had also noticed that he had looked distracted and sad in school in the last couple of weeks) and about the dynamics of the classroom. From the beginning Sophie felt that the mother's request that Jared's seat be changed was "not unreasonable," although she did not think it "appropriate" that she be able to name the specific choice of his seatmate. She ended up suggesting that the mother come up with a list of potential classmates and she would consider them in reconfiguring the seat assignments. Throughout their conversation, the tone was friendly and comfortable, and when they finished their meeting and Sophie changed Jared's seat, both of them felt satisfied. "She felt good that I'd heard her concern," recalls Sophie, "even though it wasn't solved in exactly her number-one way. She ended up trusting that I'd weighed the different factors." A few days later Sophie received a lovely note from Jared's mom saying that she had been "an amazing listener" and thanking her profusely.

Although Sophie felt pleased about the decision that they had reached and could already see a positive change in Jared's demeanor in the classroom, she was left with a haunting feeling. Afterward, she found herself thinking about the other children in the class whose lives at home might be at least as traumatic as Jared's but whose parents might never come in to report their concerns. "I know that the parents of half of my class would never approach me with these issues," she says quietly. "What do I do with the knowledge of those whose parents do not come in and advocate for their children?" Even though Sophie may be making only a mental calculation, she claims it is not a trivial shift in her stance, and it does, from time to time, lead to subtle changes in her behavior.

Sophie's attempts to balance—in her head and in her actions—the "currency of the classroom" highlight the complex and subtle calculations that teachers enact as they respond to differences and disparities in the power and resources of the families they serve. Race, class, educational background, and immigrant status conspire to produce great contrasts in the relationships that parents and teachers develop with one another. The teachers I spoke with, working in very different settings, recognize that all parents want the best for their children, and all of them look to schools as the institution that will either ensure their high status or lift them up from the low rungs of the social ladder. But the expression of their common yearning looks very different in action.

Rich parents are likely to push too hard and ask for too much. In the process, they tempt teachers to become "performers" bent on impressing them, or else they force teachers to create a "buffer zone" that will blunt their overzealousness. Poor parents are likely to retreat and avoid the humiliation of not knowing how to navigate the system or advocate for their children. This leads teachers to find ways of helping them learn how to interpret the institutional rules and navigate the school bureaucracy. Rich parents are likely to feel ownership of the school; poor parents often feel as if they don't belong there. Even though all teachers can cite parents who do not exhibit these group characteristics—poor parents who are aggressive, strategic, and entitled, or rich parents who keep their distance and treat teachers with deference—these are the patterns that they usually experience. And they are the patterns that cause teachers to constantly calibrate the distance and mark the boundaries with families that will make them feel reasonably comfortable, allow them to do their work, and offer their students the space they need to make their own mark in the classroom.

It is fascinating that these large contrasts in power, resources, and knowledge of the system—between rich and poor; black, brown, and white; well-educated and illiterate parents—lead to a similar impulse in teachers. In responding to these striking differences in parents' relationships with schools, teachers talk about the need to engage in parent education. The curriculum of this "parent pedagogy" in these very different settings is surprisingly similar. Maria Lopez sets up workshops with her parents—first-generation immigrants from the Dominican Republic, El Salvador, Mexico, and Costa Rica—to give them guidance in how to build healthier families, how to solve problems, how to discipline their children, how to communicate with their spouses. She believes that this basic training of parents will have an indirect impact on the acculturation and achievement of their children in school. Likewise, Andrea Brown describes her bimonthly parent education workshops with the middle-class white parents at her

Montessori preschool as her "political work." Like Maria, she takes a somewhat didactic stance: she reveals her values and speaks about family issues that she believes are crucial for the optimal emotional and intellectual development of their children. Andrea makes a clear distinction between the conversations that take place in parent-teacher conferences—in which she is unlikely to take a position or preach a set of values—and the exchanges in the parent workshops, where she claims an ideological position and hopes that in making her values transparent she will encourage parents to scrutinize their own.

These parent education efforts help us to realize that effective work with families across the boundaries of race, culture, and class cannot be contained in twice-yearly ritual conferences. In fact, as Maria Lopez puts it, "With my parents, the conference is definitely not where the action's at." She is speaking here about parents who are reluctant to come to conferences, either because they feel impotent, awkward, or out of place sitting in their child's classroom facing the teacher, because they do not speak the school's language, or because they do not believe that their presence will necessarily benefit their child. Maria knows that no begging will make these parents come to conferences; it is a waste of her energy even to try. So she invents another forum for parent participation, one that is more "culturally appropriate," appreciates what they need in order to become more "competent parents," and begins to break down the barriers—and build bridges—between home and school. In Maria's bilingual classroom and in a diverse range of school settings, we recognize how the typical conference can be an unproductive vehicle for building relationships between families and schools. We see the ways in which resourceful teachers create other arenas for conversation. They go to where the action's at.

As the opening to this chapter suggests, the ways teachers calculate distance and currency with parents are influenced by two important historical and cultural themes. First, as citizens we have great expectations for the role our schools play in developing and educating our children and in creating a better, healthier society, a wish list that has grown longer and more ambitious over the decades, and one that has become both overwhelming, and, I believe, unattainable. Second, we have a mutually exclusive view of schools as vehicles for mobility and equality *and* as institutions designed to maintain the status quo and reify the social hierarchies in our society. These larger cultural messages—of daunting aspirations and conflicting views on educational access, opportunity, and equality—get imprinted on parental expectations of schools and on teachers' perceptions of their roles and responsibilities. The anger parents feel, for example, when schools do not live up to their expectations and produce the results they want is seared into their dialogues with teachers, who are the school's standard-bearers and gatekeepers. The distal effects of these broad cultural currents and priorities distort and confuse the proximal spaces where the dialogues between parents and teachers occur.

It seems to me that relationships between parents and teachers—particularly those that are forged across class and racial boundaries—would be more productive if we as a society could become more realistic and modest in our aspirations of schools, and if we could become clearer and more transparent in what we really mean by claiming the goal of educational equity. By suggesting a more circumscribed agenda for schools, I do not mean reducing our expectations or lowering our standards for student learning; neither do I mean that we should retreat from holding teachers accountable for teaching *all* students. Rather, I mean that limiting the big wish list and focusing more directly on teaching and learning—the central educational agenda—will increase (rather than decrease) students' academic achievement and clarify parent-teacher relationships. We must not expect our schools to be the primary engines for creating a just and healthy society, the primary institutions on which we rely to fix our troubled cultural fabric. If we continue to expand our aspirations for the schools' role in society, we will inevitably experience disappointments when they don't meet our expectations, and these disappointments will take root most prominently and vividly in parent-teacher encounters.

Likewise, it seems to me that we as a society must face the contradictions embedded in our cultural view of the school's particular responsibility in fulfilling our nation's mandate that "all men are created equal." The confusion over whether we—as teachers, parents, and citizens—are referring to equality of access, equality of opportunity, or equality of educational outcomes creates ambiguities in our expectations and demands that have a deleterious impact on negotiations across family-school borders.

CHAPTER 5

Crossing the Line of Objectivity

The Injustice of It All

*A*ntoine, a sixth-grader, is a bright child with high intelligence. Sitting in the classroom, however, he has trouble focusing for any sustained period of time and he has poor organizational skills. Since the first grade, disappointment and failure have stalked Antoine's school career at St. Anne's Grammar. He now seems almost allergic to school, resenting every moment he's forced to be there and sabotaging himself at every turn. Antoine's mother, Fania White—who teaches at St. Joseph's, the Catholic high school nearby—remembers a moment at the beginning of third grade that seemed to seal Antoine's attitude toward school. His teacher had opened the school year with an ominous warning for the eight-year-olds: "You're not in first or second grade anymore, so we won't be treating you like little children." To Antoine, his teacher's words felt like a threat. Says Fania sadly, "That really scared my son. He felt as if his teacher was getting ready to abandon him, as if she would no longer be there for him." Fania definitely felt that it was "too early to let those little children go and turn their hands loose." A child's autonomy needs to be developed slowly, carefully, gradually, and Fania believes that if she had not stepped in at that moment to give her son huge amounts of support—"sacrificially, *and at great cost" to the parenting of her other children—he would have most certainly languished. "Here is a kid who is bright and skilled, but totally lost and angry," she says with fury in her voice.*

Each year since then, she has tried to reach out to Antoine's teachers "humbly, and without all of her emotions hanging out there." She asks them what they will be expecting of her son, and what she can do to support their work. By now she braces herself for their response. "Sometimes they look at me like 'Just do it. . . . He's got a problem, and it's his problem, not ours.' This is a kid," Fania explains, "who is super disorganized, who has a hard time remembering to carry his backpack from class to class, and is terrible at managing transitions . . . and here are teachers who refuse to help him figure this stuff out so he can have a chance of being successful.

"Lord have mercy! Pity the poor kid who has any learning difficulties," she bellows, as she compares the "joyless" experience of Antoine to the relatively smooth sailing of his younger brother, Christopher. She hates the "injustice of it all." From the very beginning Christopher just seemed to take to school, learning to read and write with ease and enthusiasm, and enjoying pleasing his teachers. "The teachers just love him up! He makes them feel great," Fania says about the equation that is often at work when school becomes mutually satisfying for teachers and their students.

Winners and Losers

FANIA'S EYES FILL with tears—tears of anger and frustration—as she rails against Antoine's teachers, who have refused to respond to his vulnerabilities, labeled him a loser, and sealed his fate. She hates that they gave up on him so soon and "created a monster out of such a sweet child." And she hates that it seems impossible to change their negative views of him. But even sadder than their branding him with low expectations is their refusal to see his strengths. Their fierce focus on his disabilities does not allow them to see how bright and creative he is, how caring he is with his friends, how beautifully he draws, how quick he is on the basketball court. All of that goes unnoticed and ignored as they blame him for his failure. It is the worst kind of "blaming the victim."

Antoine's struggles in school are magnified by the comparisons that everyone makes with his younger brother. Antoine can't do anything right at school, while Christopher seems to do no wrong. Antoine has been labeled a loser by his teachers, who feel chronically unsuccessful when—in his hardened resistance—he seems to demean their efforts. By contrast, Christopher is a clear winner, a consistent achiever who makes his teachers glow with pride—a pride in *his* industry and *their* good teaching.

Even though Fania enjoys her younger son's success and praises him for his report card full of A's, she is troubled by the labels that both of her sons live with in school. As she continues to fight for Antoine— begging his teachers to respond to his difficulties and celebrate his strengths—she also works to get Christopher's teachers to "really see him in all of his complexity." Fania knows—deep in her maternal heart, and because she is an experienced teacher—that Christopher will not always be on top, that there will not always be smooth sailing for him. And she also knows that the teachers' views of him as a "winner" who is perfect in every way may limit their ability to see the places where he might need special support, individual attention, or advocacy. When Fania goes up to St. Anne's to meet with her sons' teachers, she tries to get them to see Antoine's strengths, which are masked by his struggles and his teachers' stereotypes of him, *and* she tries to get them to recognize that Christopher is "not a saint." He too has needs and vulnerabilities that deserve their attention. To see him as perfect ultimately does him a disservice.

In his book *The Vulnerable Child*, Richard Weissbourd, a social scientist, educator, and activist, echoes Fania White's complex and generous view of the struggles and strengths she sees in her sons. Like Fania, he sees the injustice and distortion of premature labeling and confronts the danger of self-fulfilling prophecies:

> Rather than having limited expectations of children who strug-
> gle at early ages, it is critical to seize the opportunities created

by every developmental stage and to identify and pull on the strengths of every child—even, and perhaps especially, exasperating, embittering children who elicit such hostility that their strengths become invisible to adults. And rather than presuming that some children are invulnerable, it is crucial not to miss the struggles of children at different developmental stages who have many visible strengths.

(Richard Weissbourd, 1996)

Weissbourd's book challenges several of our common assumptions about the trajectory, complexity, and malleability of human development, challenges that have important implications for parents and teachers working together to support children's learning in school. First, he urges us to recognize the notion of plasticity and growth throughout the life span. In principle, there is no single period in life that should claim primacy for the origin of developmental processes. In other words, we should never assume that the first few years of a child's life are the only crucial moments for leveraging learning. We should not despair that all is lost if the child does not show very early signs of health, aptitude, and resilience. The developmental journey is full of surprises, unanticipated twists and turns, ups and downs, reversals and recoveries, and we should be vigilant about identifying the most opportune moments for intervention and support.

Second, Weissbourd urges us to see the strengths in even the most injured and scared child, and find the goodness in those who seem most difficult and delinquent. It is likely that if we are determined in our search for a child's gifts, even when they appear to be deeply buried and all but invisible, we will discover them, and the discovery will be a point of entry for supporting developmental change. Likewise, Weissbourd warns us that we should not assume that children and adolescents, who appear to be strong, achieving, and well behaved, have no problems or difficulties. Every child—every person, for that matter—has vulnerabilities and hurts, and parents and teachers must allow youngsters who appear to be uniformly well adjusted to reveal those weaknesses. No one is invincible.

Finally, Weissbourd's book challenges our assumptions about whole categories of children who tend to be labeled "at-risk" by our educational systems. After reexamining a broad spectrum of research, he finds that while poverty and prejudice contribute greatly to the disadvantage of millions of children, most of the children at risk are in fact not poor, and there is much evidence to suggest that factors such as parental stress and depression have a more powerful influence on a child's fate than whether or not there are two parents in the home or whether or not the family lives below the poverty line. Individualized problems—like social isolation, problems with hearing or vision, learning disabilities, even obesity—have far more to do with childhood outcomes than any simple formula based on the broad categories of race, income, or family structure. Teachers and parents, therefore, must not fall prey to cultural stereotypes that assume that whole groups of children—identified on the basis of the disadvantages of poverty and race and family background—will inevitably turn out losers. The evidence does not support such a claim. Rather, we must recognize that all children have strengths and vulnerabilities, and search for the origins of weakness and failure in the individual histories, temperaments, and developmental trajectories of each child.

Fania White's maternal advocacy and Weissbourd's appraisal of the research on "at-risk" children offer a wonderful point of departure for this chapter. In my conversations with teachers and parents, I heard echoes of White's and Weissbourd's challenge to our assumptions about the origins and expression of vulnerability in children. In this chapter I will, in fact, argue that parent-teacher encounters are most productive when both parties recognize that *all* children have weaknesses and vulnerabilities that need identification, attention, and work. There is no child whose intellectual, social, and emotional development is without struggle or injury. Recognizing that fact allows parents and teachers to be more candid, realistic, and pragmatic in their conversations with one another, and encourages them to be more discerning in their identification of children's needs. They will be better able to see the strengths in children who appear to be the most vulnerable, and the vulnerabilities in the ones who seem to be strong.

But it is not enough to recognize the potential strengths and struggles of all children. Those good teachers who work with students who have been identified as the most vulnerable have important lessons to teach us about working successfully with all children and their families. Parents and teachers who come together in support of a child with serious problems often develop relationships and alliances that are more expressive and productive, more focused on the special idiosyncratic needs of the student, and more mutually appreciative of one another. And the boundaries and territories that are typically drawn between families and schools are redrawn and redefined in the case of vulnerable children. The lines become less rigid, more fluid and organic; the adult roles become less distinctive and more overlapping.

The notion that successful work between parents and teachers of needy and struggling children may hold important lessons for adult advocacy of "average" or even high-achieving students is a bit of a twist on the contemporary educational wisdom. Even though Antoine never seemed to capture the benign gaze of his teachers, most teacher training programs emphasize the importance of searching for the strengths in *all* children. Teachers are taught to emphasize their students' gifts, to look on the bright side, to see the glass as half full. This optimistic perspective is understandable. It is a view designed to counteract the opposite tendency, shared by too many teachers—their almost automatic identification of weakness in whole categories of students, their wrongful assumption that if children are unlucky enough to be born poor or black or brown, or come from broken homes, that they will inevitably be at risk.

It is certainly important to counteract those negative assumptions and tendencies on the part of teachers. But this chapter argues that there is great value in being cognizant of the difficulties that all children face at some point in their school career; that being open to these vulnerabilities—both subtle and explicit, both latent and manifest—will help us to not ignore the needs of "average" children; and that advocacy for vulnerable children binds parents and teachers together in a way that is inspiring and instructive for the adult sponsors of *all* children.

Blindsided

IN CHAPTER 1, I spoke about the ghosts in the classroom that haunt encounters between parents and teachers, and about how these often-unconscious recollections are likely to refer to traumatic childhood events. When teachers identify pieces of their past that now shape how they see and interact with students and their families, they tend to refer to experiences or relationships that were hurtful and left deep scars. It is these traumatic events that are likely to hover over their teaching, not the memories of pleasure or victory. As one teacher put it, her work with children offers her the chance to heal herself. If she can give generously and empathetically to the next generation, she may be able to undo the assaults and injuries that were inflicted upon her.

The potency of ancient traumas relived is particularly important to teachers' work with children who need special, sympathetic attention. Those teachers who have suffered in their childhood seem to express a special concern for and identification with the anguish and neediness of their students. In fact, I believe that many, if not most, teachers are drawn to their work as a way of facing the lingering pain of their own old wounds, many of them inflicted at school. In their teaching, they want to do the opposite; they do not want to cause harm.

When Fania White screams, "Do you hear my cry?," her voice is full of tears. I do not know whether she is weeping for the pain and treachery of her own childhood, for the heartaches of mothering her three children, or for the weariness and frustrations that come with feeling unfulfilled and unsupported in her twenty years of teaching at St. Joseph's, a parochial school serving recent immigrant children. Fania's story traces the connections between her experiences as a child, teacher, and mother. Although she reaches back to her childhood at the end of our time together, she admits that her life as a parent and her work as a teacher have been "completely influenced" by her experiences as a little girl. When she rehearses her stories of being an elementary school student, she sees neglect and humiliation, but she also sees her resilience, her extraordinary capacity to "bounce back" and persevere.

The sixth of seven children in a poor black Fall River family, Fania mostly remembers chaos and fighting at home: angry brawls between her parents, her father staggering home stinking drunk, struggles over money, and harsh punishments the children received for minor infractions. Her mother and father did not finish high school, and Fania suspects that they probably did not go much farther than the eighth or ninth grade. When I ask Fania about her parents' work, she tells me immediately that her mother stayed at home, but she does not mention her father. I inquire again, sensing her resistance. She looks away, is silent for a long time, weighing every word, and finally says slowly, firmly, "My father was not a legitimate employee, Sara." Her eyes show the pain. "Let's just say there were lots of problems, lots of hurt, lots of danger in my family . . . minefields everywhere."

Fania's schooling—from kindergarten through college—was always defined by a central paradox. She "loved learning but always felt stupid." She went through the first six years of school in a "fuzzy haze." "Up until sixth grade, when I got my first pair of glasses, I was not able to see anything . . . and my teachers and parents didn't detect anything or do anything about it," she says, her voice almost a whisper. Fania's maiden name was Anderson, so, since the desks were arranged alphabetically, she always sat up front. Even from there she was never able to decipher the writing on the board. Every time the teacher used the board, Fania would have to get up from her seat, stand within inches of the board, and copy the words down. She rises up from her seat to demonstrate the repetitive movements that she had to make many times every day, movements that no one ever seemed to notice.

Fania knew something was very wrong, but she never blamed it on her poor eyesight. "This always made me feel so ignorant and dumb," she says incredulously. "I thought I was just lazy and stupid. I thought this had to do with my low intelligence." It was an inscription that her friend James wrote in her school yearbook that finally got her thinking that maybe she needed glasses. Beside his sixth-grade picture

James had written, "Dear Fania, I like you even though you are blind as a bat." Fania remembers the strange sensation of relief and rage that she felt at that moment as she held the yearbook right up to her eyes: relief that her problem had been identified and named, and rage that no one, especially no adult, had done anything to correct it. "Luckily," she says, sounding amazed at herself, "I never felt embarrassed by all of this. As a child, I never worried about making a fool of myself."

Fania tells me about an incident that occurred just weeks before James wrote the truth in her yearbook, an incident that underscores both the trauma and the optimism that she lived with every day. For some reason her sixth-grade teacher decided to assign her to a seat halfway back in the classroom and then refused all of Fania's pleas to sit up front. One day, when her teacher wrote the problems for the math test on the board, Fania was totally helpless. Math was her favorite subject, the one place she always felt confident, always shined. But she knew better than to get out of her seat during an exam to run to the board. So she nudged the shoulder of the boy sitting in front of her and asked him to tell her the problem. The teacher noticed the whispering and accused Fania of cheating. Fania was devastated, and for the first time in school her voice rose up in her own defense. "I wasn't cheating," she told the teacher. "I can't see the board." With that the teacher lunged toward her, picked up her desk, shoved it up against the board, and screamed, "Now let's see if you can see!" Fania's response was surprising. "That teacher," she says, smiling, "was arrogant and abusive. But I was happy and pleased because now I just knew I was going to do well on that test."

By the summer after sixth grade, when Fania was enrolled in summer school to make up for courses she had failed during the year, she finally got glasses. She finally managed to convince her parents that she was not "just whining and making excuses." In fact, her most painful childhood memories seem to be of her parents' neglect, the moments in which they did not or could not help or protect her. Her voice is a mixture of resentment and understanding. "You see, they were almost illiterate. There was no way that they could help us get organized for school or review our homework. The most involvement my parents had in my schooling was to harshly discipline me for not doing well."

All of her siblings absorbed what Fania admits was the family's "dysfunction." They got out of the house as quickly as they could and left high school before finishing. Only Fania managed to complete high school and go on to college, at Bedford State. "I have no idea how I got in!" she exclaims in disbelief. "I got absolutely no encouragement or support from my teachers or my guidance counselor." Although she now wore her thick "Coke-bottle-bottom" glasses and could see the board, her schoolwork was compromised by chronic weariness, a condition that she vaguely describes as "a fatigue problem" that had something to do with her blood. As hard as she tried, she always felt as if she was battling a terrible malaise. But, as with her poor vision, she always interpreted her fatigue as laziness, as a condition that reflected her lack of effort or ability: "I always thought everyone else was stronger, more courageous, and more intelligent." She tried mightily to push past her weariness, but to no avail. By the end of her freshman year, she had flunked out. Again she swallowed her pride and made her way to a "college program for minority students who were considered to be at risk," and for the first time in her life the counselors responded to her with support and guidance, and helped her "get back on track." Fania graduated four years later with a degree in business and a determination to become a high school teacher who would "never ever" let her students "languish right there in front of her eyes."

Fania White's childhood experiences and her determination not to inflict the same sort of injuries on her students—either through neglect or assault—make her acutely aware of the damage being inflicted on her oldest son, Antoine, by teachers who refuse to be sympathetic to his vulnerabilities or give him the special attention that he needs. Watching the teachers' impatience and frustration with her son's struggles in school brings back all of the horrible memories of her own teachers refusing to see "her near-blindness" and of how she interpreted their indifference and meanness as a weakness or laziness in herself. Fania finds the replay of her childhood injuries unbearable and aches for her son. She hates the fact that despite her most earnest efforts, she can't protect him; she can't stop the genera-tional echoes. Now there are tears running down her cheeks, and Fania makes no effort to wipe them away. "Do you hear my cry?" she bellows.

His teachers say that Antoine is about to fail sixth grade, and Fania says she feels "as if life is repeating itself all over again." But she will not force Antoine to go it alone, as she had to as a child. She is deter-mined to do everything in her power to advocate for him and get him the attention and help that he needs. But even though she is a teacher, with much more education and many more resources than her par-ents had, and even though she is fiercely motivated to do right by her son, she feels helpless and impotent. "My kids are at risk over there!" she shouts. "And I feel no support as a parent, only stress."

Just yesterday, after they received Antoine's report card—full of D's and F's—Fania and her husband, David, made an emergency appointment to see his teachers. Weeks before, Fania had suggested that they all collaborate on an "agenda book" for Antoine, a note-book in which he would copy down the homework assignment for each class, the teacher would review what he had written and sign it, and his parents would initial the work after it was complete. She hoped this book would help her son stay organized and accountable, and she hoped it would force his teachers to take some responsibility for monitoring his work and following his progress. But it was clear that by the time they received the terrible report card the agenda book idea had broken down, and at least one teacher had stopped partici-pating completely.

Fania had taken her husband along hoping to give a "weighty im-pression." Maybe if the teachers were confronted with both parents, they would recognize the seriousness of the occasion. And maybe Faith and David could modulate each other's anger, "check each other's emotionality." They had decided that since Fania was the more restrained of the two and less likely to fly off the handle, she would begin the questioning. With her heart pounding in her chest, she managed to keep her face impassive and her voice steady and make a neutral request. She began by asking his three teachers to please give them an update on Antoine's progress, to fill in "the evidence behind the report card grades." His history teacher, a plump woman with a sour face, admitted that she did not have the time to constantly check Antoine's agenda book, that by now he should have developed better organizational skills, and that they all needed to stop pampering him. Fania tried not to show the rage that was building inside her. She could not stand this teacher's laziness and irresponsibility and unwillingness to respond to the individual needs of her son.

"I would have expected much more in a Catholic school," says Fania very sadly, as if she has identified the ultimate sin. When teachers in Catholic schools choose favorites and stereotype those who fail, they are, she believes, not honoring the "gospel values." St. Anne's Grammar's mission statement, after all, says that every child is valued and worthy in the eyes of God. If the teachers took those values seriously, they would do everything in their power to help each child succeed to the best of his or her ability. They would not expend extra effort only on achieving students while letting the others fall by the wayside, as Antoine's teachers were doing now.

Reframing the Conversation

IT IS SHOCKING to Fania that the teachers at St. Anne's Grammar—a school where "God is visible in the face of every child"—would give up so easily on a child, acting as if her son were damaged property to be discarded. She thinks that it is always the teacher's responsibility to "go the distance" and work with parents to provide the necessary supports. "Teachers and parents need to be on the same side, especially with kids who are experiencing trouble," says Fania. "And parents should not be fighting for every scrap, begging for help and relief, and retreating when the teachers feel threatened."

Like Fania White, Audrey Pierce worries about "children falling through the cracks because teachers do not—or choose not to—recognize and respond to their particular needs." Over her twenty-five years of teaching in rural Maine, Audrey has changed her views about the ingredients of a productive parent-teacher encounter. "I used to feel that a successful conference was one in which I could report that no news is good news," she says, smiling at her inexperience and innocence. "Now I recognize that a successful conference is one in which I can say that the child is doing well and feels good about himself . . . one in which I can help parents see how they can become involved. But now I understand that every child has something that needs working on, some vulnerability, some weakness."

Beginning with the assumption that *all* children have "special needs" is a kind of catalyst for bringing parents and teachers together "on the same side." If you have this view, it means that no student will be neglected or ignored because he or she is merely "average," and no one will be considered perfect and invincible just because they are "high achievers." But Audrey knows that reciting a child's weaknesses is likely to make parents feel defensive and anxious. So she is careful to frame the conversation in terms that do not denigrate children or diminish their strengths. "I always try to frame things in terms of the goals we set for the student instead of talking about what he or she is not good at. . . . I want parents to feel that we're on the same team, working together, and we need to figure out how we can help their child meet the goals we have set out together." But the problem-solving includes more than the teacher and parents. The students are also involved in goal-setting, identifying the skills and qualities that need work and writing down their aspirations and expectations in their portfolios.

Audrey points to Matthew as an example of a student who has "an amazing academic record but needs improvement in his socioemotional qualities." Earlier in the afternoon I had observed Matthew in the classroom, fiercely competing with his classmates, desperate to know whether he had earned the highest grade.

Audrey is returning to her sixth graders the test papers from a recent science exam on reproduction. Eagerness is written all over their faces as they grab their tests and scan for their grades. "You guys did very well," she begins almost casually, "but you should know that I was not harsh in grading these." The students let out a collective sigh of relief. "The people who had the most trouble," she says shifting to a more serious tone, "were folks who did not follow the directions." Still holding up the exam papers, Audrey begins to ask her students to reflect on the "process" they experienced in taking the test. "Why do you think I had you do collaborative work?"

Hands are raised in the air. "So we can get more comfortable talking about these things," answers Morgan.

"So we can learn to talk to the other sex . . . and so you can see if we are being mature," says Matthew.

Audrey accepts their comments with a nod of her head, begins to return the papers, and inquires further, "Why do you think people in the same group have different grades?"

"Because some people might write more," says Cathy.

"Yes," responds Audrey. "Some people might have used more precise and descriptive language."

Before Audrey is able to continue this "process" dialogue, Matthew's voice cuts in with the most important question on his mind. "What was the highest grade?" he demands, almost shrieking.

Audrey refuses to get caught up in the hype. "You know, I won't go there," she says not even looking over at Matthew. But he is undeterred.

"Can you at least tell us," he begs, "how you graded them and what the range of grades was?"

Again Audrey dismisses his specific requests as she walks around the room answering students' individual questions. It is clear that the significance of grades and the process of "grading" have been the focus of ongoing discussion in this class. Audrey wants her students to be thoughtful and discerning about their own learning, and she uses exams for "diagnostic" purposes. She also wants to curb the competitiveness among them and get them to focus less on the product and more on the process.

From the shorthand exchange between Audrey and her students, it seems clear that they know their teacher very well and understand her philosophy and her focus. But many of them still can't resist wanting to know where they stand in the classroom pecking order. Matthew, most especially, persists in this line of questioning. Though he is speaking up for himself, he is probably expressing the sentiments of several classmates. When, after many pushy questions, he doesn't get the response he is looking for, he lets out a huge sigh of frustration and puts his head down on his desk, brooding. "This is the first year of letter grades," Audrey explains to me wearily, "so there is a lot of interest."

Later on, Audrey tells me a little bit about Matthew's background as a way of identifying the roots of his "psychological struggle." A few years ago, Matthew's father, who is Japanese, and his mother, who is Jewish American, got divorced. Since the divorce, Matthew has become estranged from his father, expressing embarrassment for the fact that he doesn't speak English fluently. At home with his mother and younger sister, Matthew "rules the roost." He is demanding, controlling, and petulant, and his mother does not seem to have the nerve, the heart, or the skills to curb his narcissistic behavior. These aggressive, demanding qualities spill over into the classroom, poisoning Matthew's relationships with his peers—who find him unbearably self-centered and competitive—and making him "not always likable" to his teacher.

When Audrey meets with Matthew's mother, she is of course delighted to report that Matthew is doing magnificently in his academics, but she dreads the conversation that they must have about his social development. "This is very tricky," she says, "because I can see that this mom just aches for her son. . . . She weeps that she and her daughter have become victims in their own home . . . and she weeps even harder at the fact that Matthew has no friends." So Audrey treads very carefully, empathizing with the mother's predicament, suggesting a few behavioral strategies that might help at home, giving the mother permission to "say no," but never trying to diminish the significance—or the pain—of Matthew's struggles.

Before parents arrive for their conferences with Audrey, they receive their child's report card in the mail. (There is no standard report card for the elementary schools in the school system, so several years ago Audrey designed a form that includes both letter grades and a detailed narrative report.) The first thing Audrey does at the conference is go over the report card, answering any questions and expanding on points that need clarification or amplification. Then she shows the parents the goals for the year that their child has set for himself and written in his portfolio, as well as his reflections on and evaluations of his own work. Immediately, the student's voice is drawn into the process and becomes important in shaping and informing the parent-teacher dialogue. Again Audrey refers to Matthew's folder full of excellent grades and evaluations. But even he recognizes his own struggles when he writes, "I need to work on my problem of seeing everything as winning and losing . . . and always having to have my own way." He also claims his primary goal is "learning to work, not compete against, a partner."

After they have reviewed the student's goals and self-evaluations, Audrey shows the parents selected samples from the portfolio, which contains a thick collection of homework, classroom assignments, and tests in math, science, social studies, and "lots and lots of writing." These samples of the students' work—spread out on the table before them—allow for a productive and specific conversation, one that is "grounded in the work," not "vague, abstract, or rhetorical." Although the review of these written materials is always "illuminating and confirming," Audrey finds that parents are rarely surprised at what they see. The constant flow of paper from school to home—teacher memos, curriculum guides, activity schedules, homework assignments—plus the occasional telephone call mean that most parents "know what's happening with their kid at school."

Not only does the portfolio allow for a conversation that is "grounded," it also stands as the most convincing evidence of the student's "real capacities." Audrey remembers an encounter with Cathy's mother in which the evidence from the portfolio proved crucial. Until she was assigned to Audrey's sixth grade, throughout her school career Cathy had been enrolled in special education classes. At the end of fifth grade, however, it was decided that she had made enough progress—academically and socially—to be declassified as a special education student. In Audrey's class, Cathy had done surprisingly well, both acclimating herself to the social milieu and managing to keep up with the academic work. When Cathy's mother received her report card that heralded the good news, she was "deeply suspicious." She simply did not believe that her daughter could do sixth-grade work, and she came to the conference full of doubt. But her questions and suspicions were answered by Cathy's portfolio. "She could see in black and white what her child had produced, and she just shook her head in amazement." Audrey was able to show her a kind of proof that was "unassailable." Using the student's work, Audrey was able to convince a skeptical parent that her child was worthy and capable, that she no longer deserved the special-needs label. The "evidence"—in black and white—was successful in challenging the "limited expectations" for Cathy, expectations that were harbored most deeply by her mother.

By the time the spring conference rolls around, the parent-teacher conference is expanded to include the student. Actually, Audrey tries to structure the meeting so that it is the student who takes the "leadership role" and the adults who become the "listeners." In order for this to be effective, Audrey meets with each student to review his or her portfolio and preview the major points that he or she would like to raise in the meeting. Most of the students embrace the opportunity to "be center stage," present their work, and "talk about their growth over time." By spring they have, in fact, accumulated an amazing amount of work, and usually made visible gains. It is a pleasure for them to have the full attention and approving response of their parents and teacher. When the students have to report weaknesses and failures, Audrey helps them plan how they will explain the problem and deliver the news to their folks, but she insists on an honest self-appraisal, and her students know that she will be there listening for the accuracy of their presentation.

Sixth grade is the first year that students are invited to join the parent-teacher conference, a prelude to their transition to the junior high school in seventh grade—the "big move to the big house." The student's presence at the conference seems to ensure that the dialogue remains focused on him or her, enhance the student's sense of responsibility and accountability, and often "amaze" the parents, who have never seen their child "be so grown-up." At some point in the conference, however, the mother or father will usually ask to have a private time with Audrey. For the most part, these requests for adult exchange are motivated by the parent's concern about the child's social and psychological development. A mother will be worried about the fact that her daughter seems to have no friends, or that the mother-daughter relationship that used to be so warm and intimate has turned into a battleground. "It is the social stuff that makes parents weep," says Audrey. "Sixth grade is a time when cliques among peers can be vicious and when kids are beginning to separate from their parents. . . . Parents suddenly feel out of it, in the dark, rejected."

The hurt they express is raw, unvarnished, and the conference seems to be a place where they do not feel as exposed as they might if they told their worries to a neighbor or a friend. They also know that Audrey will put their concerns in context and offer them a useful perspective. After all, she is a wise and experienced teacher, and she knows "what sixth graders are up to." She knows the developmental struggles and milestones of twelve-year-olds; she knows what is "normal" and what is "deviant." Most of the time, then, parents feel comforted and soothed just by "saying the hard things out loud to someone they trust" and by learning that their child's struggles and angst are not abnormal.

Occasionally, Audrey will speak to a parent about a behavioral or developmental concern that she feels is a troublesome sign. At a recent conference, for example, Audrey spoke to Morgan's mother about her daughter's "disrespectful attitude," particularly to those adults—like the paraprofessional who helps in the classroom—whom she perceives as having no power. She told the mother that Morgan is precocious academically but disdainful of any of her peers who are not as quick or facile as she. Morgan's mother listened to Audrey intently, shaking her head in agreement, and finally blurted out, "Thank God someone recognizes what I've been putting up with at home. I hate the way she speaks to me. Do you have any ideas of how I can stop her from acting this way?" Audrey smiles, remembering the relief in the mother's voice and her request for help. "She felt totally supported just knowing that someone understood what she was going through," she says.

Part of the reason that parents seem to feel so at home with Audrey, and dare to make themselves vulnerable in her presence, is that she is well known to them. Audrey has been teaching at Maple Street since 1975, and she taught many of the older siblings of the students who are now in her class. She also has a well-established reputation for being a wonderful, creative teacher, and each year parents clamor to get their children into her class. Six of her students in this year's class have brothers or sisters that she taught in former years. "I know these families very well," she says confidently. "It is much easier to communicate when you have a shared history." Audrey's comfortable relationship with families not only allows her to say things to them that may be hard to hear, it also allows them to openly express their concerns to her.

Two weeks after the opening of school, Audrey got a telephone call from Elliot's mother, Lorraine, who said that her son was having a difficult time coming to school because he felt that his teacher did not like him. Audrey was stunned by the news, because she in fact felt a "special affection" for Elliot. She had taught his older sister a couple of years earlier, developed a good relationship with Lorraine, and had looked forward to working with Elliot. Lorraine told her that Elliot reported that Audrey "never had anything good to say to him and was always scolding him." Audrey knew that Lorraine cared deeply about her kids, and she also knew that she was not a "complainer or a whiner." Her advocacy for her son needed to be listened to and taken seriously. Elliot, "a very sweet child," suffers—like his sister—from a mild form of attention deficit disorder that makes it hard for him to focus and keep his things organized. After Lorraine called, Audrey began to realize that since the day he walked in the door of the classroom she had been hounding him and trying to get him organized, so that he would establish good routines early in the school year. She did it because she wanted him to be successful and she wanted to provide the special support he needed. He, on the other hand, heard only her shrill voice and sensed her frustration with him. Lorraine's call made Audrey recognize that Elliot also needed "more celebration of what he does well." Because Audrey knew Lorraine and they had built a rapport based on mutual respect, the mother felt comfortable initiating the call and the teacher was moved to reflect on her own behavior. "I'm so grateful to Lorraine," says Audrey. "She called me early and immediately so that I was able to correct my behavior and get off on a better foot with Elliot."

Audrey's comfort with and access to the families of children in her class is also shaped by living in a small town where "everyone knows everyone else," "boundary lines are crossed," and "roles overlap." "You see parents around town all the time," Audrey says matter-of-factly. "You run into them at the hardware store, at the movies, at the dump . . . and you talk about all kinds of things, including how their kids are doing in school. . . . Aron's dad is my vet. . . . You know these folks in a number of ways. There is lots of common ground." For the most part, Audrey sees these relationships as "natural" and believes that they help to facilitate the essential trust and honesty and the telling of hard truths.

Audrey Pierce's identification of the vulnerabilities of all of the children in her class allows each child to become visible as a whole and complex human being. Her careful framing of the issues—from naming weaknesses to setting goals—discourages the blaming and defensiveness that often characterize parent-teacher dialogues. And her determination to include all voices—student, parent, and teacher—means that everyone feels a sense of responsibility and accountability to the collective enterprise of supporting the child's learning and achievement.

Asylum

EVEN THOUGH WE see the value of Audrey's reframing of the conversation she has with parents in her heterogeneous "mainstream" classroom, I think it is also interesting to explore the more rarified classrooms of children whom the school has identified as having special needs. How do parents and teachers come together in these extreme environments? What relationships do they establish? How are the boundary lines drawn and the adult roles defined when students are severely troubled? Having watched the work of an extraordinary teacher in one of these special settings, I am struck by the lessons that might be useful for parent-teacher negotiations and collaborations in "typical" schools and classrooms. I believe that the special relationships between teachers and parents of special needs children offer valuable lessons and insights that might be useful for building productive encounters in a broad range of other school settings.

In an upper-middle-class community where parents, teachers, and students strive for academic excellence, Carol Steele's program—which works with adolescents who are not able to survive the high-pressured competition—has a special and distinctive place in the school. "The Pilot Program is for students who have successfully failed the school system," says Carol bluntly. "They cut classes, don't fit in with their peers, and feel unwelcome in this environment." Currently there are eleven students in the program, supported by one full-time teacher (Carol), a full-time tutor, a quarter-time English teacher who works with them on writing, a quarter-time special education teacher, and a consulting school psychologist. Carol is very clear that the students in the Pilot Program are "plenty smart." "They are," she says, "bright, capable kids who have learning issues, and most of them come from dysfunctional families." (Carol is quick to point out that family dysfunction is not a distinctive attribute of the students in her class. She estimates, in fact, that a quarter to a third of the students at Summit High, a suburban public school, are probably from "dysfunctional families," but they somehow manage to cope with the chaos and the pain better than her students do . . . or at least their vulnerabilities are not as visibly expressed in school.)

When she characterizes the central quality that defines her students, Carol draws a clear contrast between students who come to school with clear "goals" and those who have a need to be defined by the "roles" they play. "My kids care more about their role than their goals," explains Carol, "about the slot they fill, about their fit with the environment, about a place where they will be listened to and feel safe. They need to feel that they have established a solid role . . . that they are known for who they are. . . . The relationship is critical." Absent this feeling of knowing and being known, her students feel adrift and vulnerable, unable to make connections with people or engage the academic work. Carol's classroom provides a safe haven, an asylum, a place where they can begin to "build relationships of trust." "These are kids," says Carol protectively, "who are in a lot of pain.

Trust, credibility, and integrity are extremely important to them." These qualities are also critically important to their teacher, who constantly warns her students that she will not tolerate lies, dishonesty, or subterfuge. "They know," she says, shaking her finger in my face, "that lying will push my buttons."

When students enter Carol's program the rules change, the pressure is reduced, and the pace slows. For instance, on any given day they are allowed to say that "they are not able to do something or take on a particular challenge because they are feeling too badly." Carol will talk to them about it, work it through, and give them space. But the next time that they claim their inability to "be present" and do the work, she might insist that they "at least try." She takes a long-range, generous perspective, knowing that habits and fears are hard to change, knowing that by the time adolescents reach high school the "scars are deep." "We try to take a look at what is happening to the kid that is hampering his success," she explains. "Then we begin to slowly chip away at it."

Even though patience and perseverance are central to her approach, Carol never settles for the status quo. She refuses to submit to stasis. The whole point of her program is to provide the support and the skills that will allow her students to reenter the mainstream curriculum, "to navigate the hallways" of the regular school. "They can always come home [to the Pilot Program] for sustenance," says Carol, "but moving them out into the regular school is our ultimate goal." If they cannot survive the hallways and classrooms of high school, she believes, it will be impossible for them to cope with the "real world." Intellectual skills and social competence are important for their reentry into the mainstream, but the emotional, motivational work needs to come first. "They need to develop a desire to be better," says Carol about the students who arrive at her door feeling battered and disaffected. "They have a lack of faith in their ability to do more."

In confronting her students' resistance and fears, Carol moves beyond the traditional teacher role. "Actually," she explains, "we do a lot of parenting. I'll put a finer point on it, I do a lot of mothering . . . structuring, disciplining, holding, caressing." She extends the metaphor. "This classroom is home. Food has an important place. We cook, have big holiday meals. There are always noodles available any time of day. When they get hungry, they can just boil them up. . . . Even though these kids come from families of great privilege, this is necessary nourishment." Years ago, when Carol first started teaching at Summit, she tried to draw a hard line between teaching and parenting her students. She even wore a pin that read I'M NOT YOUR MOTHER! But now she sees the line as fuzzy and does not find it wise or useful to draw such a clear distinction. Over time, her attitude has changed, and she believes that her students have "grown needier." Last week, when a girl in her class said to her, "You're more a mother to me than my own mother is," Carol took it as a compliment and recognized that her student was expressing an honest observation and her deeply felt gratitude.

The "neediness" that Carol sees in her students echoes through the generations. "The kids are expressing symptoms of greater disease that get passed down from generation to generation," says Carol. She offers a "typical"—perhaps stereotypical—example of an Irish student from a "bigoted, alcoholic family" whose grandparents and parents are very heavy drinkers. All of the adults in this child's life are "out of it." They never offer the structure, guidance, and "follow-through" that this child needs to make progress in school. "It is no surprise that this kid has become a stone 'potaholic,'" says Carol about his almost inevitable vulnerability to addiction. In this case, after repeated attempts to draw the parents in and engage their support, Carol appealed to her student. "I told him, 'I can't get your parents to change, you must do it for yourself.' I told him, 'This will be your hardest, most challenging work.'" She lets out a long, weary sigh. "So you see, I often have to become the surrogate mom, filling in the missing safety net for these kids."

Sometimes Carol's "mothering" includes "giving the parents permission to parent," letting them know that they have to establish rules and limits and insist that their children follow them. Carol's voice is adamant: "I will say to parents that they need to take their son's car away if he is driving while drinking . . . or that they must prohibit their daughter from dating the thirty-five-year-old man who she met over the Internet." When the parents look apprehensive and seem to balk at Carol's advice, she tells them to "blame it on" her: "I'm happy to be the bad guy." Carol understands their fears and their reluctance after years of struggling with very difficult children. "The parents are so traumatized and so tired. Some of them feel like just giving up." But after a lot of prodding and reinforcement for small steps taken in the right direction, many of the parents "gain bravery" and begin to take on the tough responsibilities of parenting.

Getting to We

ALTHOUGH CAROL SEES each parent-teacher encounter as "unique," she comes to every meeting with a singular motivation. "My goal," she says without sentimentality, "is to put the best plan in place for everyone involved with the kid. . . . I want the collective decisions of the group to get the kid to the next step on the ladder." She never approaches the meeting with a predetermined plan. Rather, she sees the conferences as dynamic and collaborative, and she is always hoping to get the parents to "take responsibility for their role." "I do not go to the table to say 'you must' or 'you need to.' . . . I want parents to be a part of the process, to offer their support and wisdom, to help with the homework. . . . The word *we* is the most powerful word to use. What are *we* going to do?" Carol's frequent use of *we* signals her desire to be inclusive, to underscore the responsibility and accountability that she shares with parents as well as her desire to avoid the blaming and guilt that often accompany difficult parent-teacher encounters.

Most of the parent-teacher conferences that Carol convenes include a variety of other people engaged with the child in school: perhaps the special education coordinator, other classroom teachers, a social worker, or guidance counselors. Everyone sits around the table, and Carol orchestrates the event with a firm, gentle guiding hand, remembering to use the inclusive "we," reminding everyone of their common goal of supporting the student's movement out of the program, and offering praise for each person's contribution to their collective work.

Although these group meetings are important, both substantively and ritualistically, the work of engaging parents is often much more impromptu and improvisational. It may occur when a mother or father happens to drop by the classroom or call or respond to Carol's e-mail. Carol never stands on ceremony. She knows that it is critical that she seize the opportunity when students are in crisis and parents make themselves available. She has, for example, found that e-mail has changed the way she communicates with many of the parents. She will often send homework assignments home via e-mail, or offer reminders of schedules and events, or let the parents know of something important that happened—a victory or a setback—in class that day. "I always tell the kids about it first," she says. "I tell them that it is my way of keeping an honest person honest." Even though e-mail may be an efficient way of making contact, Carol understands its limits and its potential casualties. "You have to be careful with e-mail," she warns, "because you can't read the body language, and that is always important when you are trying to interpret what someone is saying." She also worries that parents may use the information against their child. "They can abuse the knowledge and begin to harass and threaten the child." Carol believes that face-to-face contact is always better, but she also knows that making time for school visits is often very difficult for working parents, and she believes that e-mails, used wisely and with restraint, can be a useful alternative mode of communicating with parents.

Recently, for the first time, Carol experienced another technological change that altered the parent-teacher dialogue. She had called a group meeting with Steven's parents, two of his classroom teachers from the mainstream curriculum, his social worker, and his guidance counselor. As with all of her meetings with parents, the child was invited and urged to come, and he had said he would attend. Steven's parents are divorced and Steven lives with his father, but both parents were in attendance at this meeting. Carol was pleased that both parents were coming, even though she had focused most of her energies on making sure that Steven's father would be present. With divorced parents, Carol often feels that she has to be strategic and focused in her communications. This is particularly true when there is a strained relationship between the parents and their child is more successfully aligned with one of them. "I try very hard," says Carol, "to know who is the reliable and balanced parent, and I try to work with him or her more directly." She admits that "sometimes that seems unfair to the other parent," but she feels that she needs to choose the approach that has the best chance of offering support to the student. As they gathered round the table in Carol's classroom, a couple of the teachers were missing. ("They had either forgotten the meeting or been pulled away by other commitments, but they had not called to say they would not attend," says Carol matter-of-factly.) Steven was nowhere to be found. Just minutes before, when school was dismissed, Carol had seen him and reminded him of the conference, but he had disappeared without warning. "It is very hard," says Carol, "to get kids to come to these meetings. No matter how hard you try to be fair and welcoming, they tend to regard these parent-teacher conferences as put-down sessions."

The adults waited for a while for Steven to appear, but then his father had a "bright idea." He called his son's cell phone number, and after a couple of rings Steven answered the call. He refused to come to the meeting in person, but he was willing to stay on the line. "So for the first time," says Carol, laughing, "we had a team meeting with the kid on the cell phone." They ended up passing the phone from person to person so each could speak to Steven directly. When he refused to speak to his mother, she said plaintively to the father, "Please tell him I love him." And when Carol got her turn with Steven they had a lengthy exchange, the highlights of which she recorded in writing so that everyone around the table would be able to follow the conversation. Carol is shaking her head at the strange scene. "In a weird way, Steven took control of the conference." He was physically absent but more central and dominant than he might have been if he had actually been sitting around the table. Carol tells this story partly to underscore the changing venues of parent-teacher communication that are the result of technological advances. But she also wants to convey her "willingness to go with the craziness of it all," the lengths that she is willing to go in order to "keep the communication flowing" and engage parents in their children's growth and development.

In reaching out to reluctant parents, Carol is also willing to receive phone calls from them during the school day. A couple of days ago, for example, Marie said that she wanted to call her mother from school, and Carol permitted her "five minutes of privacy" in her office. Marie closed the office door, dialed her home number, and began a conversation with her mother that quickly escalated into a shouting match. When her five minutes of screaming were up, Carol entered the office, took the phone back, and asked Marie to leave. Marie's mother is a very angry and defensive person who almost never responds to Carol's calls and refuses to come to parent-teacher meetings. Carol saw the opening and seized the moment, her voice gentle and solicitous. "Your daughter asked to call you at home," she began. "I hope you don't mind. . . . What are your concerns?" Marie and her mother had been fighting about Marie's wish to quit school, and the mother sounded panicked when she said to Carol, "I want her to stay in school where she belongs. I don't want her to come home!" Thus began a two-hour exchange over the telephone between Carol and Marie's mom, a conversation that had been waiting to happen for months, and a conversation that probably would have been impossible in a ritualistic person-to-person meeting. Carol made a calculated decision that she could leave her students in the care of their tutor while she attended to what she thought was more pressing business, and she counted on her students to understand. "I assigned work to the class and returned to the telephone." says Carol "The kids were very cooperative because I rarely do this, and they know somehow that someone is being taken care of."

When she returned to the telephone—"thank God"—the mother was still on the line ("In her rage, she usually hangs up on school personnel"), and Carol began, as she always does, with a question. "Would it help to know what I have done?" she asked. "I always ask questions that communicate that I need their advice and their wisdom, and that I respect their point of view. . . . I always want to align myself with them, listen to how hard it is to struggle, to take control, to survive, to turn things around." Once she had spent a long time listening to the mother's bitterness and pain, she was able—one step at a time—to let her know that she felt, like Marie, that the Pilot Program was not serving her daughter well, that together they needed to consider other programs that would be "less restrictive," and that they all needed to collaborate on developing and executing a plan. Carol assured Marie's mother that she would not leave her in the lurch or just let her daughter walk out of school. For the first time, Marie's mother seemed to calm down and listen. She promised to work along with her daughter's teacher. She even promised to "try and listen" to her daughter's desires and needs. Carol knew enough not to claim this as a "victory" (from her years of experience, she knows that there can be promising breakthroughs followed by disappointing retrenchments, advances followed by regression), but she did leave the conversation feeling that progress had been made and she had been heard. By day's end, Carol had communicated the "gist" of the conversation to Marie. "I always talk to the kid about what I have said," says Carol, "so that they will not be in the dark, and so that we will all be on the same page."

Carol knows that spending two hours with a parent on the telephone is a peculiar privilege that she enjoys as director of the Pilot Program. With only eleven or twelve kids, all of whom she knows very well, she is able to devote an enormous amount of time and energy building relationships with their families. This is not true for her colleagues in the regular school, who may have ninety students that they barely know. "Their work with parents is inevitably more superficial," says Carol, appreciating the depth of the work that she can do with parents and the crucial nature of family-school collaboration for her students.

In keeping with her approach to parental engagement, Carol also welcomes parents who just drop by the classroom unannounced. They often arrive with a particular concern that they feel needs immediate attention. Carol is usually able to stand outside the classroom and talk with them in the hallway for five or ten minutes. Sometimes, however, Carol will not interrupt what she is doing to receive a parent—either because too much is going on in the class and she dares not leave or because the parent has been "too present" with repeated visits to school and it "begins to feel intrusive." Also, occasionally the parent's presence makes the student feel wary and uncomfortable. "The kid does not want them there. . . . While his mother is standing in the doorway surveying the scene, he is cowering in the corner." In such cases, Carol makes it clear to parents that the classroom "belongs to the kids," that it is their haven, their space to develop their own relationships and make their own mark free from the scrutiny and supervision of their parents.

Whether she is talking to parents at a ritualistic team meeting, or via e-mail, or on the telephone, Carol spends a whole lot of time actively and patiently listening, asking questions, expressing her empathy, gently challenging, and building relationships of collective advocacy for her students. When I ask her what is the most difficult message to communicate to parents, she responds without hesitation. "Drugs and alcohol are the hardest messages to give," she says firmly, "because I don't know if the parents are involved." She sees signs of abuse and addiction in her students, "red flags" that, her experience tells her, are sure signs of trouble. They begin to cut classes, their grades go down, and they entertain their classmates with war stories about wild parties. Carol knows how quickly these addictions can take hold. Often she warns her students, "It takes three weeks to develop a habit. . . . Whether it is the habit of being on time, the habit of reading, or the habits of alcohol and drugs . . . it's always three weeks." And she tells them her "duck theory": "If you look like a duck, walk like a duck, and squawk like a duck, then you are a duck."

Because Carol knows her students so well, it is rare that she makes a wrong call, and it is rare that her students deny what is going on. Their parents are another story, however. When Carol is pretty sure that one of her students is headed toward a dangerous addiction, she will approach his or her parents, and their typical response is one of denial and displacement. "Oh, I don't think so!" they will say defensively. "I'm here at home all the time, and if it was going on, I would know it." Then the parents will usually blame it on the "bad influence" of the other kids in the program. They will almost never admit to their own heavy drinking or to being out of touch with their children's lives. Carol rarely challenges them directly. This is a very tender place, a treacherous boundary between parents and teachers. She usually replies, with a calm voice, "Will you please just keep a special eye out for signs of trouble at home, and let me know if you notice anything?" She shakes her head at the casualties waiting to happen while parents indulge in denial. "You know my theory," she says to me sharply. "In Summit and other affluent communities, the houses are just much too big. Everyone goes to his corner of the house, behind closed doors, and the parents do not see the action. . . . I feel the same way about these big cars, these huge vans. The kids sit way in the back of the car and the parents have no idea what they are doing."

Honest Dialogue: Putting the Plan in Place

IT IS 12:30 P.M. on a brutally hot day in mid-June and Summit High School is almost empty of students; they have all escaped after taking final exams in the morning. Six of us gather around a large round table in Carol's classroom. Bill, the representative from Safe Haven, an employment agency for people with disabilities, arrives first, followed quickly by Tony's parents, Frank and Joan, and the head of the special education department. Carol wastes no time getting started. Her voice is steady and friendly as she addresses her opening remarks to Bill, the person she hopes will initiate and facilitate a school-work collaboration for Tony. At almost twenty, Tony is the fourth and youngest son of the Tompkins family. Although he is very bright and reads at college level, he has major emotional problems and terrible social skills that have made his life in school and in the community extremely difficult and painful. These troubles have been with him throughout his school career, and he has had to be in special programs with exceptional supports since kindergarten. He has also been under the watchful care of a psychopharmacologist and is taking medicines that require recalibration every few months. The list of medicines is long and changing, the trials and calculations are difficult and unending as Tony moves in and out of periods of "crisis." Carol's class has provided a haven and home for Tony, who is vulnerable to the cruel assaults and bullying of his peers in the regular school. They seem threatened by his strangeness—by his weird gait, his anxious perseverations, the way he mumbles to himself, and his awkward efforts to engage them—and they prey on him mercilessly. In Carol's classroom, the students, who themselves have great difficulties mixing in with the rest of the school, have over time accepted Tony for who he is. They have even learned that Tony cares about them and has useful insights to offer.

Carol offers an example of Tony's acceptance by the group. Early in the school year, he had been eating his lunch in the main cafeteria, always sitting in the corner all alone, trying to stay out of range of his peers' teasing and abuse, always fearful of the next rejection. One day Carol invited him to have lunch with her class, and after a while he began dropping in, then staying a while, and finally settling quite comfortably into the circle that "ordered out" and had lunch there every day. "So now every day it is the same," says Carol describing the noontime ritual. "BLT, extra mayo, light on the bacon." And lunch is accompanied by conversation in which Tony is an active participant, giving and receiving advice, dishing out and taking teasing. "He gives other kids decent messages," says Carol as a way of recounting how he has grown to trust his new friends and "make himself vulnerable to them," and how other kids sometimes seek out his wisdom. "He sometimes says, 'I've got a question for you guys. . . . What do you think, guys?' . . . He may not like the response, but he has opened himself up to them . . . and that is big progress." Or, says Carol, he expresses his care for them in poignant ways. He'll say, "I really care about you, Kim. And I'm really worried about you going out and getting drunk at that party. I'm worried about you protecting yourself."

Carol begins the meeting by articulating her hopes for its outcome. "We would like to begin an alliance with Safe Haven," she explains to Bill, "and begin the process of bridge-building." Although this meeting will focus on Tony, Carol is interested in making a connection with Safe Haven that will eventually serve the needs of any student from the Pilot Program who needs a transitional year between school and work. Tony is the "pioneer," the student for whom they are trying to create this special work-study program, but Carol is interested in establishing productive institutional connections. She tells Bill that she has heard great things about Safe Haven from a number of sources, about their genuine support of young people and their good follow-up. But she admits that this is new terrain for her and that she is clueless about how to proceed. "We are moving through the fog with Tony here, looking for a beacon," she says dramatically. But Tony's father, with gentle humor, corrects Carol's opening comment. "You've never been clueless, Carol," he says. "But good try."

Bill takes several minutes describing the work of the agency. His voice sounds plodding and humorless following Carol's, and the hot air in the room suddenly feels heavy. As he explains the agency's protocol, I look over at Tony's parents, whose faces are placid and expressionless, and wonder how many of these encounters they must have had to endure over the years, and how they manage to keep going and stay optimistic about what might help or work for Tony. Their faces look weary, but certainly not hopeless. As a matter of fact, it is Tony's parents who continue to raise the voice of optimism and perseverance, who often soften the hardest moments of the meeting with humorous asides. In his description of Safe Haven, Bill focuses primarily on how they try to individualize their services to the needs, capacities, and interests of the student; how they work to match these individual needs with a job; how they provide job coaching and backup support to try and ensure the student's success.

After Bill's long-winded opening statement, Carol gently cuts in, hoping to bring the conversation back to Tony. "One of our goals," she explains, "is to build in a program where Tony can feel comfortable leaving high school. Tony hates school, but he doesn't want to leave. He's very fearful, very frightened of making this transition." She leans over toward the parents and says mischievously, "I don't know which parent he gets this from, but Tony is extremely stubborn . . . and he, of course, has the right to say no." Again, Tony's father pipes up to ease the hard conversation with a bit of self-deprecation. "In our case," he admits, "the stubbornness is not additive . . . it's a multiplication." The gentle banter between Carol and Tony's parents weaves through the conference, reducing the tension and allowing each of them to face the painful moments. Their humorous exchanges are also a constant reminder of how well the teacher and parents know one another, trust one another, and share in their common advocacy for Tony.

Carol's next statement reveals how she is able to mix the good with the bad, the strengths with the weaknesses, as she describes Tony's interests. "He is very good at computers. He can really talk the talk of computers." She laughs, "Here I am getting panicked and saying to him, 'Why are you taking the cover off of that thing? You're making me nervous!' . . . But he doesn't have the people skills to go with his technical proficiency, and he can't ferret out what the problem is, give it a name, and do something about it." Tony's father can't help making a small point here, because Carol's description of Tony as "not a people person" doesn't fully square with his view. "Maybe I'm being the optimistic parent," he says slightly apologetically, but in a way that seems to reflect his temperament of always wanting to see the glass half-full and his deep devotion to his son. It is a moment he can't let go by. "I think Tony has a deep attachment and affection for people," he says softly, but with great feeling. "He is a people person, but he often finds it painful and uncomfortable, and he fears rejection." Carol shows that she understands what Frank is saying about Tony's deep connections to people and his sometimes isolating behavior, and she believes that he has shown great progress in moving from fear and isolation to acceptance and connection.

In order to make this point, she tells a tale from that morning. Tony had come in, his voice full of rage, his stance belligerent, and said—even before Carol had had her first cup of coffee—that he would not be returning to school in the fall, that he would send her a note of his whereabouts. Carol, who was feeling particularly tired on this last day of school and not in any mood to fight, responded kindly and coolly, "You know, Tony, I'm not ready to say good-bye yet. You need to return to school, so I can have my chance to do it right." Tony, somewhat caught off guard by Carol's reply, had responded immediately and simply, "Okay, I'll come back. We've got to do this thing right." This time it is Tony's mother who compliments Carol. She says in a stage whisper to me, pointing to her son's teacher, "This one is a magician."

Now the father moves the conversation along, wanting to get his wish list on the table, even if it is not attainable. "To add to our fantasy for Tony," he begins, "I'd like to find a job that, at the end of it, Tony realizes, first, that he has some competence, and second, that he knows he needs more training. I want him to feel," he says, stretching across the table toward Bill, as if his body were carrying the urgency of his request, "the cycle of experiencing success and gaining self-confidence." I listen to Frank's words and think that he is speaking for all parents when he hopes that the cycle of self-confidence and success will take hold in his son. Although this is a much greater challenge for Tony than for typical children, it must be a universal concern for parents, one of our most primal fantasies. I am impressed with Frank's articulation of his hopes for his son, particularly when I imagine that these hopes have been dashed many times before as he has tried to support Tony's growth and progress.

A good deal of information is shared as Tony's parents and teacher try to identify his interests and competencies, and his fears and weaknesses, to Bill. They begin with his obvious technical proficiency. Tony's one and only recreation is computers. He is good at data entry and creating spreadsheets. He has been responsible for and successful at doing the spreadsheets for the school store. His computer skills are accompanied by a fierce recall of events and experiences, a memory bank that amazes his parents. His father smiles, "He reminds us of things that we'd rather forget." Tony is also resilient and responsible. In all of these years of experiencing teasing, rejection, and failure in school, he has always woken up in the morning and gotten to school on time. He has been absent very little. And if he feels comfortable on a job—as he did recently when he worked side-by-side with his mother at Skyview Farm, clearing brush and spreading manure—he works very diligently and gets the job done. Finally, he has developed the ability to see other people's wounds and protect himself from being wounded. Says Carol, "He's good at making kids feel better, at giving them genuine feedback, at complimenting them on what they do well. . . . And he also has an uncanny ability to know who will be safe." The list of Tony's "gifts" impresses Bill, who sees a lot of spots where he might "fit." "Sounds like he has some good skills," says Bill quietly. This brief assessment feels like a gift to Tony's parents, who seem to draw themselves up to their full height. "Yes, he does," they chorus back.

The list of Tony's strengths is counterbalanced by an honest and hard look at his struggles and difficulties. Not surprisingly, his vulnerabilities and strengths are sometimes flip sides of the same coin. For example, Tony's proficiency with computers and his desire to be alone with them is also a retreat from social contact with others. "Given a choice," says his father, "Tony will seek isolation rather than company." Carol continues, "He doesn't like group work. If he is put in a group he withdraws, lets the other kids do all the work while he fiddles on the side." Tony's mother agrees with the view of her son as an isolate, but her voice is strong in his defense. "You see," she says, looking directly at me, "he has experienced so much rejection. Those kids out there [she points out into the hallway of the regular school] have preyed on him mercilessly, setting him up, watching him lose it . . . following after him in their cars and yelling out awful things."

The conference winds up with a lengthy exchange about how Tony and his family might initiate contact with Bill and Safe Haven; whether Tony should do it on his own or be accompanied by his mother; whether the first contact should be made by phone or should he just "casually" drop by the office (the Safe Haven office is right around the corner from where Tony's family lives); whether Tony should call from home on Friday (the day after the conference) or wait until Monday, when he could make the call from school with Carol's support. This decision seems crucial, very complicated, and loaded with symbolism. It is also shadowed by the concern of everyone around the table that Tony may refuse to contact Safe Haven at all, that he may completely withdraw from the process and totally compromise their best efforts to support him.

As the parents struggle to develop the best strategy for putting this plan in place, Tony's father stresses the need to support his son's independence, while his mother worries that he will need much more help in initiating contact. This is the first time I hear a clear difference in their perspectives, a difference that seems to have a long history and causes some frustration. Frank keeps returning to the "important" theme of "autonomy." "I see a benefit in his getting himself there. I definitely think Tony should initiate the call. The symbolism of this thing is huge. After all, his big theme is saying he won't do something that we lay out for him . . . and the social contact is important." Joan continues to worry about his fears of rejection and his still needing a lot of help in conquering that fear. "Sometimes," she says sharply, "we just have to help him put the pieces together." Carol listens patiently to these parental exchanges and chooses a moment to come in with the most pragmatic approach. "Well," she says, "let's try all of the above until one of them works."

Close to the end of the session—when the plan of action has been "more or less put in place," "contingent upon Tony's cooperation"— Frank makes a statement that resonates with his love of and advocacy for his son, moving the dialogue to an existential plane, far above the nitty-gritty. I can hear the tears in his voice. "We're trying to be imaginative. I have always thought that Tony has the gift of being unique and has the potential of being creative. Of course, the problem is that people don't always respond well to folks who are unpredictable . . . and we have to find a way to let Tony hold on to his gift and still fit in more or less comfortably." Just as I am thinking that one of Tony's "gifts" is his ability to inspire loyalty and love from others, Carol crosses the "line of objectivity" and announces her love for her student: "I know that I am a better teacher having been with Tony. He never ceases to amaze me. I know that I am supposed to be objective, but that is just impossible, especially with Tony." Now she is looking directly at Bill, and her voice is as passionate as I have heard it. She is no longer speaking as a teacher; she and Tony's parents are joined as family. "We want to find Tony someplace good, so he can have all of these wonderful additional parents supporting him," she says.

When Carol Steele announces—matter-of-factly and without defensiveness—that she is "crossing the line of objectivity" with Tony and that she is searching for other people in the community who might collaborate with her in "mothering" him, she is expressing a perspective shared by many teachers who work successfully with the parents of children who have exceptional needs. For these teachers, the boundaries between families and schools are reconfigured; the roles of parent and teacher are often blurred. The redrawing of lines and the reshaping of roles offer useful lessons for negotiating more productive relationships between the parents and teachers of "typical" children, the students who—because they do not present any particular problems or shine with any bright achievements—may not get their fare share of attention.

At Summit High, Carol creates an asylum for her students that certainly could not be replicated for students in most schools. The intensity and cost of the material and human resources that her twelve students enjoy are extraordinary. But I certainly believe that there are aspects of her perspective and practice that might be inspirational and effective for parents and teachers working together in other, more ordinary environments and with more "average" students. First of all, parent-teacher conferences are much more frequent in the Pilot Program. The twice-yearly conferences typical of most schools provide nowhere near enough contact to create the safety net needed to protect and sustain the special-needs child. Second, Carol seems to be more improvisational and resourceful in seizing the moment for communicating with parents. She is willing to do almost anything to reach out to parents and solicit their views and alliance. She interrupts her teaching to respond to a parent who drops by unannounced and spends hours on the telephone with a mother who finds it too difficult to meet with her face to face. She even participates in tracking down one of her students on his cell phone so that he can join—and ultimately take control of—the parent-teacher meeting at the school.

As part of her improvisational approach, Carol's use of daily e-mails to parents is particularly interesting, because, I think, it anticipates what may become a major shift in modes and patterns of communication between families and schools. With the presence of computer technology in classrooms across the country (particularly in those school systems that are well funded), teachers are beginning to make the transition—some with eagerness, others with reluctance— to becoming computer literate. Many are trying to figure out how to integrate the computer into their classroom as a teaching tool; others are searching for effective ways to gain access to the vast and uneven curricular content that the Internet makes available. Some are even using e-mail to continue conversations with their students after school hours, or to assist them when they run into an impasse in their homework.

But until I visited Carol's classroom, I had not heard much about teachers and parents using e-mail to be in touch with one another. Here again, I think that Carol leads the way, as she both recognizes the great potential of e-mail as a tool for immediate communication and admits the clear dangers. E-mail allows her to be in almost daily contact with parents, announcing the specifics of a homework assignment, reminding them of school events and special programs, and alerting them to a crisis, breakthrough, or victory that their youngster experienced during the day. Although this kind of communication is often effective and efficient, there are important caveats. The teacher must be careful not to tell the parents something that she has not already shared with the student. E-mail should not be used as a tool of secrecy or deception; it should not be seen as punitive, as a way to go behind the backs of students. Says Carol, "No kid should be caught blindsided when they walk in the door and get attacked by their parent because of some piece of information they've read from me on e-mail." Carol also believes that no teacher should use e-mail as a substitute for face-to-face contact. For most matters of importance—particularly those that are complex, nuanced, or difficult to discuss—it is important to "look into the parents' eyes" and read their body language. The disembodied words on the computer screen are difficult to interpret, and cyberspace can become a place to hide and retreat. So Carol's experience and her determination to "open all possible routes to communication" with the parents of her special-needs students offer a tale that holds great promise for frequent and efficient exchanges with parents at the same time as it opens up a vast array of moral and interpersonal decisions that require vigilance and restraint.

Parents and teachers of children with special needs seem to benefit from their mutual understanding that the vulnerabilities and struggles of the child are "serious and very real" and that everyone is needed if the student is going to gain in strength, health, and achievement. Very quickly, parents and teachers see themselves as allies and partners in a collective enterprise. They engage in problem solving as they try to find innovative solutions and develop individual plans for the student. In working through complex problems that rarely have simple, singular solutions and usually require several experimental trials ("There are no magic bullets," warns Carol), parents and teachers begin to see themselves "lining up on the same side" and "joined in their advocacy" for the child. "The most important word is *we*," repeats Carol like a litany throughout our conversations. "We are in the struggle together, working on behalf of the kid." Finally, the intensity and mutual investment expressed in these parent-teacher encounters seem to blur the boundaries between family and school, as parent-teacher roles get merged. Carol talks openly—even proudly—about the "maternal sensibilities" and "love" she feels for her students. She eschews the "objective" stance assumed by many of her faculty colleagues and adamantly stands by her "fierce advocacy" for her students.

In rural Maine, Audrey Pierce refers to another kind of boundary crossing in her work with a "regular" classroom full of diverse sixth graders from a wide range of social class backgrounds. Rather than speaking about "crossing the line of objectivity," she talks about the ways in which her long history of living and working in a small town and meeting parents in a variety of local settings allows for an "overlapping of their roles." Having taught many of the siblings of the students in her class and known most of the families "around town" leads to a level of trust and candor that allows her to "tell hard truths" to parents. These organic relationships also allow the parents to approach Audrey with complaints and criticisms about her work with their children, and she usually sees these parental concerns as valid and helpful in her teaching. Beyond the easy and natural crossing of small-town boundaries, Audrey has also designed a system of reporting to and conferring with parents that begins with the presumption and expectation that every child has some vulnerability, some weakness that needs work. Like Carol, with her claim that *we* is the most important word in the parent-teacher lexicon, Audrey uses collaborative "goal setting" as a way to "get everyone on the same page." The identification of individual goals for each child means that no student goes unnoticed; all children are heard and visible.

In addition, the use of portfolios that document all of the student's work and self-evaluations allows for the frequent monitoring of student progress and tracks unexpected developmental changes. The portfolio work was what finally convinced the mother of Cathy, who had been previously identified as "seriously learning disabled" and tracked in a special education class, that her daughter had made huge progress and was functioning well in Audrey's classroom. Her suspicions were quelled by the evidence from her daughter's own hand, and by the teacher's explicit assumption that the developmental journey offers many opportunities for change and growth. Audrey enacts the lessons of Richard Weissbourd that open this chapter as she keeps her mind and heart open and stays alert to the surprises and resilience shown by generations of students coming through her classroom.

Seeing the promise and strength in the students who appear to be the most vulnerable is particularly important for Fania White, whose own abusive experiences as a child give her a unique insight and sense of responsibility for the "damaged children" she teaches. The neglect Fania received from her parents and teachers, who never noticed her blindness, called her lazy, and blamed her for her failure, makes her want to protect her son Antoine from the same injustices and determined to make every student visible. She does not want to cause any child harm. But it is not just that Fania is determined that no child will suffer what she suffered, it is also that surviving her experience has left her with a deeper understanding of the resilience of children. Her reflections remind me of a poignant passage from *Voices and Silences,* the autobiography of the actor James Earl Jones, in which he speaks about the pain of being a stutterer and the ways in which—over time and with hard work—the pain was transmuted into a great, unbridled energy.

> I think a stutterer ends up with a greater need to express himself, or perhaps, a greater awareness of the deep human need for expression. Being a mute or a stutterer leaves you painfully aware of how you would *like* to say something. And I would know, as

an afterthought, how I could have said this or that. But at the moment, you are so busy making the choice to speak or not to speak, to use this word or that word. The pain is in the reflection. The desire to speak builds and builds until it becomes part of your energy, your life force. But when I was a boy, speech became a wall I could not surmount.

(James Earl Jones, 1994)

Like James Earl Jones, Fania White understands the difficulties, the work, the reflection, and the pain that go with either trying to fight through the wall constantly or adapting so the world will not see the constant fight. As a teacher, Fania hopes to help her students fight the good fight, openly, courageously, and always with her full support.

CHAPTER 6

Living Both Sides

A Huge Transformation

Melanie Allen, a veteran English teacher in a large city high school, speaks about her professional career as having "two distinct eras," before and after the birth of her son. Melanie taught for ten years before Joshua arrived. "This affected me more than anything in my life," she says, spreading her arms wide to show the "huge transformation" in her life. The impact of his birth was double-edged; it made her pull back some from her teaching as she became intensely connected to her baby (for the first few years after his birth, she worked part-time). But it also brought a new seriousness of purpose to her teaching. Surprisingly, her experience mothering both intensified and clarified her relationships with her students. "I learned through mothering that nurturing means holding on and letting go, and that my son learned when I gave him enough freedom to learn . . . to take risks, to explore, to question, to make mistakes and recover from them." She gained a new appreciation for the character and temperament that babies are born with, the ways in which they shape the worlds that they inhabit. "I discovered," she says, her voice filled with awe, "that I could not mold him into some preconceived ideal, because he was born with a personality of his own, beyond my control." The discov-

ery led to some significant changes in her teaching. She spent less time obsessing about her teaching, but she focused the time that she had differently. "I no longer thought about myself so much—what I would say and how I would appear, how I would judge and correct. Instead I thought about the students and what I could do to allow them to take more responsibility for their own learning."

But it was not only that Melanie's mothering of Joshua made her see the teaching and learning process differently in her classroom and allowed her to shift her stance from "controller of learning" to one of "wise accompaniment." It is also that the depth of her love for her infant helped her better see the relative significance of school and her place in the lives of her adolescent students. There is some embarrassment in her voice as she admits, "I felt humbled by the realization that no matter how much affection I had for my students, I probably had only a fleeting influence. I knew—and am now ashamed that I never understood it before—that my students' parents loved their kids far, far more than I ever would, and that I was not at the very center of their reality." Melanie's awe of the parental role—and her newfound humility—changed her interactions with parents. She called them more often when their youngsters were doing well in school; she no longer dreaded parent conferences as much ("Now I felt such a profound empathy for and identification with them," she says). And she grew to have a great respect for their knowledge of their children.

The Convergence and Divergence of Roles

MELANIE'S HUGE TRANSFORMATION—from being "child-free" to becoming a mother—had ripple effects that spread across the landscape of her personal and professional lives. It altered the way she spent her time and the focus and intensity that she gave to her work; it brought a passion and love to her life that she had never known before; it changed her philosophy of education and her approach to teaching; it transformed her relationship with her students and altered her communications with their parents. No other experience in her life had ever had such a cataclysmic impact; no other event had taught her so much about herself or made her reflect so deeply on her priorities and values. No other experience had required that she "reinvent" her reality in the way that mothering did. And the most surprising impact of this huge transformation in her family was on her life in school.

Melanie's story points to both the separation and the convergence of mother-teacher roles. Becoming a mother both marked and clarified the boundaries between her professional and personal worlds, *and* the ways in which the two roles became deeply intertwined and interdependent. Loving Joshua so deeply, for example, made her distance herself from her students and preserve more of her energy for parenting her son. But nurturing Joshua also taught her important lessons about human development and learning, about creating a classroom culture in which her high school students would be given more space to take risks, experience failure, problem solve, and create. Hers became a classroom in which they would learn to take more responsibility for their own learning. The lessons learned from her mothering found their way—naturally and effortlessly—into her classroom.

This paradox—of separating and merging the roles of mother and teacher—has been at the center of a long conversation among educators and social scientists, who have argued over whether these two primary women's roles should be distinct or overlapping, and whether the configuration of roles might support or undermine the learning and development of children. Fifty years ago, child psychoanalyst Anna Freud, for example, was adamant in her view that mothers and teachers should perform distinctly separate roles in children's lives, and that the boundaries between them had to be clearly drawn. She offered strong words of advice and warning to teachers who she worried might oversentimentalize or romanticize the place of "mother love" in the classroom.

> The teacher's role is not that of mother-substitute. If, as teachers, we play the part of mother, we get from the child the reactions which are appropriate for the mother-child relationship—the de-

mand for exclusive attention and affection, the wish to get rid of all the other children in the classroom. There is a difference in a child's attitude toward his mother and his teacher. He wants to be loved by his mother, and doesn't want to be taught by her. His attitude toward his mother is a demanding one based on his instinctive wishes; his attitude toward his teacher is farther removed from drive-activity, it is one of willingness to give and take in.

(Anna Freud, 1952)

Anna Freud believed that the psychological transition of the child from the all-encompassing, unmeasured love of the mother to the more circumscribed and restrained attention given by the teacher was crucial. In underscoring the contrasts between these two roles, Freud distinguished between child *care,* which is the province of the mother, and child *education,* which is the responsibility of the teacher.

According to Freud, the latter role is far more generalized and objectified in relation to children. Teachers must develop more distant relationships with their pupils and escape the dangers of rivalry with mothers, "who are the legitimate owners of the child," by taking a "more general and less personal interest in the whole process of childhood with all of its implications." Likewise, Freud warned that teachers must not slip into the therapist role and become dangerously sensitive and responsive to the emotional experiences of the child.

In emphasizing the neutral, objective role of the teacher, Freud was not only arguing that children will fare better when teachers keep them at some distance, when they do not develop intimate relationships that might cloud their judgment or limit their adult authority. She also believed that defining the more limited and formal role of teacher suggests that mother-love—with all of its passion and intimacy—stands in the way of the productive socialization of students. A mother's attachment to, and advocacy for, her child blinds her to his or her imperfections and weaknesses and makes her incapable of challenging and judging him or her in the ways that will produce optimal learning. Finally, Freud urged a division of roles and responsibilities between teachers and mothers because she believed that children must learn to make and sever relationships with their teachers every year, while their connection to their mothers lasts forever. Children, she argued, learn something important for their survival in the world when they recognize that their relationships with teachers are crucial but temporary, while their bonds with their mothers are primal and lifelong.

Freud's drawing of clear boundaries reminds us of the hard distinction that Willard Waller makes between the "particularistic orientation" of parents and the "universalistic orientation" of teachers, and his assertion that these two perspectives are inevitably in conflict. In Freud's claim we also hear an implicit statement about the ways in which the mother and teacher roles are not only distinct but somewhat at odds with one another. She seems to be suggesting a subliminal competition between them, a subtle tug-of-war between how mothers see their child, with their deep devotion, and how the teacher views the individual child, as one in a classroom of many children.

There are very few educators or developmentalists who share Anna Freud's strong view of the need to draw such stark contrasts and clear distinctions between these womanly roles. Melanie Allen's account, for example, reveals a much more complex mapping, one not of clear roles and territories of responsibility but one more like a mosaic, where boundaries are both delineated and fluid, distinct and overlapping.

Anthropologist Mary Catherine Bateson offers a point of view that directly challenges Freud's boundary-setting. She argues that the duality that Freud sets up distorts the experience of women, who, in actuality, blur, juggle, and integrate the many roles they play in their lives. In her book *Peripheral Visions,* Bateson claims that women's work across many domains is fluid and improvisational as they attend to multiple tasks and demands. And she believes that this balancing of roles has been forged in a long history of gender roles and leads to the development of a unique perspective, a way of seeing that allows women to perceive a broader frame, a deeper complexity. Even though she is not speaking specifically about mother-teacher roles and relationships, her analysis seems particularly relevant to understanding the "huge transformation"—in priorities, perspective, and insight—that Melanie Allen experienced when Joshua was born.

> Women have been trying to balance multiple claims and demands from before the beginning of history, for women's work has always embraced the array of tasks that can be done simultaneously with caring for a child. This has meant taking on whatever could be done with divided or fluctuating attention, could be set down to respond to interruptions and picked up again without disaster. It is not surprising that such work, so easily deferred and juggled, is often treated as having negligible value, yet it must be done and has always included many of the tasks that were central to survival. Women must be one thing to one person and another to another, and must see themselves through multiple eyes and in terms of different roles. Women have had to learn to be attentive to multiple demands, to tolerate frequent interruptions, and to think about more than one thing at a time. This is a pattern of attention that leads to a kind of peripheral vision which, if you limit roles to separate contexts, you may not have. Sometimes this multiplicity can be confusing and painful, but it can also become a source of insight.
>
> (*Mary Catherine Bateson, 1994*)

There is another paradox here that Bateson points to. Women's work—which has included the roles of mothers and teachers—tends to be devalued and denigrated in our society, partly because it is child centered and requires that women focus on many things at once. It is, however, just this connection to children's lives and the balancing of multiple demands that gives women a special "source of insight."

Freud and Bateson, psychotherapist and anthropologist, frame an intriguing and provocative dilemma in the relationships between the two women most directly responsible for raising the child. Freud claims that these roles, which are similar in their cultural regard and purpose, must be disentangled and made distinct. In order for the work of teachers to be productive and the conditions for learning optimal, argues Freud, mothers must distance themselves from teaching, remove themselves from close engagement in classroom life. Bateson sees it very differently. She relishes the fuzzy boundaries, the overlapping roles, the mixtures of womanly work that complement each other, and she believes that teachers and mothers—who always have children on their minds and in their view—are advantaged by their "peripheral vision," a seeing and knowing that enriches the development of children.

Most of the teachers that I talked to and observed were mothers. They possessed the "peripheral vision" that Bateson claims is a rich result of women's work, and they also spoke about the experiences of "living both sides" and having a kind of "double vision." Although I think they would all recognize Anna Freud's admonitions and concerns as legitimate, and maybe even understand the advantages of drawing clear distinctions between mothering and teaching ("I wish I could not carry my teacher-self with me when I go to a parent conference for my daughter," admitted one teacher; "that would make it so much easier"), they also see her framework as unrealistic and limiting. These teacher-mothers would certainly agree with the different weight that Freud gives to the teacher's more generalized caring and the mother's more specific love, and they might even suggest that Freud's analysis is helpful in reminding women about the primary role they play in the lives of children. But they would also argue that pushing the distinction too far produces a distortion that does not take advantage of the strength that emerges when the roles overlap, and is not optimal for the healthy growth and achievement of children.

For the teachers I talked to, embracing of both roles seemed to lead to their best work with children and their most productive interactions with parents. Each of the teachers, in a voice laced with passion and certainty, talked about the powerful and profound changes in perspective that occurred when she became a mother. As for Melanie Allen, there seems to be no more transformative experience for how teachers view their work with students and their families than becoming mothers themselves. Their views changed in three ways.

First, they talk about the ways in which mothering altered their view of parenting as the "hardest work." Once they became mothers they immediately had a new respect for the passion—the joy and the anguish—of parenting. As one teacher put it, "I finally recognized the way in which mothering breaks your heart." They also began to appreciate the more complete, holistic view that parents have of their children and recognized the narrowness of their own teacher vision.

Second, mothering let them see the development of children in a different way. It helped them see that the classroom was only one setting in the learning life of a child. They gained a new appreciation for the mysteries of learning, the individual temperament of children, and the idiosyncratic path each child takes as he or she masters the tasks and skills of school.

Finally, becoming a mother made them "gentler and more forgiving," less judgmental in their assessment of children and their families, and more ready to offer praise for the "ordinary, small achievements" of learning and parenting. "I suddenly realized after I became a mother," said another teacher, "that parenting is the great equalizer. We are all amazed and humbled in the face of it. . . . From time to time we are all brought to our knees, all made to feel inadequate. No one escapes the treachery of love. That realization made me more generous in my relationships with the mothers of my students."

Two Eras

ELIZABETH MORGAN, WHO taught first grade for five years before having her son, begins her conversation with me by dividing her professional career into "two eras"—before and after becoming a parent. "Before I became a parent," says Elizabeth, "I had no idea how narrow my view was. . . . I certainly knew the children very well in the context of the classroom. But I knew very little about their lives outside of school. After becoming a mother, I learned that it is important to ask parents questions about their child's life outside of school and to listen very carefully to their experiences, their perspectives, and their wisdom." But it was not only that Elizabeth grew to understand the importance of getting a fuller, more comprehensive view of the child she was working with in the classroom, it was also that she developed a kind of humility about offering advice and counsel to parents. "I look back now and shudder at some of the bold blanket statements I made. I was confident and unflinching in my advice," says Elizabeth about her early years of teaching. After becoming a mother, her statements were less definitive and more measured, less declarative and more collaborative, less harsh and more modulated. She listened and observed more, tolerated the inevitable ambiguities, and even learned to live with—and use—the silences that punctuate parent-teacher meetings.

It is not an exaggeration to say that becoming a mother was "earth-shaking" in its impact on Elizabeth's work with parents. "It was as if I suddenly woke up one day and saw the world as much more complicated. As far as child rearing was concerned, there were no more absolutes, no more blacks and whites." After becoming a mother, Elizabeth's teaching palette had more variations of color, many more hues. She learned to tolerate, even welcome, the ambiguities, and she began to see her work with parents as helping them manage the uncertainty of child rearing as well. Rather than tying up a conference at the end with a neat bow and a reassuring smile, she found herself ending the meetings with a question, a challenge that she asked parents to think about. Conferences became less about telling, reporting, and making judgments about her students' lives in school than about collaborative problem solving using the insights of the teacher and the wisdom of the parents.

Audrey Pierce, the sixth-grade teacher in rural Maine, also experienced dramatic changes in the way she related to the parents of her students after becoming a mother herself. Like Elizabeth, she became more modest and more humble in her judgments, listened more intently to the parents' perspectives, and identified with the "pathos and passion" that parents feel for their children. But Audrey focuses her comments on how the parenting of her own two children—now late adolescents—caused "subtle but important changes" in the ways she interacted with her *students*. Her exclamations about the impact of her mothering on her teaching are just as charged as those voiced by Elizabeth and Melanie. "It matters hugely to my teaching that I am a mother," says Audrey adamantly. Nothing has influenced the way she works with her students and their families more than being a mother herself. Her experience as a mother has made her recognize, for example, that she needs to praise her students more regularly and openly, and that she needs to more clearly express "connection and affection." "Listening to my own kids has helped me know what is important," says Audrey thoughtfully. "Children are not subtle creatures. They need to have things said out loud. They need to hear that you like them. . . . Also, after having my own kids, I began to touch my students more. I had been a little shy about making physical contact, not because I was afraid of the lawsuits but because I was just a little inhibited and reluctant. But most kids respond to a touch of reassurance." Her voice rises to a crescendo as she identifies the "most important violation of kids," a lesson she learned from her own children as well. "Above all, a teacher should never be sarcastic! That is the most hurtful, and over time that is the most damaging."

The Mothering in Teaching

TEACHERS NOT ONLY talk about the dramatic and subtle changes in their pedagogy and their relationships to children that are the result of their experiences as parents. They also speak about the mothering that begins to be woven into their teaching, both as their "maternal impulses" get expressed in the classroom and as being a mother gives them added legitimacy in the eyes of their students' parents. Carol Steele, the parent of two children in the middle grades and the director of the Pilot Program for adolescents with special needs at Summit High, an affluent suburban school, echoes Elizabeth, Audrey, and Melanie in claiming that mothering has had the "greatest influence" on her approach to parent involvement and responsibility. "Before I was a mother," she says, "I was too quick to lay the blame on parents. . . . I simply didn't understand the balancing and juggling act that is required when you are a mother, and I didn't see the ways in which schools label and categorize youngsters." She learned these lessons the hard way by watching her own daughter, now in the sixth grade, confront teacher judgments that felt unforgiving and stereotyping. Even though her daughter is an extremely bright and capable student, she struggles with her shyness, her reluctance to speak up in class, and her difficulty making comfortable and easy connections with her teachers. Carol feels that, rather than developing and celebrating her daughter's extraordinary gifts, her daughter's teachers tend to "grade her personality" and respond to the "problem of her shyness."

As a mother, Carol now identifies with the trauma that many parents experience when their children first come to school and the teacher's judgments seem shockingly ungenerous and reductive. She recalls her view of her own children before they entered school, a view unblemished by the harsh and limited judgments of teachers representing the narrow norms of the school system. "Before my children were in school," she says sadly, "all I could see was their amazing beauty. But when they entered school, I discovered that they were not perfect in everyone's eyes." Parents struggle, she believes, to hold on to that "original view" that celebrates the unique and special qualities of their child, and at the same time "help their children survive the system" by teaching them the necessary social skills, and maybe even suggesting that they repress or alter aspects of their personalities, to be successful.

Recognizing how hard it is for parents to help children negotiate the school environment (even when their children are intellectually strong and academically capable), Carol now believes that teachers who are not parents are at a disadvantage in terms of relating to their students and families. When she says, "I don't think a teacher who has not been a parent can truly understand the parental perspective," she means this in two ways. First, teachers who have never parented are not able to experience the essential qualities of parenting in their teaching, and, second, they are likely to be less empathic with the parents of their students. When a teacher crosses the boundaries that Anna Freud draws so clearly, Carol explains, "part of what you do as a teacher is parent." Mothering has taught her, as it has Melanie, about giving children more space to take responsibility for their own learning. It is a constant calibration of control and freedom, engagement and restraint. "As a teacher, you struggle with when to hold on and when to let go, when to hover and when to support independent action," she says, making a circle with her hands to indicate, "we—mothers and teachers—are all in this together." Having her own children has made her "more forgiving and more flexible as a teacher" and made her approach to parents "much more humble and generous."

Jane Cross says that mothering gives her teaching a "soft edge," but she also claims that being a "mature woman" (she is fifty-seven) and an "experienced mother" (she has two sons in their early twenties) is the primary source of her legitimacy with parents. A teacher of the nursery class at an elite independent school, Jane came to teaching late, after several years of raising her sons full-time at home. Her "primary identity" and experience as a parent give her a kind of self-confidence in the classroom that is reassuring to both the children and their parents. Even in moments of crisis—when a child gets hurt on the playground, has an accident going to the bathroom, feels injured by a classmate's teasing, or throws up at the lunch table—Jane seems to know what to do. She is adept at applying Band-Aids to skinned knees, taking out splinters, confronting bullies, and soothing hurt feelings. Her actions are quick, intuitive, and pragmatic. And when parents have a hard time leaving their screaming child at school in the morning, Jane can say—with the confidence of one who has experienced this many times herself—that they "must go right now" and that she "promises" them that the wailing will stop within five minutes of their departure. The parents feel her authority and her empathy, both qualities that reflect her "mothering self."

When Maria Lopez works with the first-generation immigrant parents of the children in her third-grade bilingual classroom, she also establishes a bond that "begins with our all being mothers." In her first written communication with parents, which lays out the procedures and rules of the classroom but also tries to convey her "educational philosophy and human values," Maria always makes reference to her experience as a parent, to the joys and struggles, the ups and downs. Likewise, in her conferences with parents, Maria is constantly pointing to all of the mistakes that she has made—and continues to make—mothering. She talks about Juan, her firstborn, with whom she was "paranoid and overprotective," and who responded to her constant hovering by "seeking out the worst dangers" during adolescence. Now twenty, Juan has survived his forays into danger. He is a handsome, strapping young man who has found new purpose in his life and is about to enter college to study business. Maria tells various versions of this story to parents because she wants them to know that she has survived the rough-and-tumble adolescence of her son, that parenting is laced with mistakes and misjudgments, and that children are, in the end, amazingly resilient. Even children who seem to have dug themselves a hole out of which they will never climb somehow manage to recover, scarred but whole. But mostly Maria hopes that her stories will allow parents to feel identified with her as a mother, and that they will feel comforted and assured by the maternal instincts that are a large part of her teaching.

Maria's mothering self, however, is most evident in the workshops that she holds for parents several times during the year. It is at these gatherings that her voice is strongest as an experienced and wise mother. These are family occasions. Maria hopes to create a warm and welcoming ambience that feels more like home than the formal environment of the classroom, which can feel alien to her students' parents. She puts on a big spread of food tempting to the "Latino palate" and chooses topics that focus on building a healthy environment at home, not on their children's achievement. The parents— mostly mothers and grandmothers—do skits and role-playing of ordinary, everyday family scenes, and Maria helps them extract useful lessons about "conflict resolution," "effective communication in the family," "problem-solving skills," and "proper discipline of children." Maria believes that the high attendance at these workshops is related to the fact that parents have a great need for support in their parenting. They come to the sessions hoping to learn the ropes of survival in their new country, a place where they are still feeling uncertain and unequipped to give their own children good guidance. But Maria also thinks that mothers come to the workshops to hear about and learn from her experience as a mother. "It is the mother wisdom that they are hungry for, that they are seeking," says Maria, "not so much my skills as a teacher."

Saving Face

Parents say that their children's teachers who themselves are mothers tend to be more empathic and easier to talk to, have a better understanding of their point of view, and are wiser about the development and learning of their children. Parents will often listen specifically for the "mother voice" of the teacher, and feel most assured and comforted by that perspective. In fact, sometimes mothers feel drawn to teachers because they themselves yearn for the maternal embrace; they want to soak up some of the teacher's mother warmth and wisdom. This was certainly true of Claudia Blake, who came to school seeking reassurance and protection for her daughter, Laura.

At six months old, Laura was involved in a terrible car accident that left her with a large scar and deformity over the left side of her face. People who saw the tiny infant never knew what to make of her strange-looking face. Whenever the family went anywhere, people would stare at Laura, and many would noticeably withdraw in terror. If Claudia was with Laura in the mall, for example, a little boy might come up close to the baby stroller and point at her face. "Oh, Mom, look at that baby!" he'd say with a combination of horror and curiosity. Some mothers, recalls Claudia, would pull their child back sharply. "Stay away from her!" they'd shout. While other mothers would try to take a more open-minded approach ("Oh, Johnny, you know that lots of people live with difference"), "wherever we went," says Claudia, remembering the constant assaults, "there was always this painful, difficult narrative in response to Laura's specialness."

It was in the neighborhood park directly in front of the Blakes' house in a lovely tree-lined neighborhood in Atlanta where the family became most practiced in facing the "cruel assaults and complex negotiations" that became part of Laura's everyday life. In this idyllic spot, with lovely gardens and a winding brook, every day Laura faced the innocent cruelty of children and the hardened prejudice of their parents. "Amazingly," recalls Claudia, "mostly Laura responded as if none of this was happening . . . as if the world belonged to her." As her parents and siblings tried to protect her from injury and make the neighborhood families feel more comfortable in her presence, Laura seemed confident and unafraid. As a matter of fact, when she was only two and a half and a precocious talker, she was already trying to reassure her playmates that they had nothing to fear. "It doesn't hurt," she would say to a child with terror in his eyes. "It was the boys" who seemed to be particularly fearful, recalls Claudia. But Laura never ran away. Instead, she responded by "developing a somewhat aggressive style toward them, refusing to let them retreat."

"Then school!" says Claudia as a prelude to the next big chapter in her daughter's life. Searching for a place to begin, her eyes fill with tears, and she suddenly looks weary. "I was always surprised," she begins, "by people's response to Laura." Because she loved her daughter so much and had so incorporated her scarred face into her view of Laura's "amazing presence," Claudia was always unprepared for the insensitive or hurtful statement that was almost certainly lurking around any corner. She remembers a family reunion in which the whole clan lined up for a picture; just before taking the shot, the photographer stopped to ask whether they might want to turn Laura around so he could record her "good side." Claudia was always stunned at these moments, "simply clueless." "I used to always say that I suffered from 'repetitive shock syndrome.' . . . I could never get this other view of Laura in my bones."

But with the coming of school, Claudia and her husband were forced to take a hard look at the realities facing her. They simply could not reassure themselves that all would be fine. In fact, they knew that surviving the school scene would be far more treacherous than negotiating the park, and they knew that, for the first time, their daughter would be largely on her own. They spent months considering their options and weighing the alternatives, constantly preoccupied with the weight of their decision. Finally, they decided to send Laura to the public school right up the street, where she would be close by, where her older sister had blazed a path before her, and where they had already built good relationships with some of the teachers. But even with all of these pluses, they knew that the transition to school would be very difficult for Laura. They especially worried about those "social spaces" that would not be closely monitored by teachers—the halls, the cafeteria, and the playground at recess. They knew, for example, that even for the most socially savvy and acceptable child, recess could be a nightmare, an arena where kids could be unbearably cruel.

The first day of school remains painfully vivid in Claudia's memory. Hand in hand, she and Laura walked up to the Worth School, through the front door, down the hall, and into the classroom. With each step, Claudia could feel her heart pounding harder. She looked for the signs of terror in Laura but saw none. At the door of the classroom Mrs. Thomas, the teacher, greeted Laura with a big, welcoming hug. Laura got settled at a table with three other children, who all stared at her wide-eyed. One little girl drew away from her and said with a scowl, "If I looked like you, I wouldn't come to school." To which Laura responded without skipping a beat, and without an ounce of defensiveness in her voice, "But then how would you learn to read?"

Laura was cool, but Claudia was completely shaken. She was tortured by a mixture of feelings. On the one hand, she wanted to strangle this little girl who had hurled the insult at her daughter; on the other hand, the girl's meanness seemed to express an anxiety that she felt was surely resident in *all* of the little children coming to school for the first time. Claudia worried that the sharp one-liner from this little girl was a sign of all the horrible assaults her daughter would have to endure at school, but she also marveled at Laura's aplomb and grace in dealing with it. "Actually," Claudia says upon reflection, "Laura's voice in that moment calmed me down for the rest of the year."

The Worth School was one of the rare public schools in Atlanta that drew students from a variety of neighborhoods: middle class and working class, both black and white. Although the school had a well-integrated faculty, it was distinguished by its core of "old-time, fabulous, black middle-class teachers," and Mrs. Thomas, Laura's kindergarten teacher, was one. Right from the beginning—even before the start of school—Mrs. Thomas and Claudia began "strategizing" about how to make Laura's transition to school as safe and as comfortable as possible. "We had expected," recalls Claudia, "that her teacher might be defensive about parents whom she perceived to be *overinvolved*. But there was none of that. . . . Instead, she wanted to know about Laura, about her birth, about her development, about the accident, about the operations and hospitalizations, about her experiences with friends in the neighborhood before coming to school. And she expected that this knowledge would help her be a better teacher, and a better advocate for Laura."

Claudia and Mrs. Thomas agreed that it was important to help the children in Laura's class talk about what they saw and how they felt when she was in their midst, and that Laura would be the best, most authoritative provider of information. They also recognized that the lessons—of tolerance and acceptance—would have to be rehearsed over and over again, that fears and prejudices, even among young children, die hard. She also believed in talking openly about Laura's scarred face so that the children might discover their own scars—both visible and invisible—that caused them hurt and humiliation. So on several occasions Mrs. Thomas's kindergarten children talked about Laura's scar and asked her questions about what had happened, how it felt, and whether it would ever go away. In addition, Mrs. Thomas was always coming up with "inventive suggestions" that might improve Laura's relationships with her classmates. For example, at Christmastime, she suggested that Claudia have the children come over to her house to make cookies, hoping that they would experience the warmth and embrace of her family and feel more comfortable coming there to play after school. With time, the classroom became a safe haven for Laura, a place where she could count on the protection and advocacy of her teacher and where the children no longer looked at her as strange.

It was different and more dangerous for Laura outside the classroom, however. "These spaces were problematic," Claudia says shaking her head sadly. In the lunchroom and on the playground at recess, when there were no teachers near by, children would try to intimidate her with threats and taunt her mercilessly. Often Mrs. Thomas would come outside at recess or scan the cafeteria to see what was happening with Laura, but she couldn't always be there, and despite her best efforts, several times a week Laura would come home with a report of some terrible encounter with a mean child. Despite the terror of these moments, Laura loved going to school because she loved Mrs. Thomas and always felt safe in her presence.

When I ask Claudia how Mrs. Thomas created a classroom space that felt like an asylum for Laura, she immediately refers to the cultural and regional traditions that must have shaped her as a woman and teacher. "I really think that her view of teaching came from the Southern, black, rural one-room schoolhouse where the teacher was in charge of and felt herself responsible for everything. In those days, if kids came to school hungry, you fed them. If they came barefoot, you found shoes for them to wear. There was always this familial feel about the classroom, not the bureaucratic feel that defines many schools today." Mrs. Thomas seemed to be the modern version of her forebears, taking full responsibility for the children's well-being, offering her "maternal" support, and taking complete control in the classroom. Claudia points to what might appear to be a contradiction in the way she ran her classroom. "Mrs. Thomas was a big screamer. She'd really yell at those kids . . . a yell that felt like the screams of a mother, not the measured tones of a teacher. But somehow there was always this incredible sense of safety."

In addition to Mrs. Thomas creating a "familial" tone in her classroom, she was also openly expressive about her Southern black religious roots. "She was a deeply religious person," recalls Claudia. "She treated Laura as if she was a special gift from God." Claudia pauses for a moment and corrects herself. It was not just Laura who was the focus of her advocacy, prayers, and grace. "This was true about her relationship to all children. She saw God in every child." And although Claudia does not think of herself as a "believer," she too was reassured by Mrs. Thomas's faith and "was drawn into her beautiful orbit." Sometimes when Claudia seemed especially down or discouraged, Mrs. Thomas would suggest that reading the Scriptures might offer her some comfort. Remembering the way Mrs. Thomas ministered to the whole family, Claudia lets the tears fall. "She was like this angel sent to us to protect us . . . a mother angel."

Laura's experience in first grade was an altogether different experience. Mrs. Thomas's kindergarten had felt like a safe haven for Laura and a welcoming environment for her parents. By contrast, Miss Green's first grade seemed like a danger zone for Laura and off-limits for her parents. Mrs. Thomas's class had a "familial" feel, as if a mother hen were protecting her young. By contrast, Miss Green seemed more "bureaucratic" in her approach: adhering to the letter—not the spirit—of the school system's rules, underscoring the boundaries, and defending the space of the classroom. Certainly, part of the difference between Mrs. Thomas and Miss Green was a reflection of their age and experience. Miss Green, a white woman in her mid-twenties, was a "hot-off-the-press" graduate of a nearby teachers' college, and this was her very first year of teaching. Says Claudia sympathetically, "She was just too overwhelmed. She had too many worries to establish with Laura the relationship that she needed." Laura's presence seemed to "really push her over the edge," requiring a "special" relationship that seemed to threaten Miss Green's ideal of order and fairness. For Mrs. Thomas, there was no such thing as an "over-involved" parent; they were all a part of one big extended family. For Miss Green, on the other hand, every parental inquiry or request seemed intrusive to the relationships she was trying to establish with her students and to the sanctity of her classroom.

Claudia remembers Laura coming home after the second week of school reporting that Susan was Miss Green's "pet." She did not even know that her six-year-old had the word *pet* in her vocabulary, and she was certainly surprised that Laura was making this claim so early in the school year. Laura begged her mother to watch the way Miss Green greeted Susan every single morning, always admiring her pretty clothes or her cute hairdo. Susan was a blond, adorable girl who wore "frilly dresses and fancy barrettes in her hair." (She was the kind of girl that Laura would later call a "girly-girl" as a way of describing the special entitlements and cliquishness that seem to go with girls who are "blond and perfect.") Susan's family lived next door to the Blakes in a big, beautiful house with a circular driveway and manicured lawns. Her parents were from the Southern aristocracy in Louisville, and Susan seemed to be the perfect reflection of their status and their privilege. The next morning—and for several mornings after—when Claudia walked Laura to school, she watched the encounter between Miss Green and Susan, and she watched her daughter's response. She listened to the teacher's profuse praise of Susan's cuteness and sweetness, and she observed that the other children received no such attention or accolades. But Miss Green's admiration of Susan had a particular sting for Laura. "It was not just resentment on Laura's part," recalls Claudia. "It was also the pain of knowing she'd never be in Susan's shoes."

Claudia thought long and hard before approaching Miss Green. After all, she knew that the young teacher was feeling besieged, and she knew in her bones that Miss Green would be "very defensive." So, over the weeks, Claudia watched carefully and gathered the evidence. She also practiced keeping her rage down and "making nonthreatening sentences." "I remember stepping very carefully," says Claudia, wincing. "I knew that she was very wary of parents' judgments." Rather than say anything that might be interpreted as accusation, Claudia gently asked whether they "might think this dilemma through together." She asked Miss Green to imagine how "anyone" (not just Laura) might feel if they watched another get special attention and favors every day. She asked her to imagine being a child caught in the shadows while Susan enjoyed the bright light. As Claudia had predicted, Miss Green became immediately defensive. Red-faced, she responded, "I find positive things to say about *all* of the children in my class. . . . Laura comes to school all the time in cute outfits that I tell her about!" Since Miss Green vehemently denied any insensitivity or wrongdoing, the conversation went nowhere. It just collapsed into a kind of stalemate, as Claudia made a polite retreat. It turned out that Miss Green's behavior toward Laura did change after Claudia's unsatisfying visit. "She suddenly started gushing over *Laura's* outfits," says Claudia, a transparent response that even a six-year-old could see through.

Claudia admires and appreciates Mrs. Thomas's motherly instincts: the way she embraces the children and their parents as family, the way she watches over Laura's safety like a fierce mother-protector, even the way she bellows at her students like an angry, loving parent. It is the mother in Mrs. Thomas that creates the asylum for Laura and makes Claudia feel reassured. In fact, Mrs. Thomas's determination to respond to the individual needs and "beauty of each child" somehow creates a classroom environment that feels fair to all children. By contrast, young Miss Green circumscribes her teacher's role, chooses her favorites based on their "girly-girl" looks, and sets up boundaries that keep parents out. She is, of course, young and inexperienced, and not a mother, so her defensiveness is not surprising. She looks for institutional protection against what she perceives to be the special and unreasonable requests of parents. Her response, says Claudia, is "bureaucratic and hierarchical," so different from the family embrace of Mrs. Thomas, whom she calls "the consummate mother."

The Tables Are Turned

ALTHOUGH THE TEACHERS that I spoke to claim that mothering had transformed and enriched their teaching and improved their work with parents, I was fascinated to hear that the opposite is generally not true. That is, being a teacher does not necessarily help them be productive and comfortable as parents relating to the teachers of their own children. In fact, most claim that interacting with their children's teachers is rarely even close to satisfactory. For the most part, their meetings feel deeply frustrating, difficult, and awkward. As she looks back on the parent conferences she has attended over the years for her two sons who are now grown, Elizabeth Morgan offers a stunning observation: She can remember only one that stands out as informative and inspiring. When her younger son, Blake, was in day care, he had a wonderful, gifted teacher named Nora. Elizabeth recalls listening to Nora talk about Blake and having the extraordinary feeling that she had learned something new about her son, and that Nora really liked and understood him. She also remembers the tone of the meeting, which was filled with moments of empathy and seriousness but also laced with humor. Elizabeth finds it very sad to think that from all those years this is the only conference that she can recall—when her son was only four—that didn't seem like empty routine or, worse, like "the worst kind of obfuscation and miscommunication."

"It was always so hard to be on the other side of the table," Elizabeth says, to hear teachers' narrow judgments and distorted views that rarely seemed to reflect knowledge of and insight about her boys. She often felt that the awkwardness and lack of authenticity in these conversations were the result of a barely masked competition between them. Somehow they found themselves competing rather than collaborating, feeling defensive rather than opening up to each other. Perhaps her children's teachers felt threatened by Elizabeth's professional knowledge and experience. Perhaps they worried that she might discover a weakness in their work, a chink in their armor.

Raising her own children and attending their school conferences has made Audrey Pierce interact very differently with the parents of the children in her sixth-grade classroom in Maine. She never wants to cause the parents the same kind of anguish that she has experienced on several occasions when sitting through conferences with her son's and daughter's teachers. "Having sat as a parent in some very uncomfortable conferences," she recalls, "it is instructive to have the shoe on the other foot." One meeting with three of her son's high school teachers stands out in particular. Her son was in his junior year, a "real good kid" but an "uninspired student." In anticipating the conference, Audrey had felt some anxiety, particularly about her boy's lack of discipline and follow-through. But she certainly expected to hear some "good stuff" as well, and she hoped to learn something about "who he is in school." Instead, she walked into the classroom and faced three stone-faced, humorless teachers on the other side of a long table. Without any warm-up or warning, they began the relentless critique. "Here they are telling me how my son is screwing up, failing in every way . . . and I keep waiting for them to say something redeeming," remembers Audrey. She could feel herself getting upset, then defensive, then sliding into "a full-scale panic attack." Finally, she heard her screaming voice cut through their negative chatter. "Doesn't anyone have anything good to say about my son?" she wailed. They stared back at her in blank silence. They could not even come up with a shred of something positive to say about her precious son. With that, Audrey stood up slowly, pushed in her chair, walked to the door, and closed it carefully behind her, never breaking the deafening silence. It was only after getting in her car that Audrey allowed herself to let go. She fell over the steering wheel and wept.

Like Elizabeth and Audrey, Jane Cross believes that although her experience as a parent informs, enriches, and legitimizes her teaching, the opposite is not true. In fact, she feels that being a teacher has made her more inhibited as a parent relating to the teachers of her own children. Admittedly, part of her feeling of motherly caution might have been the result of being a teacher in the same school where her children were students. She had followed her two sons to Northwood, becoming the school librarian after her younger son had entered kindergarten and taking on a teaching role by the time he was a third grader. Being both a parent and teacher at Northwood felt "very tricky," "full of treachery." Jane always felt as if her boys were "overexposed" and as if she were an unwelcome intruder in their space. "When you are a teacher in your children's school," she explains, "you know more than you want to know and you see more than you want to see. . . . This is when the mother-teacher roles converge in a *very* uncomfortable way."

In order to create some distance and draw boundaries ("no matter how artificial"), Jane avoided contact with her sons' teachers. At lunchtime, she would sit at a different table; at faculty meetings, she would try to sit across the room. "I didn't want them to feel that they had to say something to me about my children," she recalls. "And I didn't want to hear what they had to say." The close ("almost incestuous") proximity of roles in the same school forced Jane to draw severe boundaries between mothering and teaching—the kind of hard lines that Anna Freud recommends. When her sons graduated from Northwood after completing the ninth grade, Jane felt a "huge relief" and "a great weight" lifted from her shoulders.

Since her experience in the dual role of teacher-parent at Northwood caused her to move cautiously around the school and avoid contact with her sons' teachers, it also made her very aware of the sensitivities that her colleagues must feel when their children are in *her* classroom. When the tables are turned, she tries not to "get too close" to her colleagues, and she understands their need to avoid contact with her. In addition, she feels inhibited in their presence, not wanting to reveal any "frustrations or insecurities" about her teaching that might make them anxious about their children being in her care. Jane sums it up: "I'm extremely careful about talking about my class in front of teachers whose kids are in my classroom, very cautious indeed." She pauses for a moment and seems to discover a brand-new insight. "When teachers are also parents in the same school, the parental role *always* predominates. Mothering is the place where we feel the most anxiety and exposure, where we feel the most vulnerable."

When Jane revisits her own feelings as a parent anticipating parent-teacher conferences, she gets a knot in her stomach. "My experience was always one of terror," she shudders, "my anxiety was amazing, sky high." She is quick to point out that the news that she and her husband received at these meetings was consistently good; both of her sons were conscientious and achieving students whom teachers enjoyed having in their classes. But even though the news was generally laudatory, this did not abate the trepidation. Now—even though she describes her view of her sons' school achievements as "mellow"— she is, for the moment, feeling identified with the overzealous parents that she deals with every day. "You see," Jane says to me in great earnestness, "your child is your most precious possession, clearly a reflection of who you are." She surprises herself—and seems a little embarrassed—when the notion of child as "possession" slips out of her mouth, and she quickly amends her statement. "Children are our deepest love, and it hurts when you hear something that your child might be hurting from. My husband and I didn't care what our sons' grades were so much, but we did want them to be happy and feel good about themselves . . . and we wanted to know that their teachers had a sense of who they were and that they respected them." Again, she makes an amendment, "Actually, I longed to hear that my sons were *liked* by their teachers."

When Jane's sons finished ninth grade at Northwood, they went on to the public high school, which was considered "first rate," in the suburban community where the family lived. Although Jane had looked forward to the separation from her sons' school life, she was surprised by how removed and alienated she actually felt from the culture of their suburban high school, and how hard it was to figure out how "to be" as a parent. Her face is somber as she reflects on her discomfort. "I always had this feeling that I was just watching this all happen, as if I were not a participant. . . . Since my kids had not gone there to elementary and middle school, my husband and I had no friends in the parent body, and no one made any effort to include us. We felt like outsiders who didn't know the culture of the place. I always felt as if I was backing away, as if I had no idea how to advocate for my sons."

Jane is not proud of her "shyness," her inability to overcome her reticence even where her boys were concerned. Her reluctance to take a "proactive stance" takes her back to the one memory of her own mother's aggressive posture in relation to Jane's sixth-grade teacher in a Durham, North Carolina, public school. Jane, whose father was a college professor and whose mother was a homemaker, was a conscientious and successful student in school. "I was a middle child," she explains, "so I took care of everything. There were no struggles or problems for me in school that my parents were called in to solve." But one day her mother read something on Jane's otherwise perfect report card that disturbed and offended her. Jane's teacher had commented, as if this were a problem, that she was "a bit of a tomboy." Jane recalls her mother's immediate reaction. "I have this vivid image of my mother putting on her hat and coat, charging down to the school, and storming into the classroom."

"I'm so glad that my daughter is a tomboy," she said, and turned on her heels to exit.

Jane shakes her head in admiration at her mother's advocacy and assertiveness. "My mother did not hold back!" In retrieving this childhood memory, she is underscoring the contrast between her mother's activism and her own reticence, a contrast that still "puzzles" her and causes her some lingering guilt, even though her sons have both made it safely and successfully through high school.

Jane's reluctance or shyness or holding back is a stance so different from that of the parents she deals with each day at the Northwood School, who have no trouble being assertive and aggressively advocating for their children, and from the moment when her own mother put on her hat and rushed up to the school to defend her daughter. Perhaps her reluctance is a remnant from the time when her sons were students at Northwood, and she had to avoid contact and conversation with their teachers in order not to be overly intrusive. Back then, Jane had thought it was better not to know too much; she had not wanted to violate the boundaries of professional courtesy, and above all she had been determined not to crowd her growing children. Perhaps this reluctance and caution had become habit, a more comfortable approach to encounters with her son's teachers that always seemed to cause anxiety in her anyway. "I was always afraid of getting myself in the middle of something. Especially since I didn't have a clue about how to advocate for my sons." Jane's voice trails off. "Somehow I always ended up feeling sidelined, like a passive bystander."

Andrea Brown's response was just the opposite of Jane's. Andrea jumped into the middle of the action. She refused to stand on the sidelines when she saw things going on in her daughter Heather's school that caused her concern. In fact, there was nothing that inspired her skilled activism more than "being a mom advocating for my daughter's education." This was where she brought all of her experience as an organizer. "After I became a mom, I pledged that I would never let my kid go to a teacher who did not see her as a gift!" says Andrea about how her attitudes toward Heather's teachers reflected the same devotion to her child's healthy development that she promised to the parents of the children in her Montessori school on the North Shore. She expected nothing less for her daughter than she gave to her students. "I brought to Heather's teachers that they have the most precious gift in my life. I needed to hear back from them that they felt that way too." In fact, her passionate voice of maternal advocacy seemed to reflect an even deeper concern for the harm and abuse that might befall her daughter. The urgency in her voice also echoes with generational connections; protecting and loving a child always offers the parent a second chance. Says Andrea, rehearsing one of her "personal litanies," "Having Heather was having *me*! . . . It was my opportunity to heal Andrea."

Of course, this expectation and standard—that Heather's teachers see her as a "precious gift"—was rarely met throughout her daughter's school career, but this never discouraged Andrea from voicing her demands. In fact, the opposite conditions usually prevailed: Heather was not valued or respected by her teachers, and Andrea would have to fight to protect her. As a matter of fact, advocacy for Heather often felt like a full-time job, requiring every bit of Andrea's political skill and emotional subtlety. "For the twelve years that Heather was in school, I gave it my all. I worked assiduously at it," recalls Andrea, clenching her fist. "I would get ferocious . . . and my way of getting ferocious is to get involved."

The troubles started early. As the token child of color (her father is white and she thinks of herself as biracial) in the neighborhood, Heather stood out among her schoolmates and experienced the sting of racial slurs. Andrea will never forget the day when six-year-old Heather was called a "nigger" by children on the school bus, and that was just the beginning of the racial assaults, which were usually more oblique and subtle, but nevertheless deeply wounding. But Andrea believes that the more serious discrimination against Heather in school was less a response to her color than to her intelligence and experience. Andrea's voice reveals the pain that she still feels when remembering the scars her daughter still carries and the huge differences between Heather's childhood experiences and those of her peers on the North Shore. "She was so bright, and she came from two parents who were worldly and sophisticated. She was born in Denmark, began studying the violin at two and a half and performing at five. . . . Her parents were travelers, went to the opera, had dinner parties. . . . So the cultural differences were a bigger issue than the racial differences. . . . It was what came out of her mouth in class that was troublesome in their eyes."

Andrea remembers working for months with a parent group that she had organized, trying to get the elementary school to offer a foreign language, and the unbelievable response from the principal. "It was like he was from another planet. He finally said to me in exasperation, 'Why would *any* child in Beach Head want to learn French, or any other foreign language, for that matter?' " As Andrea recites the several ways in which her daughter was disadvantaged by her privilege, she suddenly recognizes themes repeated from her own childhood in western Pennsylvania. "It was like me growing up," she exclaims. In her lonely and alienated childhood, Andrea's parents' ambitions and her own dreams put her far ahead of her peers and left her friendless. Heather was rehearsing the cruel paradox of academic achievement and social dislocation.

But Andrea's involvement as a parent advocate was never limited to protecting her daughter, even though Heather's background and experience were indeed unique. She always recognized that, in comparison to other children in her class, Heather was privileged by her talents, her experience, and her parents' education and sophistication. "Despite all of the race and class discrimination—all of the ways in which Heather seemed to threaten the status quo—I always knew that she would make it. . . . I knew she had the skills, the intelligence, the courage, and her parents' full support. . . . I felt it was wrong to focus all of my energies on only protecting my daughter." So Andrea's efforts were devoted to improving the lot for *all* of the children in the classroom, and her strategy was always focused on supporting the teachers' work. "I was always trying to figure out what the teacher needed to make her classroom a better place," says Andrea.

There are three aspects of Andrea's approach as a parent that seem unusual to me. First, when she saw that Heather's teachers were not acting in her best interest, her response was one of rage. But the rage quickly turned into engagement and activism, into becoming more involved rather than more distant and adversarial. Second, when Andrea deepened her involvement, she acted on behalf of all of the children. She didn't just defend her precious daughter and fight for special privileges that might put Heather in a more competitive position vis-à-vis her peers. Third, her involvement was always focused on trying to find ways of helping the teacher, offering support and resources, and participating in problem solving.

She is determined that Heather's teachers will see her daughter's strengths and celebrate her gifts, treating her with respect and reverence. But this is the way Andrea believes that *all* children deserve to be treated. So she expands her focus and fights for educational improvements for all of the children in Heather's class. She organizes other parents in collective action. She works to provide the teacher with the resources and support that she needs in order to do better work, and she refuses to retreat. "Do you know that wonderful United Nations poster that says, 'Women hold up half of the world?' " Andrea asks me, smiling. "Well, that is a huge understatement and it does not begin to describe our many roles, our passions, our powers, or our responsibilities." Now she is leaning toward me with fire in her eyes. "Women—mothers and teachers—are at the epicenter, balancing the claims on our lives, juggling all kinds of demands, engaging in the hard work of raising children." Andrea's words echo Mary Catherine Bateson's observations about the nature of women's work: crossing boundaries, merging roles, tolerating interruptions, and responding to multiple demands. It is work that both crosses boundaries and remains at the center. It is labor guided, in part, by women's peripheral vision.

It is clear that living both sides does not provide a comfortable and balanced "double vision" for teachers. Mothering enriches their teaching, but being a teacher does not necessarily help when they move to the other side of the table and enter the school as mothers. On the one hand, mothering informs and complicates a teacher's view, and inspires more generous and productive relationships with her students and their parents. With alacrity, they cross the boundary line that Anna Freud draws between "child education" and "child care," and the merging of roles enriches their teaching in a way that all of them describe as powerful and transformative. On the other hand, teachers who are mothers are not equally advantaged in taking their teacher selves into the parent-teacher conferences of their own children. Their experience as teachers is more likely to lead to competition rather than identification with their child's teacher; more likely to deaden rather than enliven the conversation; more likely to enact the scenario that Freud recounts of a struggle over "the rightful ownership of the child."

When teachers take on the parent role in parent-teacher conferences for their own child, they discover how much more powerful and passionate mothering is than teaching; how much more raw and exposed they feel; and how much more of their own identity and well-being is riding on their child's back. Mothering always trumps teaching; it is the place where women feel the most vulnerable and know the most heartbreak. They also discover—often to their great surprise and dismay—that their maternal view of their child—as special, as beautiful, as strong—is not necessarily shared by their child's teacher, whose perspective is likely to be narrower and more reductionistic, whose eyes notice and judge their child's imperfections and weaknesses. So teachers who are also mothers find themselves struggling to hang on to their original, primal image of their child as they confront their fellow teacher's contrasting portrayal. At the same time they know that it is their responsibility to help their own child learn to survive in an environment that is unlikely to see his or her "amazing beauty" or celebrate his or her unique gifts.

Andrea Brown's advocacy for her daughter Heather offers an important insight and a valuable lesson. She is unusual in having found a way to work productively as a mother in her child's public school. She comes to the parent's side of the table prepared to embrace the "universalistic perspective" of the teacher, even as she holds fast to her loving and particular view of her daughter. Just as her maternal instincts enrich her teaching, so does her teaching experience and perspective make her more generous and expressive in her encounters with "the other women" in her child's life.

Borderlands and Crossroads

Mirrors and Metaphors

SCHOOLS HAVE ALWAYS been the arena where the cultural and historical dramas of our society get played out. Joseph Featherstone's view of schools as society's "theater" not only recognizes that schools mirror societal priorities, values, and conflicts, but also the ways in which—in vivid microcosm—they magnify and intensify them. We look inside schools—and at the relationships between the schools and the communities they serve—and see vivid reflections of our society's struggles to enact democracy, to reduce inequalities, and to open access and opportunity for our diverse citizenry. We witness the political and intellectual arguments surrounding bilingualism and multiculturalism. We hear the rancor in the competing perspectives on immigration, assimilation, acculturation, and indoctrination. Schools as theater reveal—in bold relief—the dissonance between our professed values and our behavior, between, for instance, our societal claims that "children are our most precious resource" and what we are actually willing to expend and sacrifice in order to assure their safety and development.

At the borders of families and schools, parent-teacher meetings become the tiny stage on which these broad cultural priorities get translated into dialogue. Beneath the polite surface of what appears to be a civilized and polite ritual, we hear the adult actors' voices shaping a poignant and powerful drama that is rich with emotion. Between the lines of orderly, structured text of a practiced script, we notice the chaos and emotion of a subtext that is often inaudible to the participants. This subtext—more powerful because it is largely unconscious and unnamed—is shaped by both intergenerational and autobiographical experiences and broader historical and cultural narratives.

Every time parents and teachers come together, their dialogue is to some extent related to their early childhood experiences, which get rehearsed and replayed in the classrooms of their children. As parents and teachers sit facing one another they are drawn back in time, to the time when they felt small and powerless, to the specters from their youth. These ancient ghosts invade the classroom, crowd into the conversation, and often make it difficult for the adults to place themselves in time and space. It is as if there are two plays being enacted simultaneously: one in which the adult actors speak rationally and clearly about the young person for whom they are responsible, and a second drama that goes on inside, where adults reenact scenes from their own childhoods.

These two plays compete and converge to produce the doorknob phenomenon. At the end of the conference, just as he is about to leave, the father suddenly unleashes the anguish that he has managed to ignore and repress during the meeting. He warns the teacher that he is determined that the trauma he experienced as a fifth-grade student will not be inflicted on his son. He will do anything to protect his boy from a repetition of the same pain. One of the great challenges facing teachers and parents is to recognize the presence of these autobiographical echoes—the ghosts in the classroom—that reverberate through the conference, and then to be careful not to let them drown out the dialogue that should be focused on the student. There are both important insights and dangerous distortions carried in these ancient echoes, and bringing them to consciousness helps parents and teachers distinguish the good from the bad.

Teachers who are aware of this "double channel" going on in the parents' heads find ways of helping them unravel the knots of converging narratives. Elizabeth Morgan, for example, speaks about her use of "wait time," a purposeful pause in the dialogue that opens up space for inchoate feelings and formless reflections. She uses these "silences," generously and strategically, to make room for the wandering, improvisational talk that often leads to new insights and interesting discoveries. "I'm very good on the back roads," she says about the comfort she feels in letting the drama unfold. She gathers the pieces of the jagged conversation together, "giving it back to the parents in a form that makes sense and moves the conversation forward." All the time, however, Elizabeth works to keep the child in focus. The travel along the back roads must be in the service of carving out a more straightforward and productive path for the child. The adult reflections and retrospection that the silences permit must be in the service of moving the student forward.

It is important to recognize that these ghosts inhabit the psyches of both teachers and parents, and that most of the ancient material in both refers to experiences of trauma, not moments of victory and achievement. In fact, every teacher I spoke to needed to begin with their early childhood experiences as a way of describing the origins and motivations of their work with families. And every childhood narrative was charged with disappointment and pain, a pain that radiated into the present, a pain that these teachers were determined not to pass on to their students, a pain that, for some, seemed to be the major reason they chose teaching as a career. As one teacher put it, in a voice that gave thanks, "You know, teaching gives me the chance to heal myself."

But the drama of parent-teacher conferences is not only composed of these autobiographical scripts—the haunting laments of the psychic ghosts—it is also fueled by broader historical and cultural narratives. In the small scene of parent-teacher dialogue we see reflected a long-running play about, for example, how our society deals with the hierarchies of race, class, and gender. Or we see the enactment of our deep cultural ambivalence about whether schools should challenge or reinforce these pervasive inequalities. Or we hear the actors express the great expectations that we as a society hold out for our schools. Then we listen to the inevitable disappointment and cynicism that follows when schools don't come close to meeting these ambitious goals. Each of these larger cultural dilemmas and social conflicts gets played out in schools, the most visible of our social institutions, whose very transparency allows us to see the unfolding drama. But, as this book attests, it is in the places where families and schools meet—in the conversations between parents and teachers—where the drama reflecting these cultural themes is most vividly manifest.

Once again, there are two plays converging in the heads of parents and teachers, a text and a subtext that illuminate the tiny stage. The first is a conversation about the individual experiences and development of the student in school. Here the parents discuss their expectations and aspirations for their child and the teacher offers judgments about his or her learning and development. The second reflects the broader social and institutional backdrops that frame parental expectations and aspirations for their children and help to define our society's perspectives on childhood. No conversation between families and schools seems to fully escape the press of these cultural preoccupations; no contemporary dialogue is not, to some extent, shadowed by powerful historical antecedents.

When Elizabeth Morgan, a middle-class African-American teacher who is the principal of an elite independent elementary school, is confronted by the angry upper-class white parents of kindergarten children who disagree with a hiring decision she has made, she is overwhelmed by the vehemence of their rage. The fathers are relentless in their verbal assaults, and Elizabeth feels suddenly impotent and becomes uncharacteristically mute. Even as she struggles to find her voice and resist their badgering, she knows that this is not just a discussion about the wisdom or viability of her administrative decision or even about its impact on the educational experience of their children. It is also—perhaps primarily—a power struggle with race and class at its center. The aristocratic white parents do not seem to be able to stand this middle-class black woman in authority, and this conversation is intended to keep her in her place.

But Elizabeth experiences another layer in this unfolding narrative, an older story in which this contemporary struggle is embedded. This is not only a battle over the institutional and interpersonal forces that shape disparities and conflicts in race and class. For Elizabeth, this is an even more troubling and ancient drama—the enactment of the master-slave relationship. In this northern Virginia town, where the vestiges of the Southern plantation are still evident, these parents' voices echo the abusive assaults of the master punishing his uppity slave, and Elizabeth's silence and passivity is a response carved out of a bloody and horrible history. When she does not pick up the telephone that rings and rings during their conference, she comes close to endangering her own son, who is in crisis.

Throughout the narratives in this book, we see the interplay of larger cultural and historical dramas that shape and inform the play-within-a-play that is the parent-teacher conference. The presence and power of the larger framework are particularly troublesome when parents and teachers are trying to communicate across the chasms of class, race, and ethnicity, or navigate the disparities in educational background or immigrant status. When there is an asymmetry of power and status between schools and the families they serve, when prejudice, ignorance, and fear expose broader social and economic hierarchies, then parent-teacher encounters are more likely to become the sites of misunderstandings and conflict. Teachers and parents must work extra hard not to let these broader cultural biases obscure their clear sight of one another and distract them from focusing on the well-being of the child.

In *The Vulnerable Child,* Richard Weissbourd warns us about the power of the deep-seated prejudices that hover over family-school encounters and give adults a distorted view of the strengths and capacities of children. He reminds us, for example, of the danger of the self-fulfilling prophecy that assumes that children who come from impoverished communities are necessarily the most vulnerable and the least likely to be successful in school. And he challenges our expectation that whole categories of children should necessarily be labeled "at risk" because of their socioeconomic or racial backgrounds. Weissbourd finds instead that while poverty and prejudice may contribute to the disadvantage of millions of children, that there is much evidence to suggest that other factors, such as parental stress and depression, have an even more powerful and deleterious impact on a child's educational fate. In fact, it is the individual problems of children—their difficulties with hearing and vision, learning disabilities, and social isolation—that have far more to do with learning and developmental outcomes than any simple formula based on the broad categories of race, income, ethnicity, or family structure.

Weissbourd also speaks about the plasticity of human development, the many opportunities for growth and learning that occur across a person's life span. He urges us to recognize the strengths in even the most scared and delinquent child, and the vulnerabilities and weaknesses that lurk below the surface of children who appear to be strong and successful. All of Weissbourd's warnings underscore the ways in which our cultural preoccupations and prejudices can intrude upon our clear-sighted view of children and distort relationships between families and schools. Meaningful dialogues between parents and teachers, and authentic assessment of children's capacities, necessarily means resisting the prophecies of prejudice deeply ingrained in our culture and history, and focusing instead on the individual qualities and trajectories of children.

Many of the teachers I interviewed spoke about their efforts to resist these broader societal forces, to resist the mirrors and magnification of the broader cultural drama. When Andrea Brown meets with the striving middle-class parents at her Montessori preschool, she challenges the societal forces of competition and materialism—what she calls "the constructions of capitalism"—that shape the values and behaviors of parents and influence the expectations they hold and the ways they advocate for their children. This "value frame" that parents bring into their meetings at the school is not only about money. It is about all of the qualities of life that emerge when accumulation of personal wealth and the pursuit of social and economic power are primary life goals. Andrea believes that these parental preoccupations work against the kind of dialogue that she hopes to develop with them. In working with families, she wants to "create a space" for a different, more "organic and fluid" kind of conversation that supports a process of inquiry and discovery. She is clear that in creating these spaces for dialogue about children, she is "purposefully and strategically resisting" the press of contemporary culture, which she believes rules the lives of families who live in "a world of entrepreneurship and profit."

Like Andrea Brown, Sophie Wilder, a fifth- and sixth-grade teacher in an alternative public school, "resists" the hierarchies of power and the unequal distribution of resources that she witnesses each day as her students—from widely diverse racial and social class backgrounds—enter her classroom. Sophie loves the fact that her school is deeply committed to parental involvement and sees families as vital to the education of the whole child. But over the years, her enthusiasm has been quelled by the unequal patterns of parent participation she sees that privilege her affluent students and too often cause the least advantaged children to be ignored. Not surprisingly, it is the highly educated white parents who tend to be the most actively involved and the most demanding of teachers, while the poor and working-class minority parents are much more reluctant to be engaged in schools and aggressively advocate for their children. In the last year, Sophie has tried to "resist these hierarchies of participation" by balancing what she calls "the currency of the classroom." When the more assertive parents come to her and ask for special favors for their children, she tries to "mentally advocate" for the children whose parents are not there. Sophie muses about a strategy that she is still in the process of figuring out. "I am trying always to be disciplined in my thinking. . . . I've heard the views and demands of the vocal parents. Now, what would the other parents say or need me to do if they were here?" These kinds of mental calculations require energy and vigilance, and Sophie worries that it is hard to translate "her head trip" into her interactions with children and families. But she believes in the kind of intentionality of resistance that is embedded in the corrective actions she takes, and she knows that over time her efforts will make her classroom feel less like a mirror and magnification of the worst aspects of society.

Children at the Center

Children should be present—and given a voice—at parent-teacher conferences. They are the only people who know both the family and the school domains. They are the best interpreters of, and authorities on, their own experience. Their presence helps the adults stay focused on their primary reason for coming together in the first place: to support the learning and the development of the child. And student participation should not be reserved for the teenage years; it should begin when children are very young. Of course, they must be old enough to use and understand language, sit relatively still, and attend to what is going on. Molly Rose's first graders are present and vocal at all of the parent-teacher meetings; they tell their parents about their own experience in school, about what they have learned and what things are still hard for them. Their portfolios—filled with their work and reflecting their growth and their progress—offer the evidence that supports their presentation. Molly sees the child at the center of the conference and the adults as audience, listening attentively and responding appreciatively. In fact, she believes that a major benefit of including children in the ritual is that they begin to develop the skills of self-evaluation. They learn how to present and take responsibility for their ideas and their work. And for the first time, many of their parents are able to see their children with new eyes. They are surprised and pleased to see their growing competence and self-assurance.

Molly is one of those rare teachers who manage to get 100 percent attendance at parent-teacher conferences. She does this year after year in a city school with a large immigrant population, with a majority of students from single-parent homes, and with families who are poor and often illiterate. Certainly her unbridled enthusiasm and persistence, her willingness to meet parents, grandparents, and caregivers ("whomever the children call their family") any time and any place (and not "take it personally" when they don't show up or cancel at the last minute), and her weekly communications that keep them abreast of classroom activities encourage their attendance at the twice-yearly conference. But I also suspect that parents come to these ritual meetings because they look forward to hearing their children hold forth; they relish the chance to watch them perform. Their child's participation in the meeting is a big draw. After all, no parent wants to disappoint a child who has worked hard to prepare for his or her most important and appreciative audience.

There are, of course, occasions when teachers and parents need to speak privately and in confidence; when the news may be too painful, difficult, or complex for children to hear; when the adults need to strategize on the child's behalf; when the conflict between the adults would make the child feel conflicted or unsafe. At these moments, children should be out of hearing range and out of harm's way. But I believe that these adult-only conversations should be the exception, not the rule. If the typical ritual is presumed to be three-way—parent, teacher, and child—then the adults will become more and more comfortable with the youngsters' presence and discover that their voices enrich and inform the encounter.

Carol Steele's story about Steven, one of the special-needs high school students in the Pilot Program she heads—who had promised to attend the meeting with his divorced parents, the learning specialist, and the social worker, but who at the last minute disappeared from school—is a tale about the lengths that Carol will go to get students to participate in and take some responsibility for the problem solving and decision making that will affect their learning and healing. It was actually Steven's father who had the bright idea of tracking down his son on his cell phone. Steven answered the call, knowing it was from his father because he saw the number on the phone screen. He must have been at least ambivalent about joining the conversation, both wanting and not wanting to endure the discomfort of what was sure to be a difficult scene. But, at the last minute, Steven's voice was not only incorporated into the conversation, it became the dominant voice. Carol laughs at the irony: His long-distance participation didn't marginalize him, it put him at the center. Six grown-ups sitting around the table at school hanging on every word of one adolescent tuning in from his car. Carol tells this story both to underscore the importance of student participation in parent-teacher meetings and to emphasize that adults must be willing to improvise, to go the extra mile, to reach out and include them. This is particularly important for adolescents, who want to assert their independence and who are likely to see the conference as an ambush, with the adults lying in wait to expose their weaknesses, hurl criticisms at them, or put them down.

But even if adolescents are not worried about being ganged up on by the most powerful adults in their lives, there is a tendency for parents to respond to their teenager's need for more autonomy—and the secrecy and silence that often accompanies that—by becoming less involved in the school scene, by deciding that their presence at parent-teacher conferences is no longer as crucial as when their children were young. Parent participation certainly recedes as children grow older. Some studies show a precipitous decline in parental involvement during the teenage years by as much as 50 percent, for example, between grades six and nine. Even though adolescents may turn surly and rebuff their parents' efforts to stay connected to their school life, and even though parents may feel awkward not knowing exactly how to advocate for someone who suddenly feels like a stranger to them, it is important for parents to remain vigilant, particularly since the academic decisions their children are making are likely to have real consequences for their future lives.

Steven's willingness to respond to his father's telephone call, despite his disappearing act, speaks to another reason why children should be included in parent-teacher meetings. However hard it may be to attend the conference and risk hearing criticism, it is even harder to be completely outside of the conversation, to be sitting somewhere knowing that your teachers and parents are having a conversation about you without being there to defend yourself, or even to lap up all of the wonderful praise. Molly Rose makes such a big point of including her first graders in the grown-up conversation because she has vivid and painful memories of the two evenings each year when her parents would hire a babysitter and drive off to her snazzy private school to rendezvous with her teacher. Molly would wait at home racked with anxiety, desperate to know what they were saying, playing over in her mind the possible scenarios. Even though she was a high-achieving student whose report cards were full of A's and "Excellents," and even though she enjoyed the admiration of her parents and teachers, being excluded from this essential conversation made her feel exposed and vulnerable. And it made her both yearn to hear all the good stuff and worry about not having the opportunity to correct or explain the things that the adults might be misinterpreting. After all, even at a very tender age, Molly recognized that she was the only one who knew both the home and school scenes. Only she knew what it took to navigate across the family-school border. I believe that even when students seem to be reluctant, even resistant, to attending parent-teacher meetings, there is a part of them that wants to be a part of the conversation. It feels worse to be excluded and given no voice in the conversation than it does to be included and forced to listen to things that are hard to hear.

Learning About the Other:
A Teacher-Parent Curriculum

IT IS IMPORTANT to remember that the teachers whose work is documented and celebrated in this volume are not typical in the ways they engage and communicate with parents. In fact, I chose to watch their good work and I listened very carefully to what they had to say because I believe that their voices carry important lessons and valuable wisdom, and because I believe that too much of the educational literature is focused on recording the deficiencies of teachers, the pathologies of families, and the weaknesses of schools. Too often the literature's focus on pathology ignores the goodness that is there in schools, offers us few lessons about how to make things better, leads to a kind of chronic cynicism and despair, and ends up blaming the victim. Without denying education's problems and failures, or romanticizing and idealizing evidence of progress and productivity, I think it is most instructive to examine what is good enough and to excavate and identify the useful lessons.

The teachers in this book, then, were chosen because they are unusually good at joining forces with parents on behalf of children.

They are rare in how they are able to build relationships with the families of their students, relationships that are collaborative and authentic, relationships that seek symmetry and alliance. They see parents as the first educators, are respectful of their experience and perspective, and listen carefully to their observations and insights about their children, which will help them be better teachers for these children. It is not that these good teachers are perfect or flawless in the ways they forge relationships with parents. Their encounters are not always productive and smooth. In fact, all of them are able to recall scenes where miscommunication erupted into angry accusations; where unconscious prejudices caused fear and defensiveness; where they were left feeling bruised and raw or racked with terrible guilt about the hurt that they caused.

So these caring and compassionate teachers are considered rare not because they are perfect. Negotiating family-school borders is, at best, an imperfect and delicate enterprise. Rather, they are unusual in the value and focus that they place on parental engagement, and in the way they see parents as essential to the child's healthy development and optimal learning. They are unusual in the many ways they reach out to parents, in the creativity and improvisation that define their approaches. They always search for what works best, tolerating—even welcoming—conflict that seeks clarification and problem solving to move past moments of impasse. And they are unusual when compared to the majority of teachers, whose relationships with parents tend to be defensive and formulaic, who look to the institutional bureaucracy to shield or buffer them from what they see as the intrusions of families.

But the teachers whose stories are told here are *not* unusual in the lack of formal preparation and training they have received for working with families and in the criticisms they offer for this "hole in their curriculum." Most of what they do well results from trial and error and from the learning that follows failure, from intuition and accumulated experience, or from witnessing and absorbing the ways in which their own parents and teachers encountered one another. Several of them even speak about their strengths in working with families as growing out of temperamental inclinations. "I love working on the margins of institutions," says one. Another speaks about relishing the "complexities and difficulties of relational work." A third says that teachers need to have the personality and skills of "ethnographers." She muses, "I feel as if it has been a lifetime of watching the way my mom and dad dealt with people and relationships in the world. . . . This is the first and most important informal training that I received." But ultimately she admits that she was "largely self-taught," leading with her "intuition, imagination, and developing ideas." So even though all of these teachers manage to invent a productive, even imaginative, approach to working with families, they all lament the absence of a curriculum that explicitly and deeply prepared them for this important part of their professional role.

Across the country, and in a wide variety of educational settings, teachers receive almost no training or support in developing relationships with the families of their students. Graduate and undergraduate teacher training courses do not help students anticipate or prepare for—conceptually or pragmatically—their work with parents. And once new teachers are hired, they receive almost no guidance, support, or supervision from their administrators or colleagues in this area. They make it up as they go along, usually relying on perspectives and practices that they learned as children watching their own parents and teachers. Those who have good memories tend to want to reproduce and incorporate those values and behaviors into their adult repertoire. Likewise, many teachers with childhood memories of unease and conflict on the family-school borders try to do the opposite of what they observed and experienced as youngsters.

I believe that a core part of the curriculum of teachers in training needs to be focused on productively relating to the parents of their students. First, they need to learn to value the authority and wisdom of parents and recognize the contributions that they can make to the child's success in school. Second, they need to develop a wide-angle view of the broad ecology of education, be able to envision a map of the several institutions where children are socialized, and develop an appreciation of how students individually and collectively navigate the terrain between home and school. And third, teachers in training need to develop strategies, tools, and skills for supporting productive dialogues with parents. They need to learn to listen—patiently, intently, and respectfully—to parental perspectives on their children. They need to develop their powers of observation so that they will be able to see, and then document, the important evidence, illustration, or anecdote that will help them offer a vivid portrayal of the child's life in school and help them convey to parents that they know their child and care for him or her.

Once teachers finish their training and join the faculty of a school, they need to receive mentoring and supervision from administrators and senior colleagues about communicating effectively and building productive relationships with parents. They must be socialized into a community of colleagues who value the knowledge and perspective of parents and see it as essential to supporting their students' development, and they must receive their collective wisdom about the best practices in working with families—practices that are shaped by and responsive to the surrounding community. Newcomers to a school faculty should never be left to simply figure it out on their own, and their knowledge of the families and community must not be reduced to the snippets of gossip—often pejorative—that they might hear in the teachers' lounge.

Teachers need to learn about building productive relationships with families, but parents also need support and guidance in figuring out the scope and dimensions of their role. Even when the rhetoric and policies of the school seem to support parental engagement and participation, many parents feel as if they are trespassing when they cross the threshold of the school, as if they are treading on territory where they don't belong. This makes them feel ill at ease, off-balance, and often defensive. Other parents—particularly those who speak a different language, who are poor, or who themselves were school dropouts—feel excluded by an institutional bureaucracy that seems opaque and unwelcoming, hard to understand and difficult to navigate. And they feel demeaned by a subtle message that they are inadequate parents who have not prepared their children to succeed in school. Still other parents feel ill equipped to play their roles productively and strategically. They are unclear about how to best advocate for their children, how best to strike a balance between engagement and intrusiveness, between accompanying their children and giving them the space to develop independence. And they feel alone and at sea, afraid to reveal their anxiety to teachers and even to other parents. They are fearful of doing the wrong thing and reducing their child's competitive edge.

Whether parents' discomfort comes from not knowing how to navigate the bureaucracy or from their response to subtle institutional barriers that make them feel as if they are trespassing, or whether they just have no clue about the appropriate dimensions and limits of their role, I believe that parent-teacher conferences would be far more productive if schools became clearer and more explicit about their expectations, made the rules and rituals of parental engagement more transparent, and marked the boundaries and defined the common ground more clearly. This means that teachers and school leaders need to spend some time at the beginning of the school year educating parents about how to make their dialogues with teachers more productive, about how to prepare for and what to expect during these encounters, about what to listen for and good questions to ask, and about those aspects of school life in which they should not be involved.

Jane Cross, the teacher of four-year-olds at a progressive private school, talks about the conflicts and tension between families and schools that arise when the limits of parental authority are not defined clearly. This is particularly problematic in a school where influential and highly educated parents want to be involved in every decision that might impact their child's successful climb to the top. Even though Jane works to create "a seamless connection" between home and school by welcoming the parents into her classroom each morning and keeping in close touch with them about their child's progress, she also feels that the school needs to be much clearer with parents about what things are not open for discussion, about areas of educational jurisdiction in which they should not have a voice. To spend years haggling with parents over whether French should be offered—along with Spanish—to four-year-olds is, in Jane's judgment, a waste of everyone's time and sends a message to parents that Jane feels is disingenuous. It is a message that pretends that teachers value their opinion on these curricular matters, a message designed to make parents feel as if the school is "endlessly flexible and open to their views." Teachers chafe at the intrusion into their "professional territory." Much of the tension and exasperation that is felt by both teachers and parents might well be lessened, if not resolved, if the school helped parents understand the appropriate limits of their involvement and responsibility.

It is also important for parents to make good and wise and strategic decisions about the nature of their involvement in schools. There are so many ways in which parents can make their presence felt in the life of the school: from making cookies and brownies for a bake sale, to becoming active in the parent-teacher association, to chaperoning school trips, to sitting on boards of directors, to helping out in the classroom on special projects, to attending parent-teacher conferences, to assisting their children with homework. Although each of these ways of engaging the school may be important to providing needed resources and supporting the school community, those activities that are fairly remote from the child's learning experience seem to contribute less to successful relationships between parents and teachers, and, more important, seem to have less impact on learning and achievement.

Researchers who have studied the types and levels of parental participation and their impact on achievement patterns of children make a distinction between the proximal and distal engagement of parents in school. They find, for example, that children are likely to do better in school when parents are vigilant in helping their children with homework, when they are conversant with the classroom curriculum, and when they regularly communicate with the teacher about the child's experience in school. Likewise, learning will not necessarily be enhanced for students whose parents primarily focus their efforts on institutional maintenance, on those aspects of school life that do not engage the teacher or the child directly.

Joyce Epstein, a researcher at Johns Hopkins University, has spent the last twenty-five years exploring the dimensions and impact of family-school engagement. She finds that parental involvement in a child's education—more than the family's educational background— can be one of the strongest predictors of academic success. But which kinds of activities parents become engaged in matters a lot. Sitting on steering committees or running capital campaigns may make parents feel committed, but, says Epstein, they are likely to have a negligible effect on children's achievement. Much more fruitful, for example, are the connections parents make at home with their children, discussing and reinforcing the classroom activities.

Molly Rose, the first-grade teacher in a city school serving poor and working-class children, seems to do the most thorough job of engaging parents in a way that is likely to have an impact on their children's success in school. Each week, for example, parents receive *The Rose Room Report,* a newsletter that describes what is going on in her classroom—the class trip to the aquarium, the planting of avocado pits, the working on vowels, learning to count by twos—and it also suggests activities that parents and their children might engage in together at home to reinforce their child's learning in school. Molly believes that these weekly communications help parents understand what is going on in their child's world and give them access to a part of their child's life that is usually invisible to parents. "Most kids," says Molly, "will reveal very little about what is going on at school when their parents quiz them directly. This allows the parents to open up the conversation in a very specific way, and it gives them a context and a language." It also gives parents confidence in approaching Molly. Armed with knowledge of the curriculum and classroom activities, ready with common points of reference, they feel better prepared to engage in a real conversation with their child's teacher.

All Children Have Special Needs

CONVERSATIONS BETWEEN parents and teachers are often least productive when they are discussing a child who is considered "average": a student who does not have any visible or identifiable deficiencies or any obvious and compelling strengths, a student who does not stand out, cause trouble, or make waves. "Average" children tend to get lost in the shuffle. Those teachers who work successfully with the most vulnerable children have a lot to teach us about the kind of focused and empathic attention that *all* children should receive. Carol Steele, who runs the Pilot Program, sees parents as necessary allies and collaborators. In an odd way, the adults benefit by their awareness that they can't do without one another's support. Without a joint effort, the youngsters will languish. And parents and teachers of special-needs students are more likely to see themselves as responding to real problems that require complex remedies, persistent problem solving, and a discerning and honest accounting of the student's vulnerabilities and strengths.

Although very few schools and programs can afford the kind of time, energy, and resources that Carol has at her disposal, there are lessons here for teachers and parents in more "average" and ordinary settings—lessons about listening and alliance, about identifying and naming the deficiencies and celebrating the strengths, about not indulging or making excuses for the student's vulnerabilities, and about pushing him or her toward independence. "I'm always intent upon moving them out of this protective asylum, helping to make them strong enough to withstand the rigors of the regular school," says Carol.

When we watch Carol's extraordinary vigilance—her commitment, creativity, and truth-telling—it is important to recognize that her attentiveness is supported by a federal mandate called the Individuals with Disabilities Education Act (IDEA), signed into law in 1975. IDEA focuses specifically on the families of children with special needs. In fact, this is one of the few arenas where public policies in education support the good works of teachers who choose to enact the spirit of the law with caring and compassion. (There are, of course, many special education professionals who may follow the letter of the law but still manage to exclude and diminish parents and stereotype and limit their children.) Though the IDEA may be translated differently from state to state and district to district, it is the only federal law that is specific in its requirements for parental involvement in the decision-making process about their children. Parents have a right to be part of an IEP (Individualized Education Plan) team along with a special education teacher, a regular education teacher, an evaluation specialist, and any other specialists who are involved with the student's education. The IEP team decides on a plan for teaching and providing special services to the child.

Not only are parents legally entitled to participate in writing the IEP, they also have a number of rights regarding the extent and frequency of their involvement and their input into the decision-making process, and their rights of appeal about decisions with which they disagree. There are "procedural safeguards," including the need for informed parental consent, the right of parents to appeal decisions through a mediator, and the right to request evaluations and reevaluations of their child. In her conference with Tony's parents, other special education specialists, and the social worker from the employment agency, Carol Steel enacts—with discernment and humor—the spirit of IDEA. The discussion is open, collaborative, and inclusive, using the wit and wisdom of all of the participants. And the highly educated, deeply concerned parents know their rights and responsibilities so that they can be effective advocates for their son.

Even when there is an explicit law in place, however, it is often hard for parents to fully and effectively participate in developing the IEP. They may be made to feel stupid by teachers and specialists who withhold or do not sufficiently explain crucial information. They may find the requirements and regulations of the law too complex and opaque to decipher. Audrey Pierce, who teaches sixth graders in a heterogeneous classroom in a small town in Maine, works closely with the parents of special-needs children who are primarily poor and illiterate and who "don't have a clue" about their rights and responsibilities under IDEA. She enjoys her role as translator and advocate for these parents. As she works to make their rights understandable to them and walks them through the bureaucratic and legal steps, she is determined not to speak down to them or make them feel infantalized. Audrey knows that the law is an empty instrument that must be filled with knowledge and goodwill, and must be made usable and understandable to parents.

But Audrey does more than help illiterate, undereducated parents translate the letter of the law into understandable rules of practice. She does more than help them navigate the complicated bureaucratic regulations. Her understanding of the notion of "special needs" extends beyond the few children in her class who have been so classified. She believes that every child has strengths and weaknesses, even those who appear to be thriving and achieving in the classroom, even those whose "very averageness" causes teachers to almost ignore them. In order to recognize the individuality of all of her students and make every child visible in her sight, Audrey reframes the conversation that she has with students and their families, so that it begins with the assumption that *all* of the children in her class have "particular challenges" that stand in the way of their full and optimal development. They all have dimensions of their intellect, their character, and their skills that need special attention and improvement. And it is a reframing that forces everyone—teachers, parents, and students—to articulate goals for each student and measure progress not only in relation to a uniform collective standard, but also in relation to the individual student's trajectory.

In reframing the conversation, however, Audrey is careful not to denigrate children's strengths or focus exclusively on their weaknesses. The blunt naming of vulnerabilities out of context and without an appreciation for the counterbalancing strengths causes parents undue anxiety and makes them become defensive. Instead, Audrey frames things in terms of "goal setting," a process in which the students are deeply involved. It is the students who identify the skills and qualities that need work and improvement and who record their aspirations in their individual portfolios. Matthew, a high-achieving student whose competitive stridency left him friendless, wrote in his portfolio his most important goal for the year: "I need to work on my problem of seeing everything as winning and losing . . . and always having to have my own way." Once the student has identified and named the challenges he or she faces, parents and teachers can join together in mutual support and help him or her reach those goals.

Creating New Spaces for Conversation

THE NARRATIVES AND reflections of the teachers and parents in this book express an intriguing paradox: We need to make conferences both weightier and lighter, both more serious and more casual, more structured and more improvisational. Encounters between families and schools need to be richer, more productive, and more meaningful, and yet we should not overburden them with unrealistic expectations. Likewise, they need to be seen as central to the educational experience of children, yet the significance of the family-school relationship must never overshadow our focus on the development and learning of the student. Managing this balance—of giving parent-teacher conferences our full attention and not letting them dominate the scene—requires shifts in the values, practices, and purview of educators, and in the responsibilities and commitments of parents.

First of all, the traditional two parent-teacher conferences each year is nowhere near enough time for teachers and parents to stay in touch or communicate with one another productively. Meetings need to be more frequent, and they need to last longer than the usual twenty minutes typically reserved in a crowded schedule during an evening open house at school. More time and more frequent contacts would, of course, require a major shift in the value that schools place on parental engagement. The school's attitude cannot continue to be one of defending against the intrusions of parents or seeing them as competitors, or even enemies. The conference must not be reduced to a reporting out of test scores and a recounting of innocuous platitudes. Rather, there must be a stance of welcoming parents, seeking their alliance, listening to their perspectives, honoring the ways in which they see and know their child, and seeing them as a valuable and essential resource for working successfully with their children. This stance of alliance rather than competition, of bridge building rather than boundary drawing, must not be seen as a distraction from teaching and learning—the central agenda of school—rather, it must be seen as a necessary dimension of building successful relationships with children that will ultimately support their academic success.

Not only is it important for parents and teachers to meet more frequently and be allowed more time to swap stories, share information, problem solve, and suggest remedies, it is just as important that teachers develop alternative ways of communicating with parents about the progress of their child and about the classroom curriculum.

Molly Rose's weekly newsletter—simply written, but never "talking down"—allows parents to see into her classroom, makes her expectations "transparent," provides a model for carrying on the classroom curriculum at home, and gives parents a language for talking with their children about school. A brief note accompanies the newsletter to parents about their child's experience that week. The notes are often just one-liners reporting a new friendship with a classmate, or a wonderful observation on a science experiment, or a struggle on the playground at recess. But these one-liners allow the parents to see the their child's growth over time and force Molly to take stock of each individual student's progress. It also, she admits, helps her recognize the "good things" that children are doing on a daily basis and gives her the chance to report the "good news" to parents. So much of the communication from teachers to parents focuses on the weaknesses, problems, and pathologies of the student—the things that need attention and remediation. Molly's practice of capturing "something special" about each child each week does not avoid identifying the problems that some children are having, but it does allow every child to be in her sight and it allows goodness to be more often revealed.

Molly Rose's system of communication with parents is deliberately structured to give all parents equal access to the school experience of their child. The system is purposely designed to be "just, inclusive, and transparent." Once her parent communication model is in place, her face-to-face meetings with parents become more productive and meaningful. They seem more like continuations of an ongoing conversation than like anxiety-laden, bigger-than-life events. The frequent communications about the individual progress of the child and the collective experience of the class support and inform the parent-teacher meetings. "There are rarely surprises," says Molly about the conferences that are made richer by the regular and frequent exchanges of information.

If Molly manages to build bridges through a well-developed model of communication, Carol Steele, by contrast, has developed a highly improvisational way of offering the parents of her adolescent special needs students access and seek their support. She brags about "going to any length" to lure parents into the circle of support for their youngsters. She is open to parents visiting the classroom unannounced, as long as they don't abuse the privilege and as long as their presence does not begin to feel intrusive to their son or daughter. She will stay on the telephone for hours with a parent who has been endlessly evasive or reluctant to meet with her face-to-face. "Timing is everything," she claims as she seizes the moment for a connection with a family that has been eluding her all year. She will even allow a student to participate in a meeting by using his cell phone. Carol is undaunted and endlessly creative in offering parents the opportunity to solve problems and join in the decision making about their child. And she is relentless in helping them understand their responsibility in following their child's progress and building an alliance with the school. Carol's communications with parents have been extended by daily e-mails, in which she reports on the progress of a classroom project or announces upcoming events or activities or lets parents know about a problem that has arisen that day with their teenager. She enjoys the efficiency and ease of communicating through e-mail, and she understands that the busy, upper-middle-class parents of her students appreciate the daily updates and immediate rapport. She believes that e-mail messages should never replace face-to-face contact; real communication about complex and intimate issues demands that she see the expressions and gestures of the parents to whom she is speaking. "I need to look deep into their eyes, and they need to see how much I care," says Carol, when she talks about the courage it takes to deliver painful news. E-mails allow people to hide out, to mask their emotions—or even fabricate their identities—behind a flat written response that usually lacks nuance and dimensionality. Likewise, she worries about the ways in which teachers and parents might use e-mail to "keep the student out of the loop" or "catch the student in the act of doing something wrong or dangerous." So everything that Carol writes in an e-mail to parents she also discusses first with her students. She never wants them to be blindsided by a parent who has received information from school about which the student is unaware or misinformed.

Carol Steele's use of e-mail represents a growing phenomenon in school systems across the country, particularly in relatively affluent communities where families have computers at home. In many suburban districts, for instance, where dual-career families commute long distances to work and feel detached from their children's school life, schools have created Web sites and instituted voice-mail systems that allow parents to receive up-to-date information about school activities and programs. Some Web sites give parents information about their youngster's attendance, grades, homework assignments, and scores on standardized tests. This kind of quantifiable, discrete information keeps parents abreast of the academic progress of their child, and it may even help them begin a conversation about his or her experience in school. With something specific to talk about, parents may be better able to push past the silence that so often greets them when they ask their youngster, "How was school today?" But I believe, as Carol Steele does, that parents need to remember that the Web site offers only a partial view, and one that is defined by those dimensions that can be quantified and measured. It does not include those aspects of a student's experience that are not reducible to numbers but may, in fact, be the most significant to the child's development and learning. And parents and teachers must also remember that while e-mail communications may be a useful supplement to face-to-face meetings, they should not be seen as a replacement for them.

Even though schools need to be welcoming and teachers need to be vigilant in their efforts to encourage parents to attend and fully participate in parent conferences, it is important to recognize that in some communities the ritual of individual face-to-face meetings with families may not be the most productive and meaningful way to relate to them. In communities where parents are collectively reluctant or uncomfortable about attending parent-teacher conferences, schools need to create other arenas for parental engagement. Maria Lopez, a third-grade bilingual teacher in an inner-city school, dutifully follows the school system's mandate of two conferences each year, but even with all of her notes and telephone calls and prodding, only a handful of parents show up for the meetings. "That's not where the action's at for them," Maria says without an ounce of defensiveness in her voice. These immigrant families—recent arrivals from Costa Rica, El Salvador, Mexico, and the Dominican Republic—feel awkward and estranged when they cross the threshold of their child's school. The institution feels opaque and difficult to navigate, the rules unclear, the rituals unfamiliar. "They are," says Maria, "strangers at the gates." Even though Maria sees herself as "one of them," and even though she and they share the same mother tongue, there is something about the conference that underscores their feelings of inadequacy, reinforces their foreignness, and makes them fall mute.

Maria's family workshops are designed to do the opposite: make parents feel engaged, challenged, powerful, and supported, and help them better understand their new country and the role that they might play in supporting their children's education. The workshops are communal events that welcome all comers. Everyone feasts on good Spanish food. There is warm conversation, storytelling, role playing, laughter, and harmless gossip. Maria believes that the workshops offer nourishment and knowledge to the parents whose needs must be met before they can provide support and guidance to their children. And she knows that she needs to create a "space that feels culturally familiar" to them. When parent conferences are experienced as irrelevant, when the ritual seems restrictive and foreign, schools and teachers must be ready to develop alternative arenas and scenarios. They must create places and spaces where the institutional and cultural boundaries that inhibit communication can be eased to create new forms of alliance and collaboration.

Connections and Constraints

THIS SHIFT IN attitude toward a more inclusive and communicative stance with families does not mean, however, that schools should be without boundaries. The teachers in this book are good at the complex and subtle negotiations that both welcome families and limit access to their classrooms. Andrea Brown, for instance, who calls herself a "yes" woman because she almost always responds to parental requests with openness and generosity, makes the barter explicit. Parents can visit her Montessori preschool classroom whenever they want, but they are not allowed to participate; they must be observers, sitting quietly on the edge of the activity. They must not interrupt the flow and texture of the classroom culture. And Jane Cross, the teacher of four-year-olds in a progressive independent school, wants to create a "seamless connection" between home and school so that the children will feel comfortable in making their first transition to school, and so that parents will be able to understand and trust what is going on behind the classroom door. So each morning the parents come to the classroom and hang around for half an hour, giving extended good-byes to their children, reading them one last story, talking to one another about their common challenges and expectations, and exchanging useful pointers.

Even though Jane Cross seeks this easy and fluid rapport with parents and wants them to feel "warmly welcomed and completely at home," she also knows that the school needs to set limits and needs to be clearer to parents about those agendas and arenas in which they should *not* be involved. Parents need to be told—in no uncertain terms—about those places where their participation is likely to be uninformed and intrusive, where their presence may even be injurious to their children's successful acclimation to school and inhibiting to the development of their autonomy. So, like Andrea Brown, Jane Cross is involved in a subtle negotiation with parents. Her message is double-edged and differentiated, a balance of connections and constraints, reaching out and resisting. And she looks to the school, and its policies and practices, to help her draw the line, to help her find a firm clarity in defining this fluid, treacherous landscape.

Willard Waller's image of parents and teachers as "natural enemies" is helpful in underscoring the different perspectives each brings to the table. He helps us see the contrasts between the universalistic relationship of teachers, who focus on the collectivity of students—seeking to create a just classroom that offers equal resources to all children—and the particularistic relationship of parents, who are protective of their own child and tend to advocate for special favors for him or her. Waller's "natural enemies" metaphor is also helpful in pointing to the productivity of these contrary adult perspectives and how these contrasting relationships with children support their development and learning. Children need both: the distance and the intimacy, the objectivity and the advocacy. But Waller's image of adult enmity is also distorting and misleading. It conjures up a picture of static roles, rigid boundaries, and hierarchies of power between families and schools. It does not embrace the contradictions embedded in productive, symmetric relationships, nor does it appreciate the coexistence of boundaries *and* bridges, of open access *and* closed doors. And, importantly, it misses the essential ingredients of empathy and respect that define successful parent-teacher encounters.

Productive dialogue requires, in fact, that both teachers and parents push past the constraints of their universalistic and particularistic roles and see the necessary and crucial claims of each other's position. Each must respect and value what the other knows and sees; each must attend carefully and listen deeply to the perspective and wisdom that the other brings. The only way to remove the sting of enmity, I believe, is to replace it with empathy. By empathy, I do not mean a gushing sentimentality or an exaggerated rhetoric of appreciation. By empathy, I mean putting yourself in the other person's shoes, seeing the world from the other person's vantage point.

There are three images that appear in the narratives of this text, offering useful contrasts to Waller's notion of "natural enemies" and making room for the development of an empathetic stance between families and schools. The first is one that does not put parents and teachers on opposite sides of a physical or metaphoric boundary; it does not place them at odds with one another. Rather, positions them "on the same side of the table," joined in their support of the student, coordinated in their efforts to problem solve, open in their expression of needing one another. In her work with special-needs adolescents, Carol Steele offers up this image of parents and teachers "on the same side of the table," facing the complex and difficult challenges together, in alliance against the dangers—both internal and external—that their adolescents are facing. As a matter of fact, her meetings with parents—which usually include a large cast of social workers, tutors, counselors, and regular classroom teachers—do not allow people to line up on either side of the table. She purposely seats people around a large circular table, an arrangement that does not easily permit the drawing of sides or the hierarchies of power and authority.

As Carol works to get parents and teachers on the same side of the table, she is trying to change the pronouns that define their positions. She wants to transpose the language from one in which positions are staked out in the first person singular of "I" to one that respects their collective quest on behalf of the student. "*We* is my favorite word," says Carol adamantly, referring to the alliance she believes that this alliance is crucial for communicating successfully with families and necessary for supporting her students. Having watched Carol work with parents, I also know that the "we" is punctuated with a soft but incisive humor that is never cynical or self-serving, a humor that is slightly self-deprecatory and pokes gentle fun at parents (with whom she is deeply identified), easing the tension and helping to quiet their fears.

The other way in which Carol builds alliances with parents and obliterates strict roles and hard boundaries is to "cross the line of objectivity." By this she means that a teacher's role in supporting her student must not be constricted by rigid distance or detachment, by always taking a universalistic pose. Rather, she believes that there are moments when teachers need to cross over the line and become "nurturing mothers." In these moments—carefully chosen—teachers must express their advocacy through deep identification, connection, and intimacy. Carol is unapologetic when she claims this "totally unobjective" place in the conversation—when she dares to speak about her "love" for her student, when she joins with her students' parents in emotional, passionate engagement. At the culmination of her meeting with Tony's parents and the representative from the Safe Haven employment program, for example, Carol's voice rises in a crescendo that feels both totally natural and completely strategic. "I'm carrying the torch trying to find someplace good for this amazing boy . . . trying to find other people who will mother him like we have."

The second image that offers an alternative to Waller's notion of parents and teachers as natural enemies is one that also draws a line between families and schools but gives the boundary a different, much softer definition. It was Sophie Wilder, a fifth- and sixth-grade teacher in an alternative public school, who suggested the wonderful, old-fashioned picture of parents and teachers coming together like "neighbors chatting over the back fence" as a way of conveying the mutuality of their concern for the child. The conversation between good neighbors honors the fence that separates their families, but it also marks their collective responsibility for all of the neighborhood children, their need to look out for each other's well-being. It is a conversation that is easy and natural and that anticipates living side-by-side for years to come. Sophie calls this collective, community-based concern "a loose kind of love" that allows for the forging of deep connections and the marking of boundaries. "Good fences make good neighbors," Robert Frost reminds us.

A third image that speaks to the development of empathy between teachers and parents, and offers a vivid contrast to Waller's assumption of enmity between families and schools, extends the theater metaphor that opens this chapter. The great performance artist Anna Deavere Smith stretches our conventional view of empathy. She draws a distinction between "getting the character to walk in the actor's shoes," the acting tradition that Smith herself was trained in, and "getting the actor to walk in the character's shoes," which is what she is aiming for in her work. The distinction is both subtle and huge. In the former case, the characters reside in the experiences and parameters of the actor, while in the latter the actor must travel outside of his or her range to find the character. The second approach requires a greater stretch, a deeper identification, some risk taking, and a leap of faith. As Smith puts it, "the spirit of acting is the *travel* from the self to the other." Her conception of this "deeper empathy" speaks to the challenges and possibilities in parent-teacher dialogues. It means that teachers and parents—working to support the learning and development of children and devoted to a discourse that will capture their different perspectives—must move beyond their frame of reference, and travel the distance to "the other."

Each of these three images—sitting on the same side of the table and getting to "we," neighbors chatting over the back fence expressing a loose kind of love, and walking in the other's shoes and traveling the distance to inhabit the character—offers an alternative conception of parent-teacher encounters. Each suggests a dialogue that develops out of a growing trust, a mutuality of concern, an appreciation of contrasting perspectives, and a deep empathy. All three images also suggest the risk taking and courage required to navigate the tender and treacherous terrain between families and schools, a terrain full of surprises and minefields. The terrain is difficult because the signposts are not always clear and because productive encounters require the balancing and embracing of stark contradictions. In seeking meaningful alliances, parents and teachers must build bridges *and* mark boundaries; they must reach out *and* resist; they must find points of mutual identification *and* hold fast to their different perspectives.

In *Borderlands/La Frontera,* Gloria Anzaldúa describes the frontiers in which these contradictions get played out, where the dialectics of difference make way for intimacy. Borderlands, says Anzaldúa, are "present wherever two or more cultures edge each other, where people of different races occupy the same territory, where under, lower, middle, or upper classes touch, where the space between two individuals shrinks with intimacy." By this definition, the parent-teacher encounter can certainly be termed a borderland. The participants in this space may very likely be of different cultures, races, and classes, but the borderland—separating and joining contrasting orientations—is there in *any* family-school arena. Through a personal narrative of prose and poetry Anzaldúa, a self-described Chicana "border woman," witnesses the treacherous and contradictory negotiations that take place when we live in the borderland.

> *In the Borderlands*
> *you are the battleground*
> *where enemies are kin to each other;*
> *you are at home, a stranger,*
> *the border disputes have been settled*
> *the volley of shots have shattered the truce*
> *you are wounded, lost in action*
> *dead, fighting back*

To survive the borderland, Anzaldúa claims that we must embrace still another contradiction. We must learn to live *"sin fronteras"*— without borders. We must "be a crossroads." The borderland that Anzaldúa sketches, then, is full of oppositional forces, which are stark and persistent. And it is a place where each person plays multiple roles. Enemies are kin and kin are enemies; people are both strangers and familiar. They are the crossroads, existing and acting without borders. I believe that the borderland is a powerful metaphor for parent-teacher meeting spaces. The natural enemies are also intimates, family, sharing much in common and also strangers. Those who make these encounters meaningful and productive are those who can cross boundaries and live in both the contested terrain and the common ground.

The images of battleground and crossroads hold deep peril and exciting promise. The battleground is where the conflict is played out— each parent and teacher *is* the contested terrain, the flashpoint for the struggle over issues creating contrast, opposition, and discord. At the same time, each parent and teacher *is* the crossroads, offering multiple paths and choices, presenting ways out to new places and uncharted territory. These images give a great deal of power and creativity to the participants in these encounters. In their hearts, minds, and actions they hold the conflict and the resolution, the problem and the solution, the battle and the peace.

CONTRIBUTIONS TO THE CONVERSATION

Anzaldúa, Gloria. *Borderlands/La Frontera: The New Mestiza*. San Francisco: Spinters/Aunt Lute Book Company, 1987.

> *Borderlands* is both Anzaldúa's personal account of her life as a "border woman" and a history of the Chicano people told through poetry and prose. Anzaldúa describes the borderlands as being "present whenever two or more cultures edge each other, where people of different races occupy the same territory, where under, lower, middle, and upper classes touch, where the space between two individuals shrinks with intimacy." Her image of the borderlands as a place where relationships are characterized by intimacy and distance, connection and restraint, helps us recognize the complex, often paradoxical engagement between parents and teachers at the institutional boundaries between families and schools.

Bateson, Mary Catherine. *Peripheral Visions: Learning Along the Way*. New York: HarperCollins, 1994.

> Through "stories and reflections," anthropologist Mary Catherine Bateson explores ways of thinking, feeling, and interpreting that involve incorporating a "multiplicity" of perspectives and

vantage points simultaneously in order to achieve understanding. What Bateson calls "learning from experience" involves appreciating "ambiguity" and "improvisation," and expanding one's range of vision rather than seeking to simplify and constrict one's sight. Her observations about engaging complexity and welcoming ambiguity, and about seeing things from a variety of perspectives, speak to some of the qualities teachers and parents identify as essential to successful relationship building. Bateson puts it this way: "Many tales have more than one meaning. It is important not to reduce understanding to some narrow focus. . . . Openness to peripheral vision depends on rejecting such reductionism and rejecting with it the belief that questions of meaning have unitary answers."

Dewey, John. "My Pedagogic Creed," originally published in *The School Journal,* vol. LIV, no. 3 (January 16, 1897).

In this provocative and incisive series of essays, Dewey lays out his core beliefs and guiding principles about education, teaching and curriculum, child development, and the relationship between school and society. His convictions are stated powerfully and unequivocally, a refreshing contrast to the more neutral language of most contemporary educational researchers and commentators. Dewey believes that the close and "unsentimental" observation of children, and a recognition of their individual needs and capacities, are essential ingredients of good parent-teacher dialogue and necessary for the optimal development of children.

Epstein, Joyce L. *School, Family, and Community Partnerships: Preparing Educators and Improving Schools.* Boulder, Colo.: Westview Press, 2001.

In this useful and comprehensive volume, Epstein, the director of the Center on School, Family, and Community Partnerships at Johns Hopkins University, gathers together twenty-five years of insight based on her research on parental involvement in schools. The text offers a theoretical framework for parent and community engagement in schools as well as practical applications, guidelines, strategies, and templates to help schools create successful programs for partnerships with parents. At the foundation of the work is Epstein's theory of "overlapping spheres of influence," in which family, school, and community all function internally and interact externally to have an impact on student learning and development. She delineates "six types of involvement" that schools should develop in order to create effective partnerships with communities: parenting, communicating, volunteering, learning at home, decision making, and collaborating with community.

Fraiberg, Selma, with Edna Adelson and Vivian Shapiro. "Ghosts in the Nursery: A Psychoanalytic Approach to the Problems of Impaired Infant-Mother Relationships." *Selected Writings of Selma Fraiberg,* edited by Louis Fraiberg. Columbus: Ohio State University Press, 1987. Article originally published in the *Journal of the American Academy of Child Psychiatry* (1975), 14:387–421.

Psychoanalyst Fraiberg combines case analysis, developmental theory, and metaphor to examine the persistent—and often unconscious—influence of past experiences and "long-gone individuals" on the present relationship between mothers and their infants. The "invasion" of these "ghosts in the nursery" is such that, at times, "a parent and a child may find themselves reenacting a moment or a scene from another time with another set of characters," creating the "repetition of the past in the present." Fraiberg's notion of "ghosts" carrying powerful intergenerational echoes offers a powerful image for considering the ways in which early childhood experiences and traumas shape the encounters between parents and teachers, often causing a confusion between past and present, and between their own childhood experiences and those of their children.

Greene, Maxine. *Teacher as Stranger: Educational Philosophy in the Modern Age.* Belmont, Calif.: Wadsworth Publishing Company, Inc., 1973.

Who we are, what we've experienced, where we've been, and the context in which we work profoundly affect how we think and what we do. In *Teacher as Stranger,* philosopher Maxine Greene explores this idea in connection to the work of teachers, challenging the more prevalent traditional view of teachers as lacking an inner life and personal history relevant to the work of teaching. She suggests that teachers need to develop a "heightened self-consciousness and greater clarity" by "doing philosophy," questioning their actions, beliefs, and purposes. Ultimately, Greene believes that this kind of self-scrutiny and self-reflection will better equip teachers to develop more productive and authentic relationships with their students and their families.

Hiatt-Michael, Diana B., ed. *Promising Practices for Family Involvement in Schools.* Greenwich, Conn.: Information Age Publishing, 2001.

This volume brings together essays and articles by a number of educators, practitioners, and policymakers working in the field of family-school relations. The first in an annual series of monographs devoted to current research and practices in the field of family-school involvement, this book is useful in offering theoretical perspectives, research findings, evaluations of programs, and policy recommendations.

Jencks, Christopher, and Marshall Smith; Henry Acland; Mary Jo Bane; David Cohen; Herbert Gintis; Barbara Heyns; Stephan Michelson. *Inequality: A Reassessment of the Effect of Family and Schooling in America.* New York: Basic Books, 1972.

In a penetrating analysis, Jencks and his colleagues examine the concept of "inequality" across a variety of domains, looking particularly closely at how policies that attempt to give people greater opportunities for mobility seem to do very little to eliminate poverty. For example, movements to deal with economic inequality often center "on helping workers in poorly paid jobs to move into better paid jobs" rather than attempting "to reduce wage disparities between highly paid and poorly paid workers."

Jenck's investigation of the relationship between social class and educational attainment exposes a central contradiction between our cultural rhetoric and the reality facing students matriculating through school. On the one hand, we claim that education is the great equalizer, that all children have the right to equality of educational access and opportunity, while on the other hand, in reality schooling has served to reify existing social class hierarchies. Parent-teacher encounters are shaped by the conflicting messages embedded in this central contradiction.

Klein, Alexander, ed. *Natural Enemies? Youth and the Clash of Generations*. New York: J. B. Lippincott, 1969.

Klein compiles an assortment of articles, chapters, excerpts, interviews, and short pieces from an eclectic range of authors—Margaret Mead, Kenneth Clark, Benjamin Spock, James Baldwin, Robert F. Kennedy, R. Buckminster Fuller, Robert Coles, Erik Erikson, and the Beatles, among others—to examine the place of the younger generation in society and the roots and nature of the conflict between generations. An important insight from Klein's work is that "natural enemies" emerge where there are inherent clashes in culture, style, values, and perspectives, with those clashing defining themselves and their goals as much in terms of what they're not, what they don't want, and who they don't want to be as in terms of what they are, what they want, and who they want to be. In this way, he argues, there can be both mutuality and individuality, interdependence and independence, contention and cooperation, among "natural enemies." These contrasts and dialectics—in positioning and perspective—are useful in thinking about the encounters between parents and teachers as well.

Lawrence-Lightfoot, Sara. *Worlds Apart: Relationships Between Families and Schools*. New York: Basic Books, 1978.

Before I published *Worlds Apart* twenty-five years ago, social science investigations had tended to emphasize a conceptual dichotomy between research that examined socialization in families and research that documented education in schools. My book was an effort to challenge and correct this dichotomy and bridge these realms, offering an analysis of the institutional and relational connections between these two primary arenas of child development and learning. Using sociological, historical, political, and economic lenses, I offered a broad-scaled examination—illustrated through case studies and ethnography—of the roots of conflict and connection between families and schools, recognizing as well those situations when conflict is clarifying and productive, and those times when it leads to animosity and distrust.

Martha, Minow. *Making All the Difference: Inclusion, Exclusion, and American Law.* Ithaca, N.Y.: Cornell University Press, 1990.

Minow, a Harvard Law professor and child advocate, focuses on the complexities of how the law treats those who are different in some way from the "norm," the accepted, the standard. For example, a part of her analysis deals with children with disabilities, and the challenges of the law to protect the rights of children with disabilities to education, services, accommodations, etc., while also avoiding the stigmatization of those children as different in ways that will impede their ability to live their lives and succeed in society. In one passage Minow writes:

> With both bilingual and special education, schools struggle to deal with children defined as "different" without stigmatizing them. Both programs raise the same question: when does treating people differently emphasize their difference and stigmatize or hinder them on that basis and when does treating people the same become insensitive to their difference and likely to stigmatize or hinder them on *that* basis?

This complex conundrum, which Minow calls "the dilemma of difference," can become a source of tension and misunderstanding between teachers and parents as they seek to distinguish between identifying the individual needs and vulnerabilities of children in order to better serve them on the one hand, and the potential for stereotyping that labeling often implies on the other.

Nemerov, Howard. "September, the First Day of School," in *Gnomes and Occasions: Poems by Howard Nemerov.* Chicago: University of Chicago Press, 1973, p. 42.

In his poem "The First Day of School" Nemerov speaks about the anxiety, loss, and childhood echoes that consume the father when he takes his child to the first day of kindergarten. When he drops his son off at the classroom door, at the beginning of the poem, the tears he sheds recall his own weeping as he separated from his parents when he was a child beginning schooling.

> *My selfish tears remind me how*
> *I cried before that door a life ago*
> *I may have had a hard time letting go.*

At the end of the poem, it is clear that part of the deep pain that the father experiences comes from seeing the first day separation as the beginning of a lifetime of estrangement—the classroom door will be closed to him forever.

> *. . . . My child has disappeared*
> *Behind the schoolroom door. And should I live*
> *To see his coming forth, a life away,*
> *I know my hope, but do not know its form.*
> *Nor hope to know it. May the fathers he finds*
> *Among his teachers have a care of him*
> *More than his father could.*

Vandenbroucke, Russell. *Truths the Hand Can Touch: The Theater of Athol Fugard.* New York: Theater Communications Group, 1985.

A white South African playwright, Fugard examines the struggles of people living under the oppression of apartheid, exploring the political and social relationships between and among racial groups. His powerful plays, produced worldwide, include *Master Harold . . . and the Boys, Blood Knot, Boesman and Lena,* and *A Lesson from Aloes.* Vandenbroucke's text closely analyzes Fugard's plays and places his work in political and historical context. Although Fugard's characters are driven by and profoundly affected by the larger political and social context, he makes his purposes clear, trying always to reveal the "truths the hand can touch": "If there have ever been 'universals' in my writing, they have had to look after themselves. I concern myself with the 'specifics.'" The search for specifics—for detailed observations, evidence, and anecdotes—is at the heart of productive parent-teacher encounters.

Waller, Willard. *Sociology of Teaching.* New York: Russell and Russell, 1961; originally published in 1932.

In his sociological analysis of schools, Waller examines the concept of the school as a social entity unto itself, as a "social organism" existing and functioning independently of other societal institutions. Looking within schools, Waller explores the roles that people play, the relationships among people, and the culture that exists, all functioning to create an institution that is unique and distinct from all that is outside of the school. One aspect of Waller's analysis centers on the relationship between parents and teachers, whom he describes as "natural enemies predestined for the discomfiture of the other." This animosity and antagonism, according to Waller, is rooted in the differences—contextually, emotionally, and relationally—between the ways parents see their children and the ways teachers regard their students. Waller views the goals of "parent-teacher work" in schools as gaining "for the school the support of parents; that is, getting parents to see children more or less as teachers see them." However, Waller also asserts that "it would be a sad day for children if parent-teacher work ever really succeeded in its object." In this sense, the ongoing conflict between parents and teachers is inevitable and complex, being potentially beneficial and potentially damaging for the child.

Weissbourd, Richard. *The Vulnerable Child: What Really Hurts America's Children and What We Can Do About It.* Reading, Mass.: Addison-Wesley Publishing Company, 1996.

In a wide-ranging analysis of social programs, policies, and research, Weissbourd explores the myths that society holds about children who are seen as "disadvantaged" and the ways in which our labeling of them not only distorts their strengths and capacities but also limits their chances. These presumptions and biases that lead to labeling and categorization are particularly pernicious inside schools. Weissbourd challenges our assumptions about human development and the roots of vulnerability and failure in children by examining the issues on individual, structural, and systemic levels. He concludes by offering descriptions of programs and institutions that are successfully working to support the healthy development of children. His description of model programs offers important practical lessons for teachers working with students and their families.

About the Author

SARA LAWRENCE-LIGHTFOOT, a sociologist, is a professor of education at Harvard University, where, since 1972, she has studied the culture of schools, families, and communities. She is the author of seven books, including *I've Known Rivers* and *Balm in Gilead,* which won the 1988 Christopher Award for "literary merit and humanitarian achievement." In 1984 she was the recipient of the prestigious MacArthur Prize. In 1993 she was awarded Harvard's George Ledlie Prize for research that makes the "most valuable contribution to science" and is to "the benefit of mankind." She is the first African-American woman in Harvard's history to have an endowed professorship named in her honor.

About the Type

This book was set in Sabon, a typeface designed by the well-known German typographer Jan Tschichold (1902–1974). Sabon's design is based upon the original letter forms of Claude Garamond, and created specifically to be used for three sources: foundry type for hand composition, Linotype, and Monotype. Tschichold named his typeface for the famous Frankfurt type founder Jacques Sabon, who died in 1580.